SONS OF ANARCHY

EST 1967

REDWOOD ORIGINAL

VOLUME FIVE

SONS OF ANARCHY Volume Five, May 2016. Published by BOOM! Studios, a division of Boom Entertainment, Inc. Sons of Anarchy ™ & © 2016 Twentieth Century Fox Film Corporation and Bluebush Productions, LLC. All Rights Reserved. Originally published in single magazine form as SONS OF ANARCHY No. 19-22. ™ & © 2015 Twentieth Century Fox Film Corporation and Bluebush Productions, LLC. All Rights Reserved. BOOM! Studios™ and the BOOM! Studios logo are trademarks of Boom Entertainment, Inc., registered in various countries and categories. All characters, events, and institutions depicted herein are fictional. Any similarity between any of the names, characters, persons, events, and/or institutions in this publication to actual names, characters, and persons, whether living or dead, events, and/or institutions is unintended and purely coincidental. BOOM! Studios does not read or accept unsolicited submissions of ideas, stories, or artwork.

A catalog record of this book is available from OCLC and from the BOOM! website, www.boom-studios.com, on the Librarians Page.

BOOM! Studios, 5670 Wilshire Boulevard, Suite 450, Los Angeles, CA 90036-5679. Printed in China. First Printing.

ISBN: 978-1-60886-824-7, eISBN: 978-1-61398-495-6

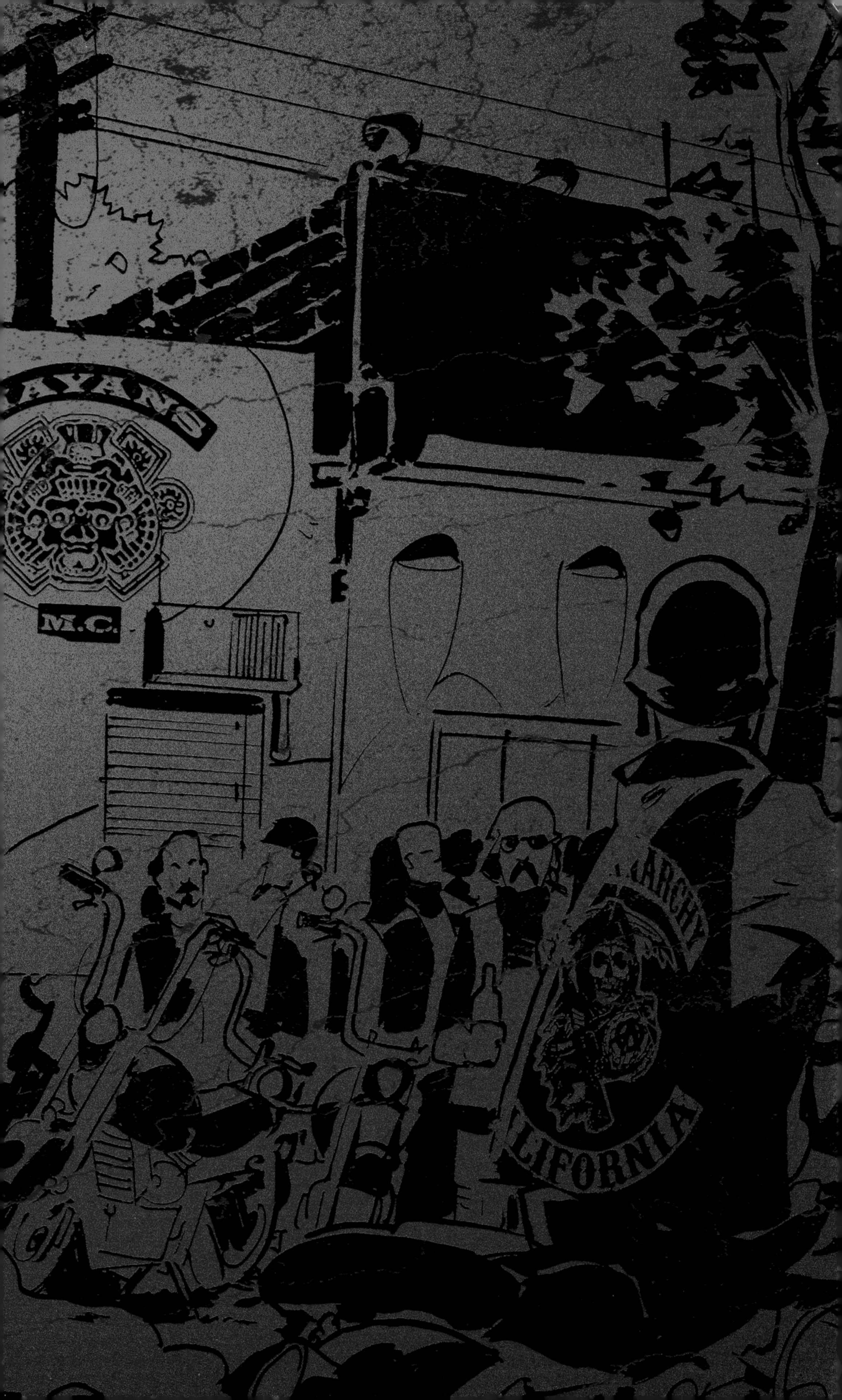
AYANS
M.C.
LIFORNIA

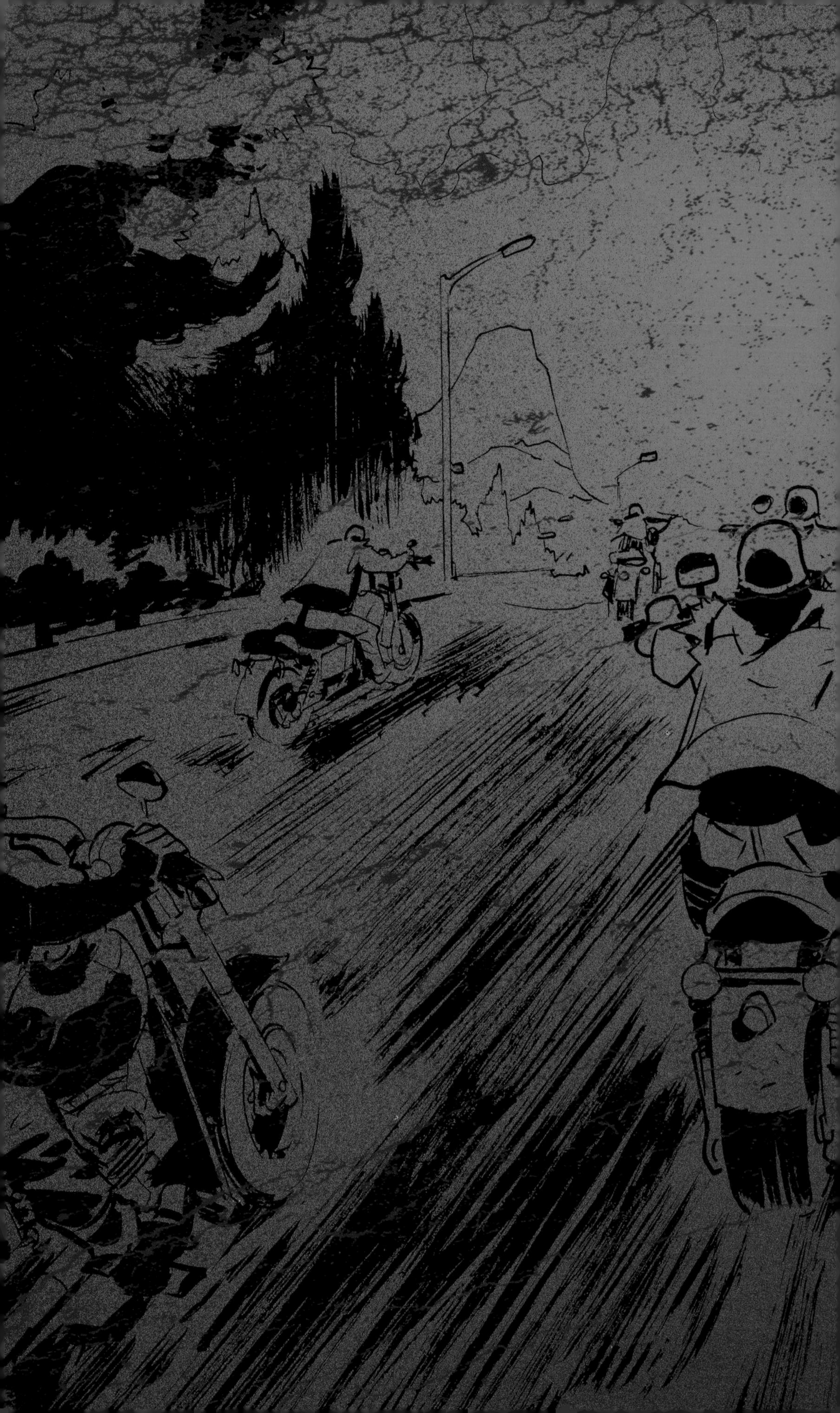

WRITTEN BY
RYAN FERRIER

ILLUSTRATED BY
MATÍAS BERGARA

COLORS BY
PAUL LITTLE

LETTERS BY
ED DUKESHIRE

COVER BY
TONI INFANTE

DESIGNERS
KELSEY DIETERICH & SCOTT NEWMAN

ASSISTANT EDITOR
MARY GUMPORT

EDITOR
DAFNA PLEBAN

SPECIAL THANKS TO
NICOLE SPIEGEL, MARIA ROMO, JOSH IZZO,
JOHN BARCHESKI, KURT SUTTER AND THE ENTIRE SOA FAMILY

BOOM! STUDIOS MC: ERIC HARBURN, EDITOR • BRYCE CARLSON, MANAGING EDITOR • MATT GAGNON, EDITOR-IN-CHIEF

CHAPTER 19

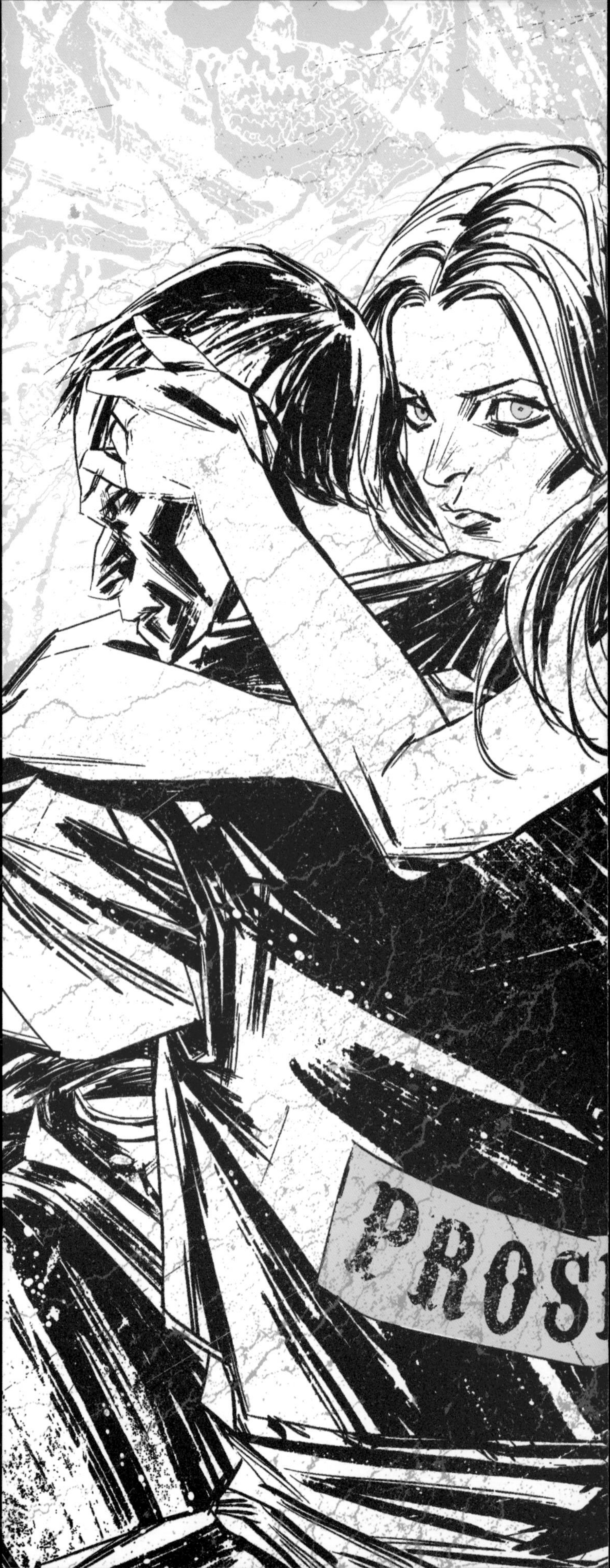
PROS

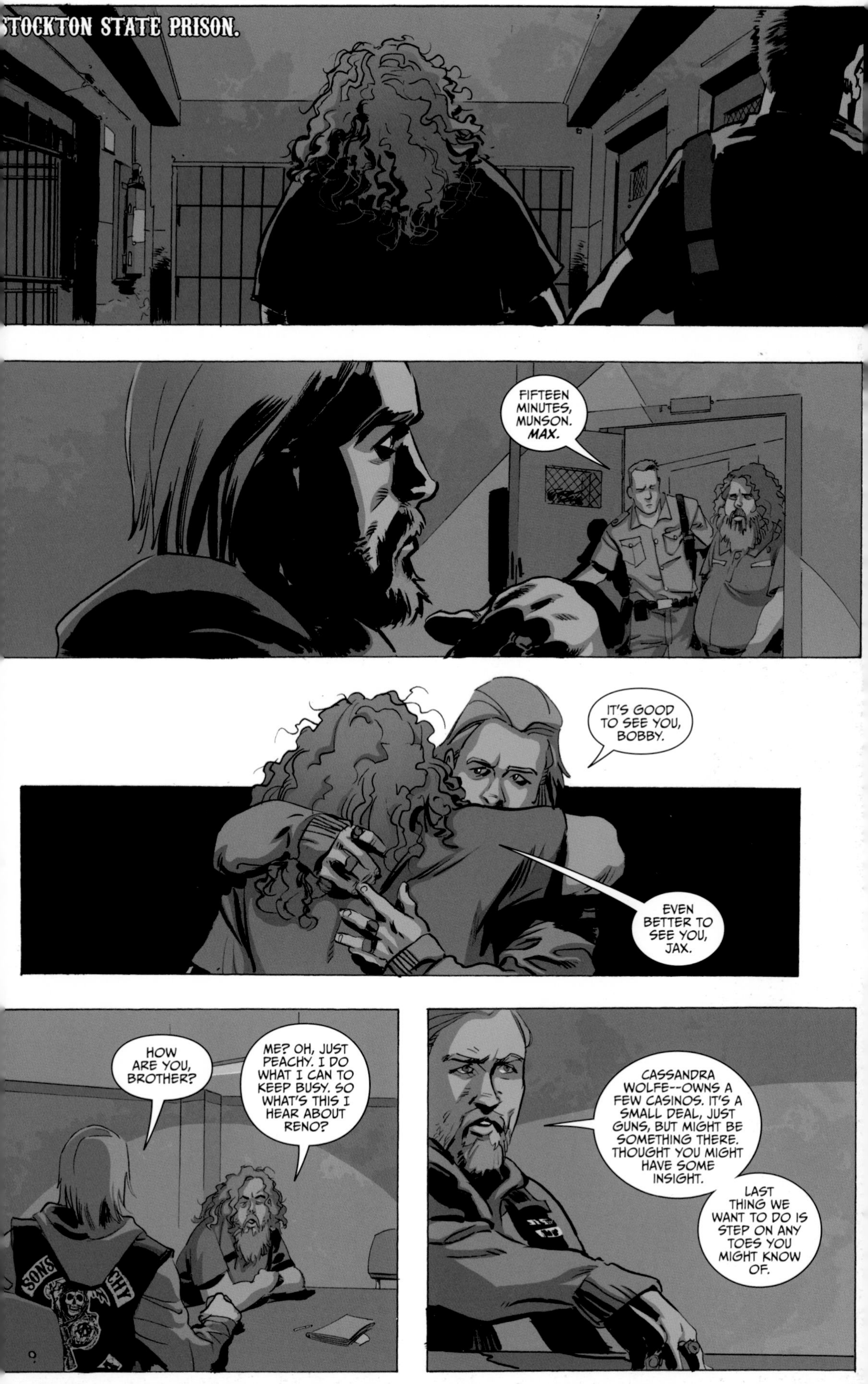
STOCKTON STATE PRISON.
FIFTEEN MINUTES, MUNSON. MAX.
IT'S GOOD TO SEE YOU, BOBBY.
EVEN BETTER TO SEE YOU, JAX.
HOW ARE YOU, BROTHER?
ME? OH, JUST PEACHY. I DO WHAT I CAN TO KEEP BUSY. SO WHAT'S THIS I HEAR ABOUT RENO?
CASSANDRA WOLFE--OWNS A FEW CASINOS. IT'S A SMALL DEAL, JUST GUNS, BUT MIGHT BE SOMETHING THERE. THOUGHT YOU MIGHT HAVE SOME INSIGHT.
LAST THING WE WANT TO DO IS STEP ON ANY TOES YOU MIGHT KNOW OF.

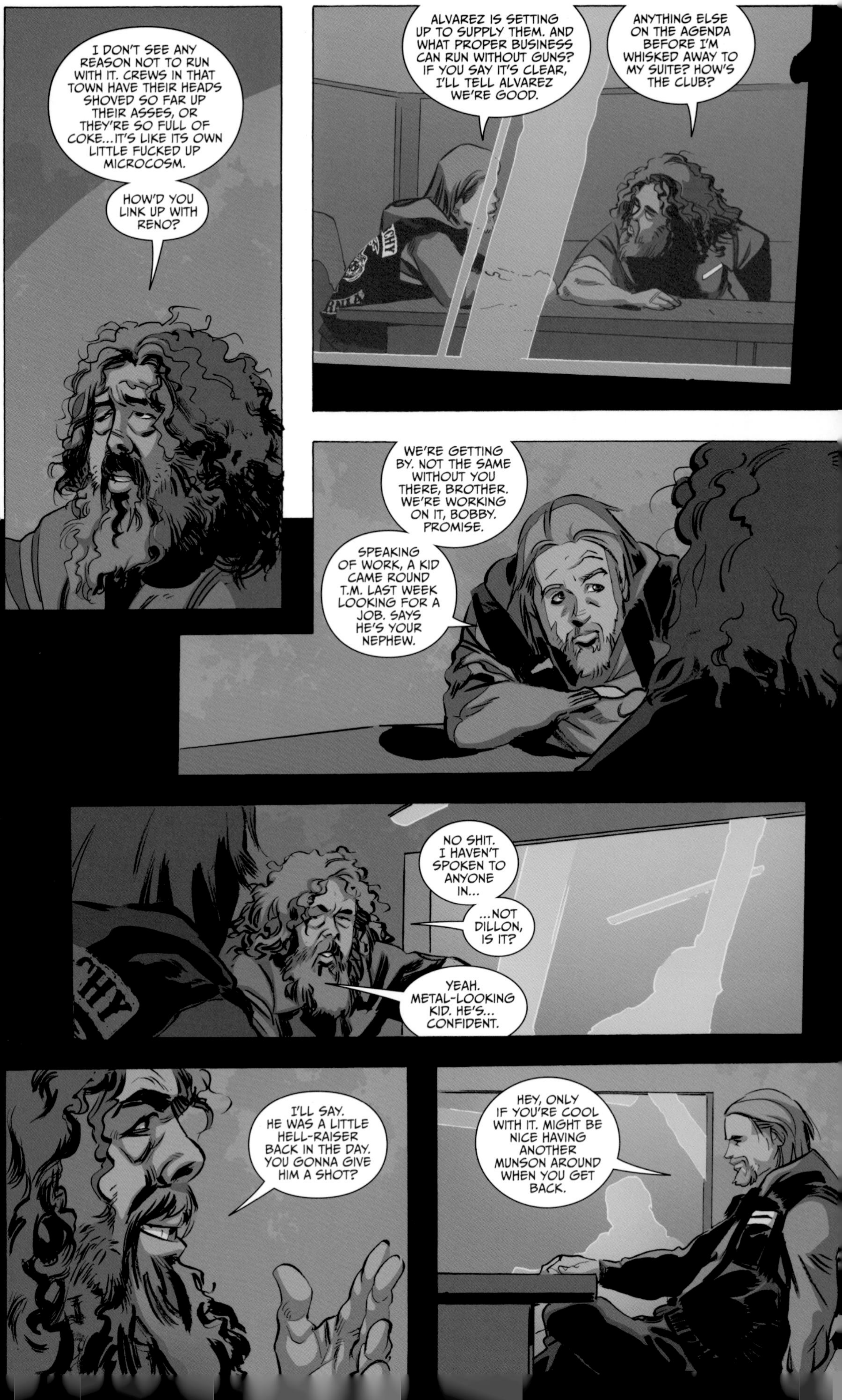

I DON'T SEE ANY REASON NOT TO RUN WITH IT. CREWS IN THAT TOWN HAVE THEIR HEADS SHOVED SO FAR UP THEIR ASSES, OR THEY'RE SO FULL OF COKE...IT'S LIKE ITS OWN LITTLE FUCKED UP MICROCOSM.
HOW'D YOU LINK UP WITH RENO?
ALVAREZ IS SETTING UP TO SUPPLY THEM. AND WHAT PROPER BUSINESS CAN RUN WITHOUT GUNS? IF YOU SAY IT'S CLEAR, I'LL TELL ALVAREZ WE'RE GOOD.
ANYTHING ELSE ON THE AGENDA BEFORE I'M WHISKED AWAY TO MY SUITE? HOW'S THE CLUB?
WE'RE GETTING BY. NOT THE SAME WITHOUT YOU THERE, BROTHER. WE'RE WORKING ON IT, BOBBY. PROMISE.
SPEAKING OF WORK, A KID CAME ROUND T.M. LAST WEEK LOOKING FOR A JOB. SAYS HE'S YOUR NEPHEW.
NO SHIT. I HAVEN'T SPOKEN TO ANYONE IN...
...NOT DILLON, IS IT?
YEAH. METAL-LOOKING KID. HE'S... CONFIDENT.
I'LL SAY. HE WAS A LITTLE HELL-RAISER BACK IN THE DAY. YOU GONNA GIVE HIM A SHOT?
HEY, ONLY IF YOU'RE COOL WITH IT. MIGHT BE NICE HAVING ANOTHER MUNSON AROUND WHEN YOU GET BACK.

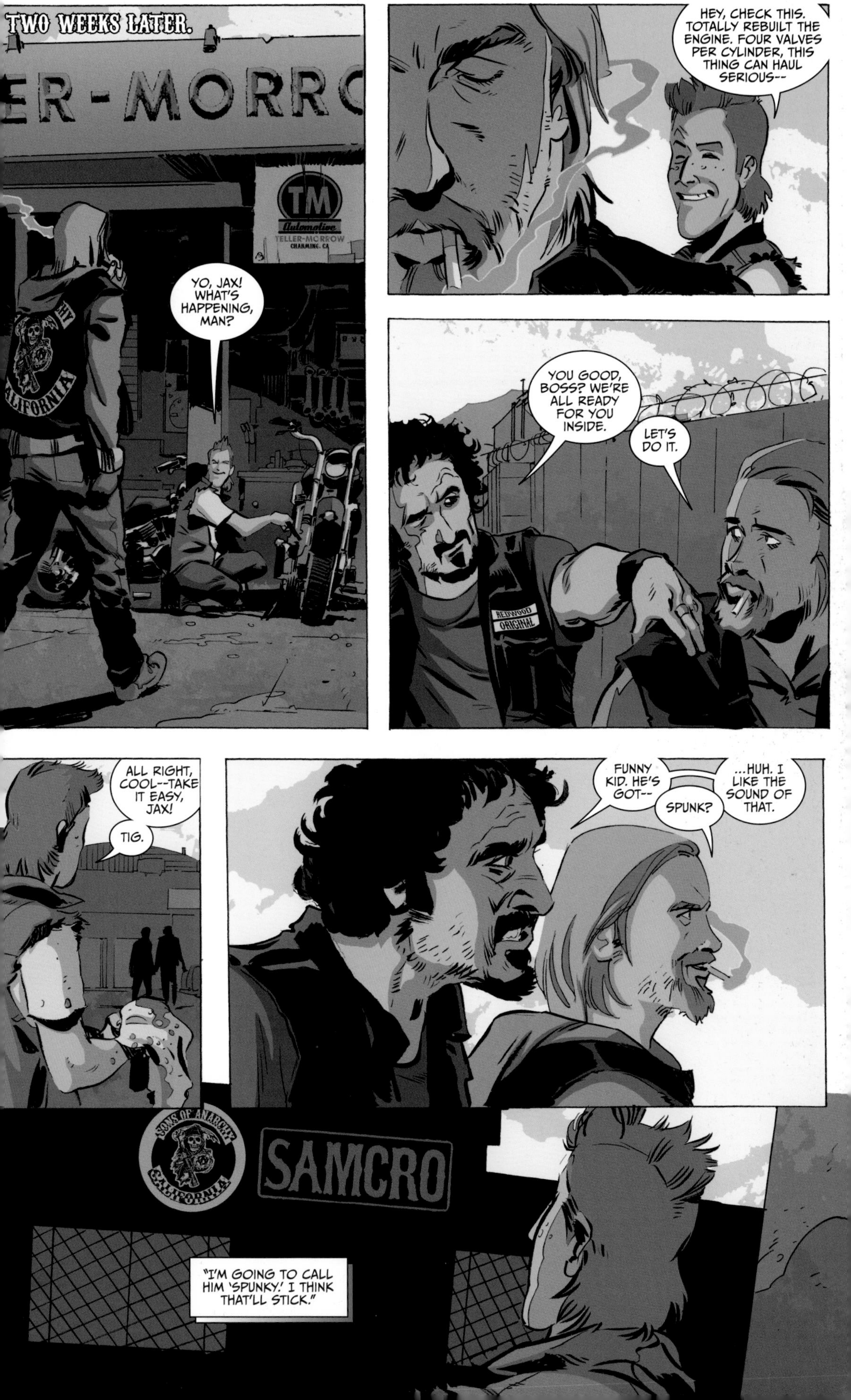
TWO WEEKS LATER.
ER-MORRO
TM Automotive TELLER-MORROW CHARMING, CA
YO, JAX! WHAT'S HAPPENING, MAN?
HEY, CHECK THIS. TOTALLY REBUILT THE ENGINE. FOUR VALVES PER CYLINDER, THIS THING CAN HAUL SERIOUS--
YOU GOOD, BOSS? WE'RE ALL READY FOR YOU INSIDE.
LET'S DO IT.
REDWOOD ORIGINAL
ALL RIGHT, COOL--TAKE IT EASY, JAX!
TIG.
FUNNY KID. HE'S GOT--
SPUNK?
...HUH. I LIKE THE SOUND OF THAT.
SONS OF ANARCHY CALIFORNIA
SAMCRO
"I'M GOING TO CALL HIM 'SPUNKY.' I THINK THAT'LL STICK."

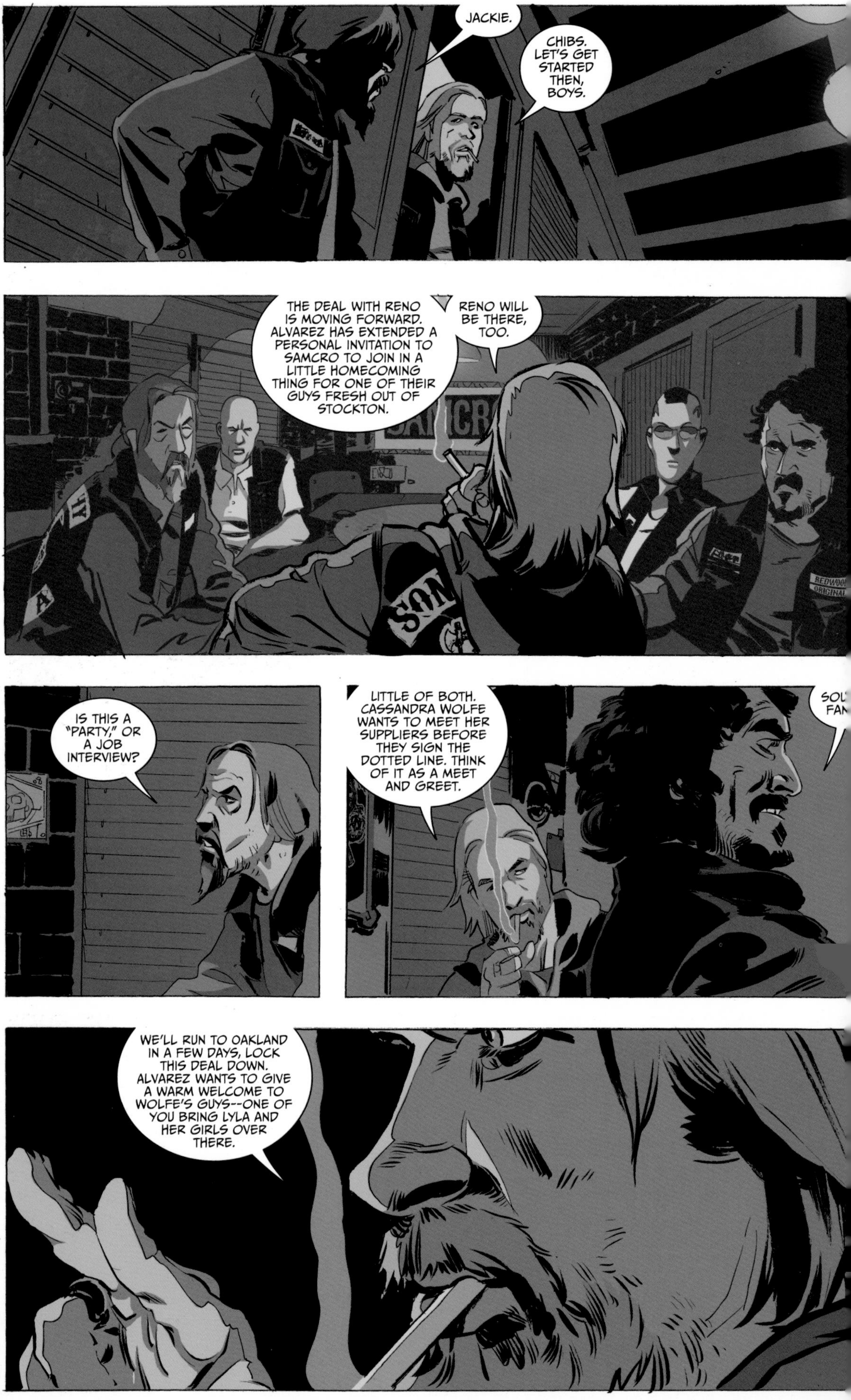
JACKIE.
CHIBS. LET'S GET STARTED THEN, BOYS.
THE DEAL WITH RENO IS MOVING FORWARD. ALVAREZ HAS EXTENDED A PERSONAL INVITATION TO SAMCRO TO JOIN IN A LITTLE HOMECOMING THING FOR ONE OF THEIR GUYS FRESH OUT OF STOCKTON.
RENO WILL BE THERE, TOO.
IS THIS A "PARTY," OR A JOB INTERVIEW?
LITTLE OF BOTH. CASSANDRA WOLFE WANTS TO MEET HER SUPPLIERS BEFORE THEY SIGN THE DOTTED LINE. THINK OF IT AS A MEET AND GREET.
WE'LL RUN TO OAKLAND IN A FEW DAYS, LOCK THIS DEAL DOWN. ALVAREZ WANTS TO GIVE A WARM WELCOME TO WOLFE'S GUYS--ONE OF YOU BRING LYLA AND HER GIRLS OVER THERE.

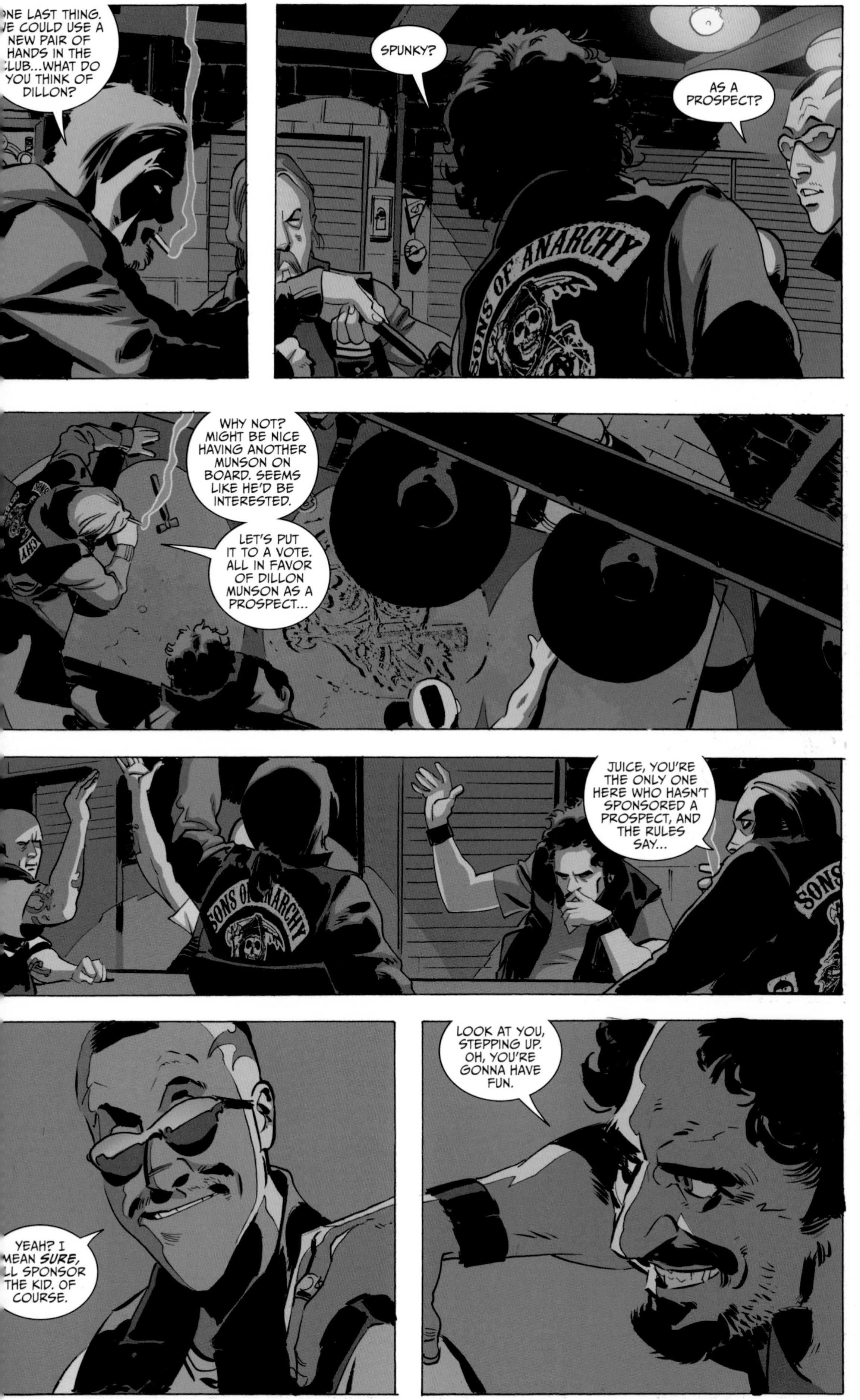
ONE LAST THING. WE COULD USE A NEW PAIR OF HANDS IN THE CLUB...WHAT DO YOU THINK OF DILLON?
SPUNKY?
AS A PROSPECT?
SONS OF ANARCHY
WHY NOT? MIGHT BE NICE HAVING ANOTHER MUNSON ON BOARD. SEEMS LIKE HE'D BE INTERESTED.
LET'S PUT IT TO A VOTE. ALL IN FAVOR OF DILLON MUNSON AS A PROSPECT...
JUICE, YOU'RE THE ONLY ONE HERE WHO HASN'T SPONSORED A PROSPECT, AND THE RULES SAY...
SONS OF ANARCHY
YEAH? I MEAN *SURE*, I'LL SPONSOR THE KID. OF COURSE.
LOOK AT YOU, STEPPING UP. OH, YOU'RE GONNA HAVE FUN.

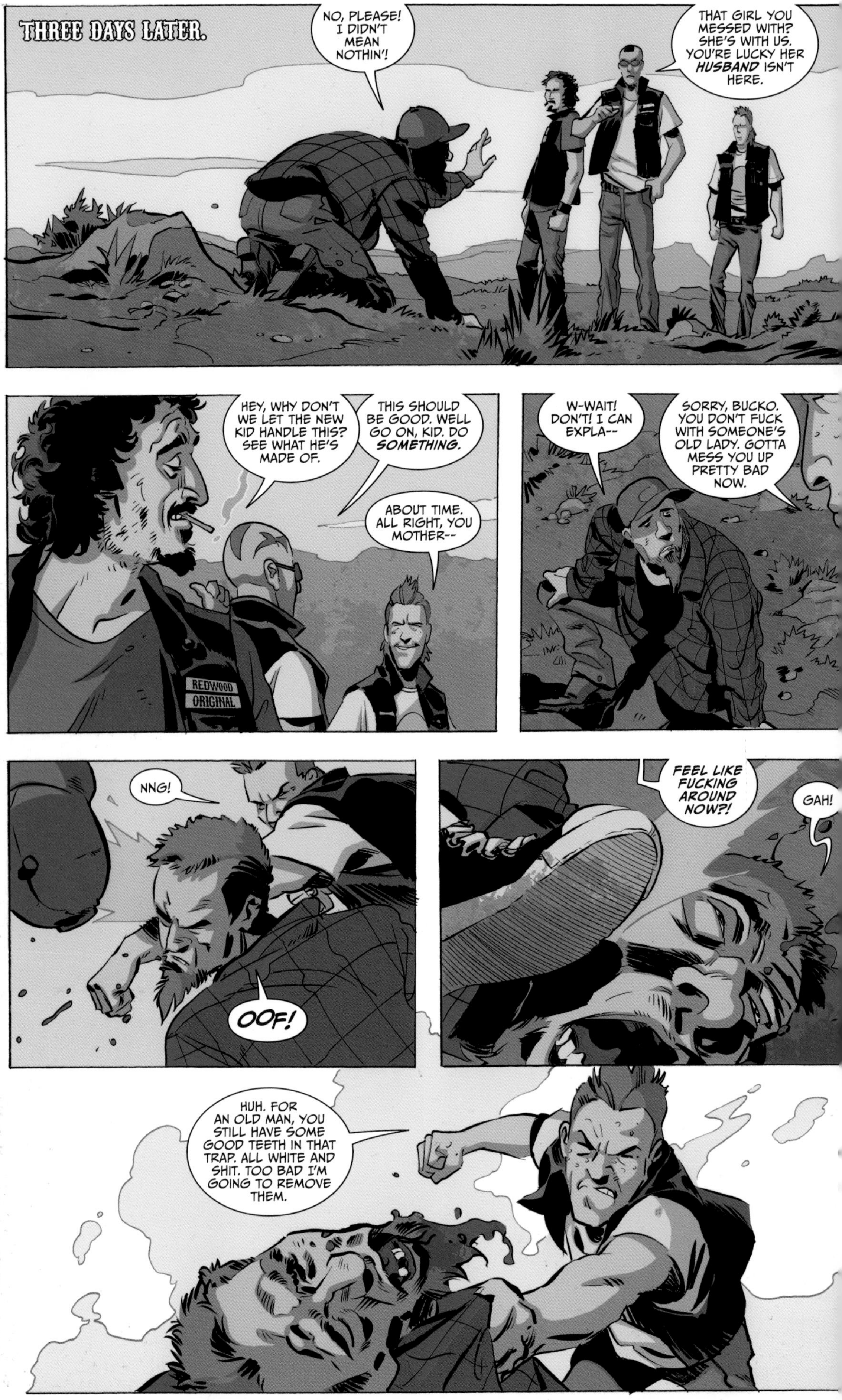
THREE DAYS LATER.
NO, PLEASE! I DIDN'T MEAN NOTHIN'!
THAT GIRL YOU MESSED WITH? SHE'S WITH US. YOU'RE LUCKY HER HUSBAND ISN'T HERE.
HEY, WHY DON'T WE LET THE NEW KID HANDLE THIS? SEE WHAT HE'S MADE OF.
THIS SHOULD BE GOOD. WELL GO ON, KID. DO SOMETHING.
ABOUT TIME. ALL RIGHT, YOU MOTHER--
REDWOOD ORIGINAL
W-WAIT! DON'T! I CAN EXPLA--
SORRY, BUCKO. YOU DON'T FUCK WITH SOMEONE'S OLD LADY. GOTTA MESS YOU UP PRETTY BAD NOW.
NNG!
OOF!
FEEL LIKE FUCKING AROUND NOW?!
GAH!
HUH. FOR AN OLD MAN, YOU STILL HAVE SOME GOOD TEETH IN THAT TRAP. ALL WHITE AND SHIT. TOO BAD I'M GOING TO REMOVE THEM.

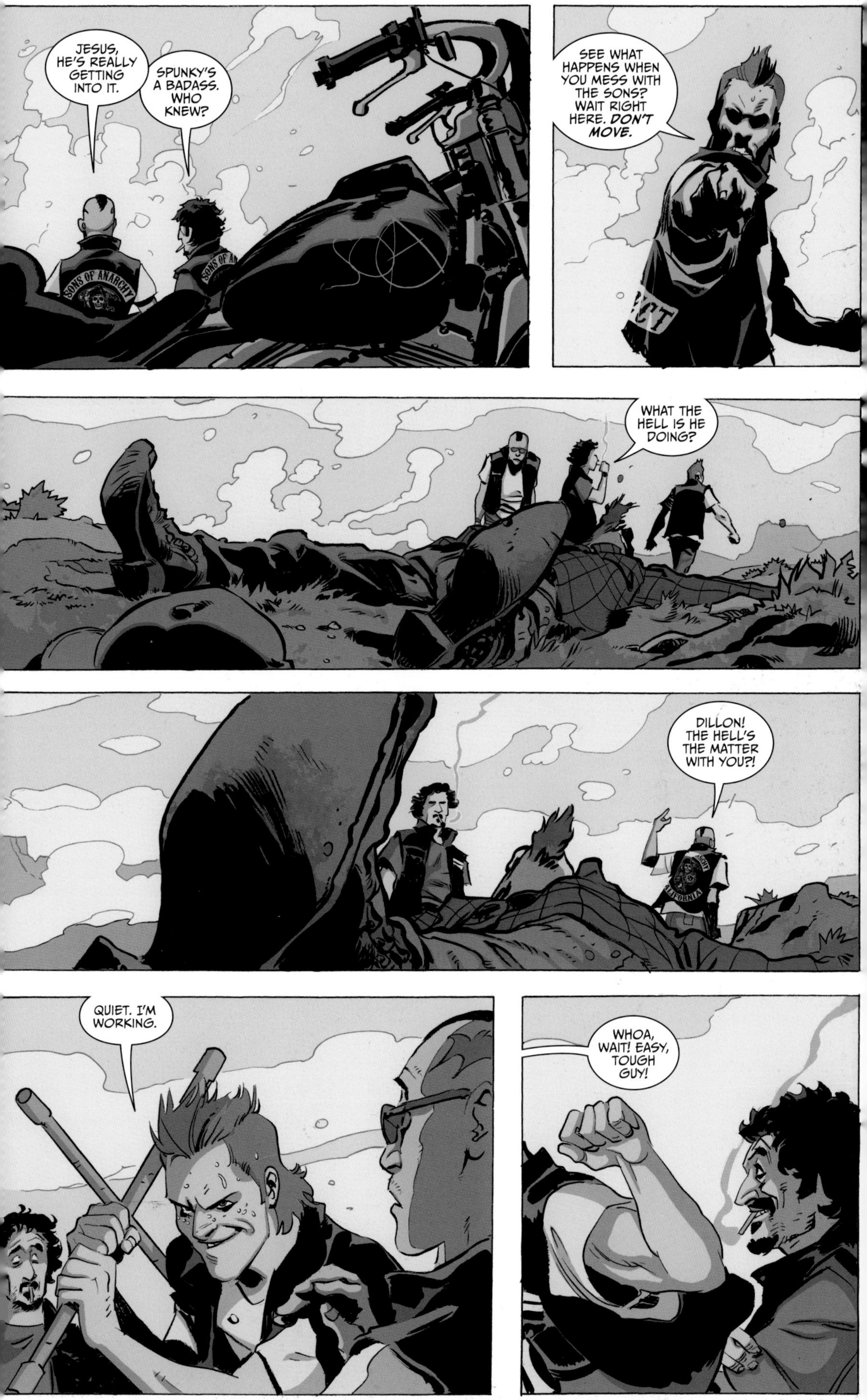
JESUS, HE'S REALLY GETTING INTO IT.
SPUNKY'S A BADASS. WHO KNEW?
SONS OF ANARCHY
SEE WHAT HAPPENS WHEN YOU MESS WITH THE SONS? WAIT RIGHT HERE. *DON'T MOVE.*
WHAT THE HELL IS HE DOING?
DILLON! THE HELL'S THE MATTER WITH YOU?!
QUIET. I'M WORKING.
WHOA, WAIT! EASY, TOUGH GUY!

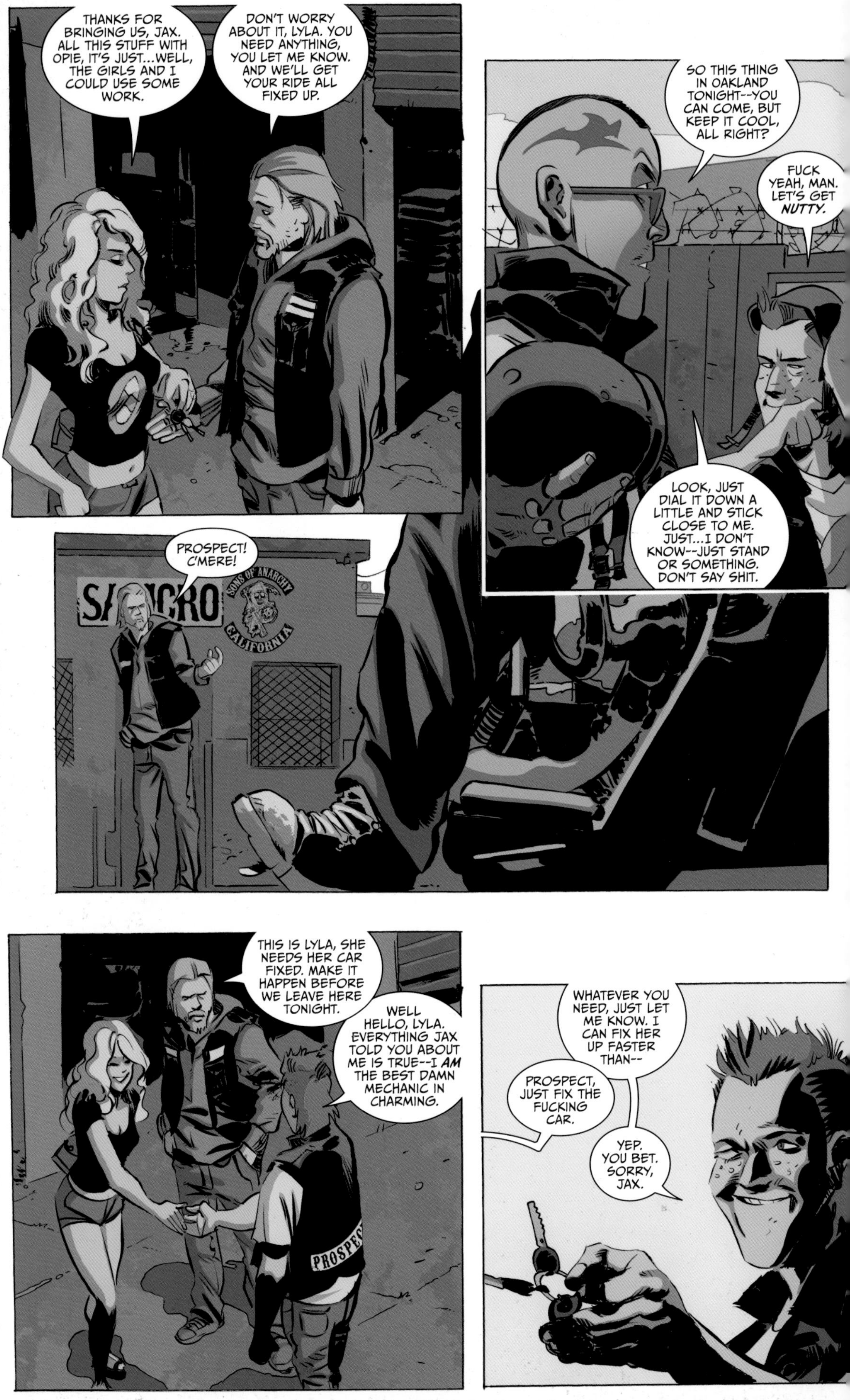
THANKS FOR BRINGING US, JAX. ALL THIS STUFF WITH OPIE, IT'S JUST...WELL, THE GIRLS AND I COULD USE SOME WORK.
DON'T WORRY ABOUT IT, LYLA. YOU NEED ANYTHING, YOU LET ME KNOW. AND WE'LL GET YOUR RIDE ALL FIXED UP.
SO THIS THING IN OAKLAND TONIGHT--YOU CAN COME, BUT KEEP IT COOL, ALL RIGHT?
FUCK YEAH, MAN. LET'S GET *NUTTY.*
LOOK, JUST DIAL IT DOWN A LITTLE AND STICK CLOSE TO ME. JUST...I DON'T KNOW--JUST STAND OR SOMETHING. DON'T SAY SHIT.
PROSPECT! C'MERE!
SONS OF ANARCHY
CALIFORNIA
THIS IS LYLA, SHE NEEDS HER CAR FIXED. MAKE IT HAPPEN BEFORE WE LEAVE HERE TONIGHT.
WELL HELLO, LYLA. EVERYTHING JAX TOLD YOU ABOUT ME IS TRUE--I *AM* THE BEST DAMN MECHANIC IN CHARMING.
WHATEVER YOU NEED, JUST LET ME KNOW. I CAN FIX HER UP FASTER THAN--
PROSPECT, JUST FIX THE FUCKING CAR.
YEP. YOU BET. SORRY, JAX.

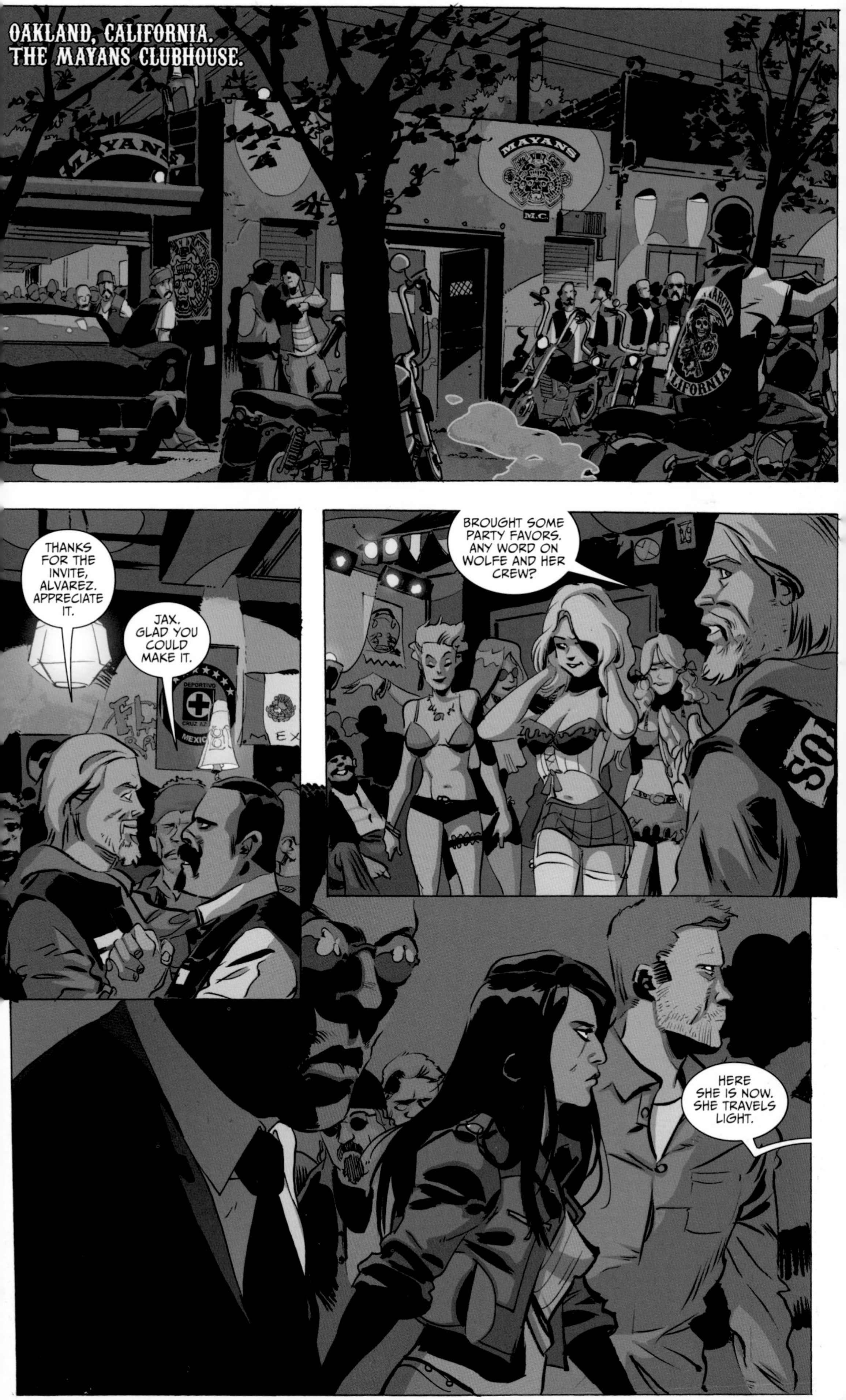
OAKLAND, CALIFORNIA. THE MAYANS CLUBHOUSE.
MAYANS
MAYANS
M.C.
THANKS FOR THE INVITE, ALVAREZ. APPRECIATE IT.
JAX. GLAD YOU COULD MAKE IT.
BROUGHT SOME PARTY FAVORS. ANY WORD ON WOLFE AND HER CREW?
HERE SHE IS NOW. SHE TRAVELS LIGHT.

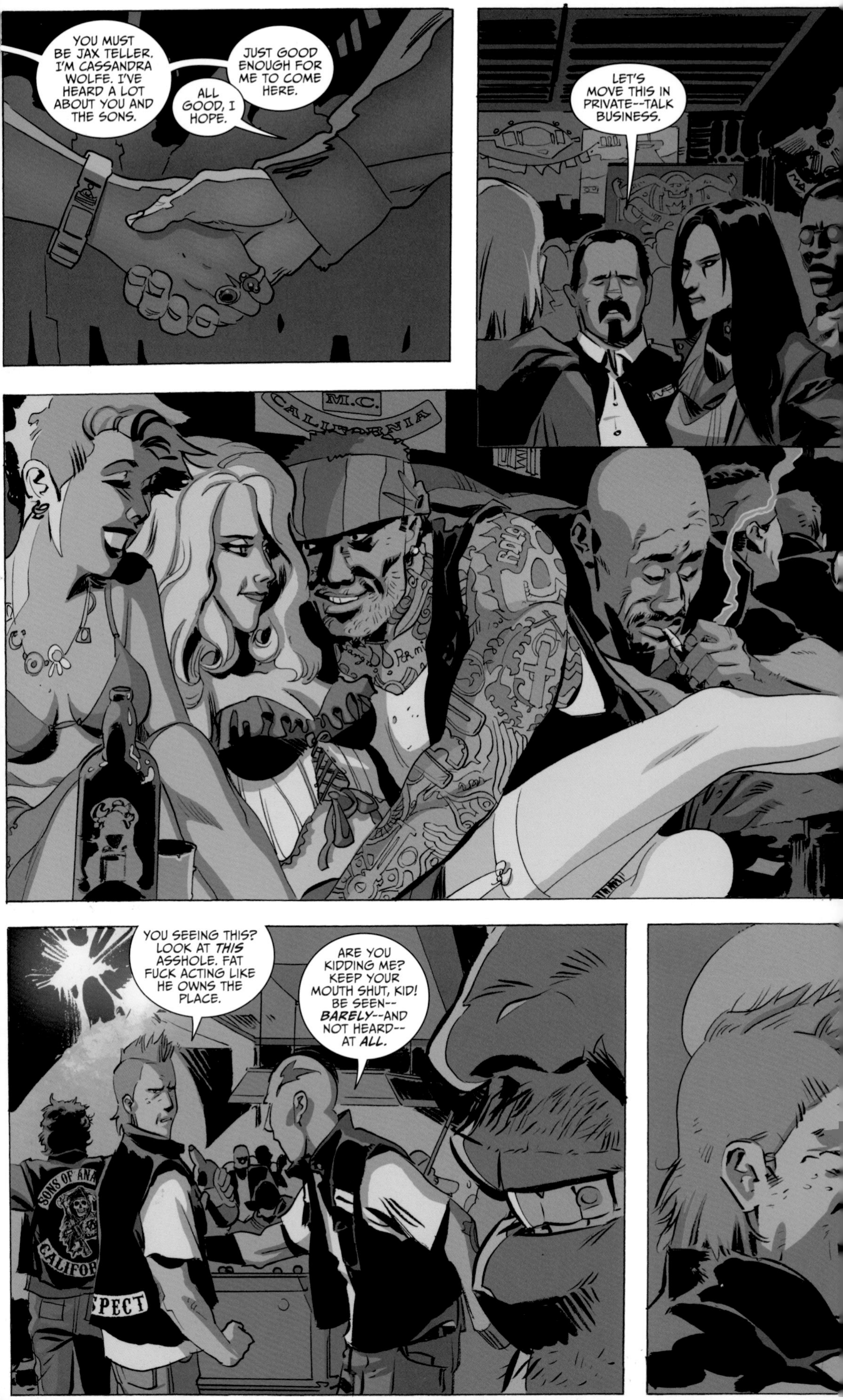

YOU MUST BE JAX TELLER. I'M CASSANDRA WOLFE. I'VE HEARD A LOT ABOUT YOU AND THE SONS.
ALL GOOD, I HOPE.
JUST GOOD ENOUGH FOR ME TO COME HERE.
LET'S MOVE THIS IN PRIVATE--TALK BUSINESS.
M.C.
CALIFORNIA
YOU SEEING THIS? LOOK AT THIS ASSHOLE. FAT FUCK ACTING LIKE HE OWNS THE PLACE.
ARE YOU KIDDING ME? KEEP YOUR MOUTH SHUT, KID! BE SEEN--BARELY--AND NOT HEARD--AT ALL.
SONS OF ANA
CALIFOR
SPECT

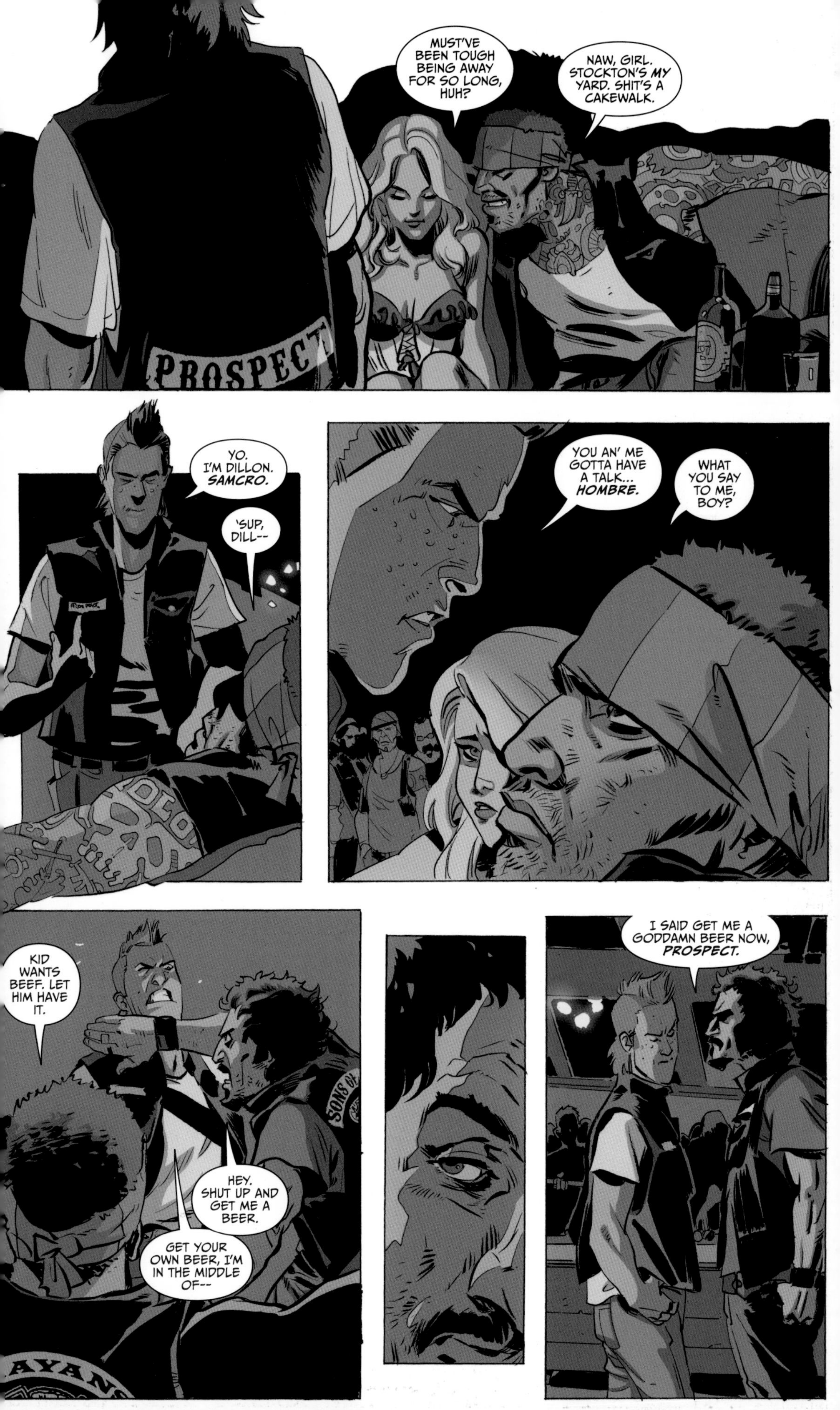
MUST'VE BEEN TOUGH BEING AWAY FOR SO LONG, HUH?
NAW, GIRL. STOCKTON'S MY YARD. SHIT'S A CAKEWALK.
PROSPECT
YO. I'M DILLON. SAMCRO.
'SUP, DILL--
YOU AN' ME GOTTA HAVE A TALK... HOMBRE.
WHAT YOU SAY TO ME, BOY?
KID WANTS BEEF. LET HIM HAVE IT.
HEY. SHUT UP AND GET ME A BEER.
GET YOUR OWN BEER, I'M IN THE MIDDLE OF--
I SAID GET ME A GODDAMN BEER NOW, PROSPECT.

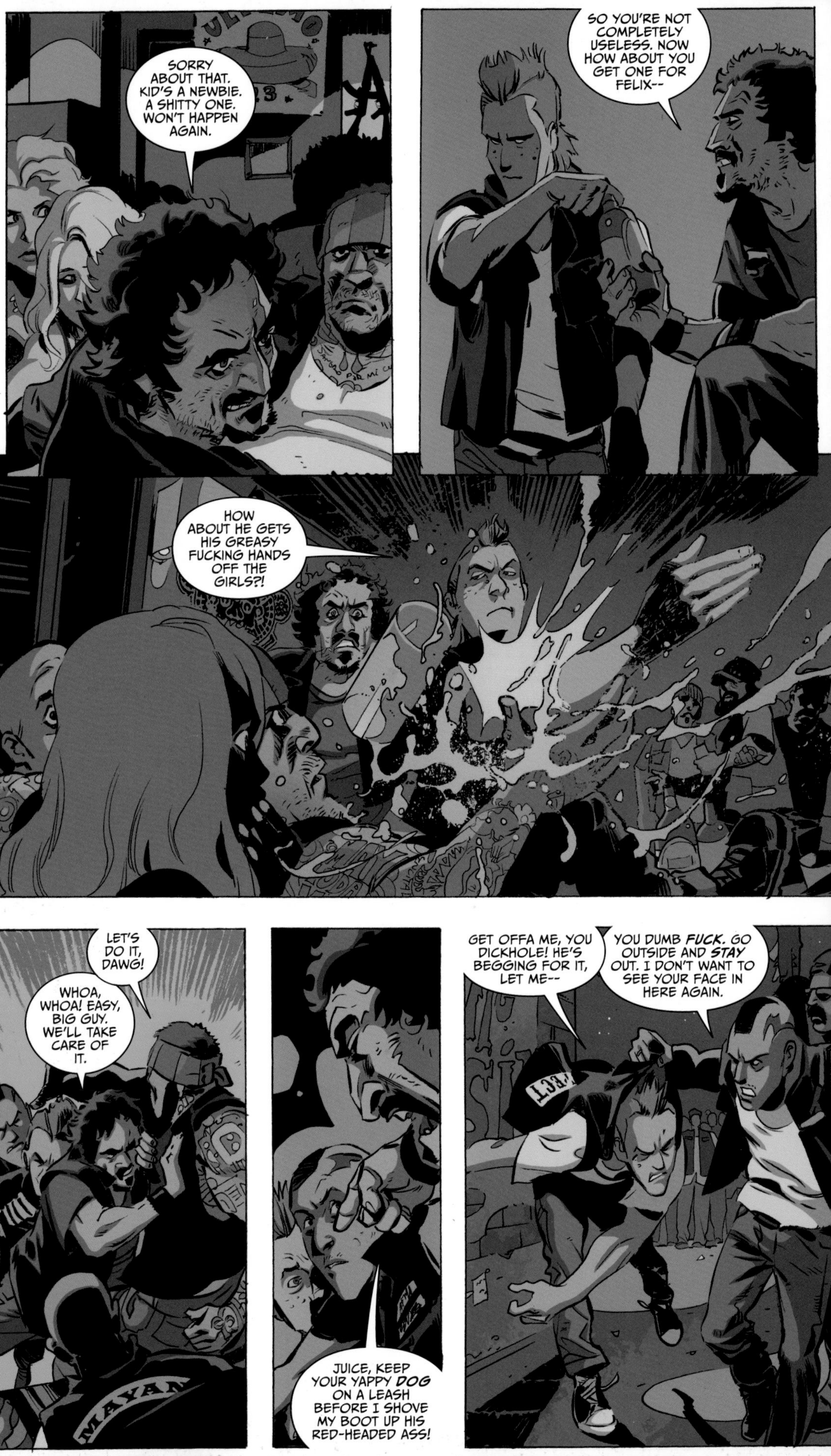
SORRY ABOUT THAT. KID'S A NEWBIE. A SHITTY ONE. WON'T HAPPEN AGAIN.
SO YOU'RE NOT COMPLETELY USELESS. NOW HOW ABOUT YOU GET ONE FOR FELIX--
HOW ABOUT HE GETS HIS GREASY FUCKING HANDS OFF THE GIRLS?!
LET'S DO IT, DAWG!
WHOA, WHOA! EASY, BIG GUY. WE'LL TAKE CARE OF IT.
MAYAN
JUICE, KEEP YOUR YAPPY DOG ON A LEASH BEFORE I SHOVE MY BOOT UP HIS RED-HEADED ASS!
GET OFFA ME, YOU DICKHOLE! HE'S BEGGING FOR IT, LET ME--
YOU DUMB FUCK. GO OUTSIDE AND STAY OUT. I DON'T WANT TO SEE YOUR FACE IN HERE AGAIN.

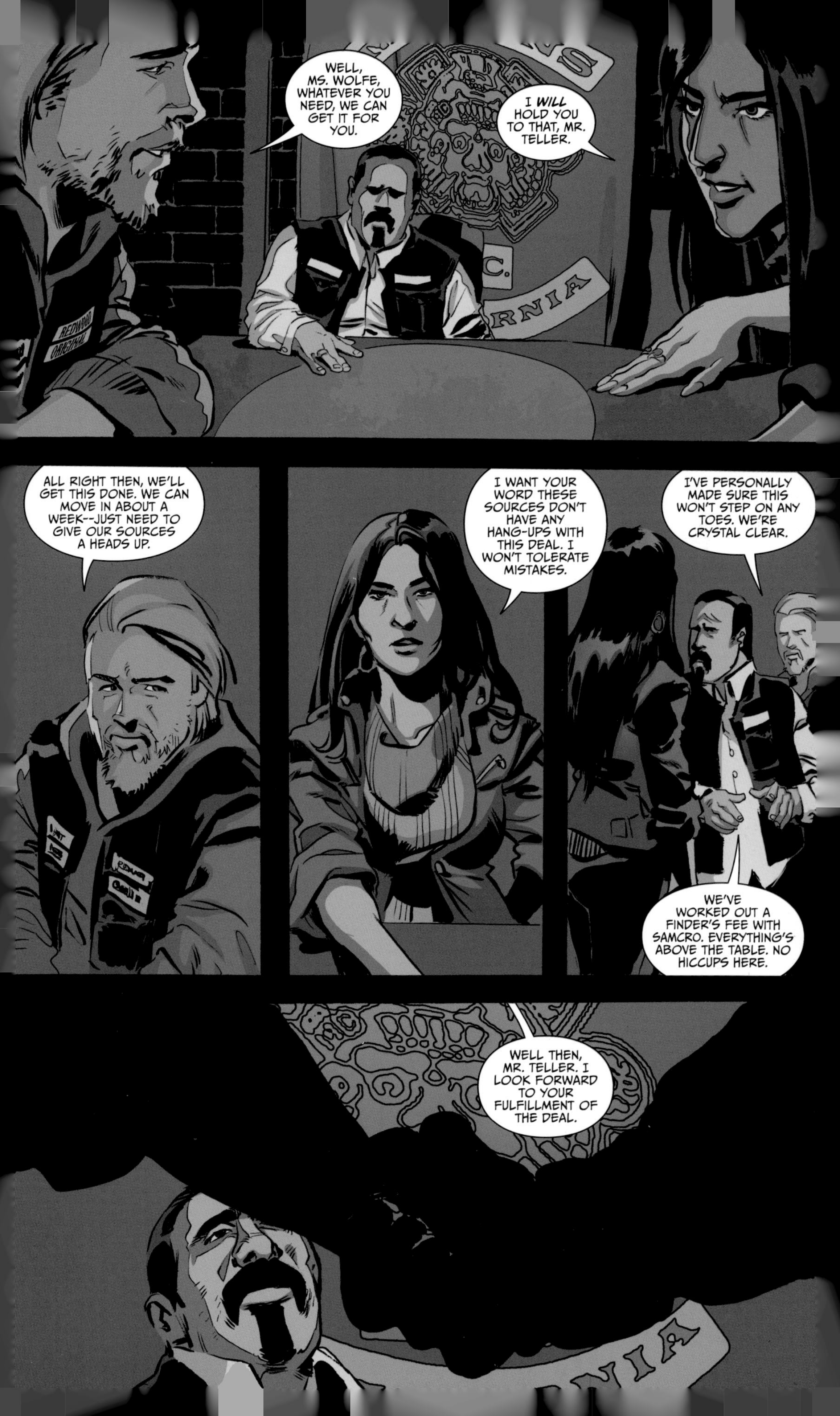
WELL, MS. WOLFE, WHATEVER YOU NEED, WE CAN GET IT FOR YOU.
I WILL HOLD YOU TO THAT, MR. TELLER.
ALL RIGHT THEN, WE'LL GET THIS DONE. WE CAN MOVE IN ABOUT A WEEK--JUST NEED TO GIVE OUR SOURCES A HEADS UP.
I WANT YOUR WORD THESE SOURCES DON'T HAVE ANY HANG-UPS WITH THIS DEAL. I WON'T TOLERATE MISTAKES.
I'VE PERSONALLY MADE SURE THIS WON'T STEP ON ANY TOES. WE'RE CRYSTAL CLEAR.
WE'VE WORKED OUT A FINDER'S FEE WITH SAMCRO. EVERYTHING'S ABOVE THE TABLE. NO HICCUPS HERE.
WELL THEN, MR. TELLER. I LOOK FORWARD TO YOUR FULFILLMENT OF THE DEAL.

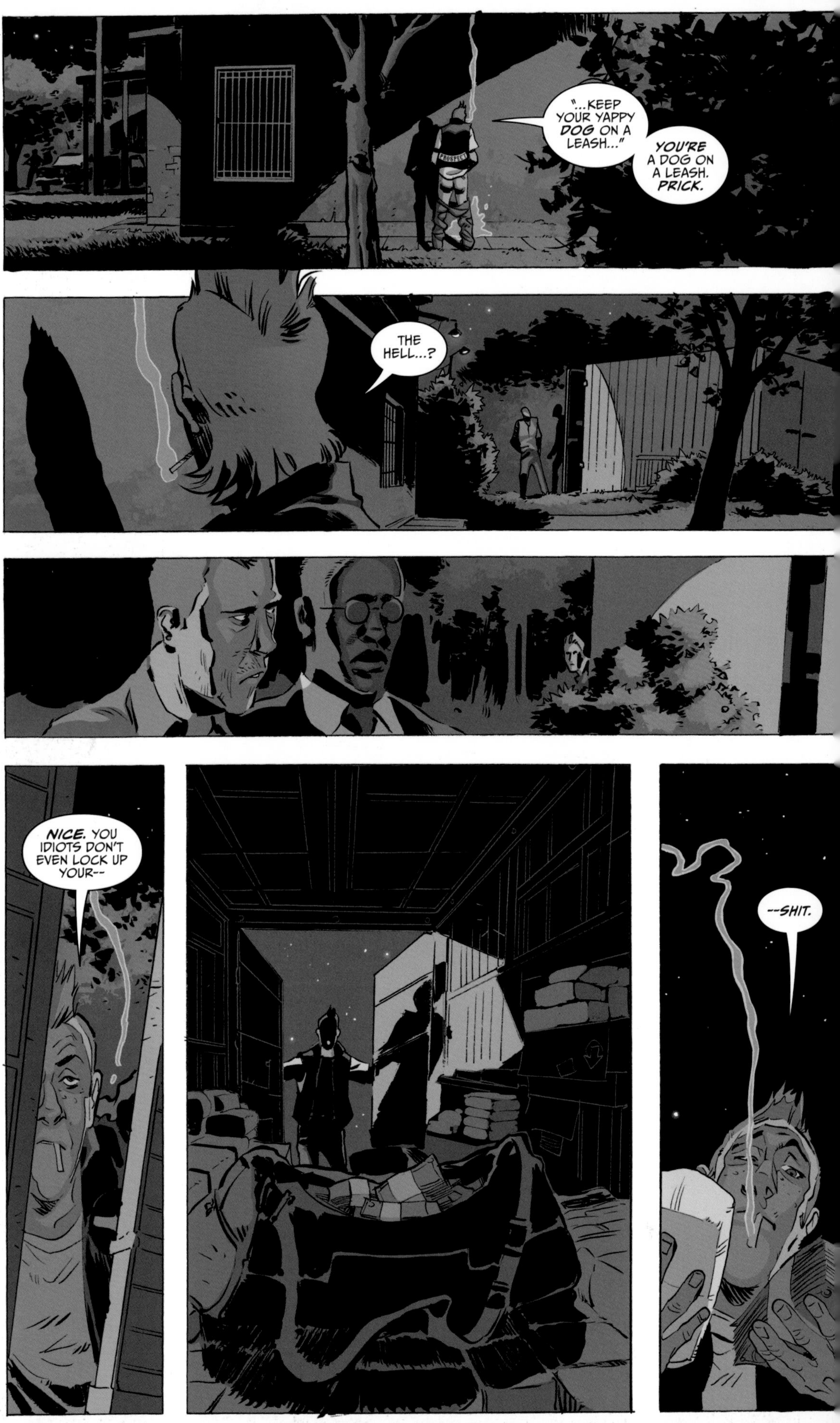
"...KEEP YOUR YAPPY DOG ON A LEASH..."
YOU'RE A DOG ON A LEASH. PRICK.
PROSPECT
THE HELL...?
NICE. YOU IDIOTS DON'T EVEN LOCK UP YOUR--
--SHIT.

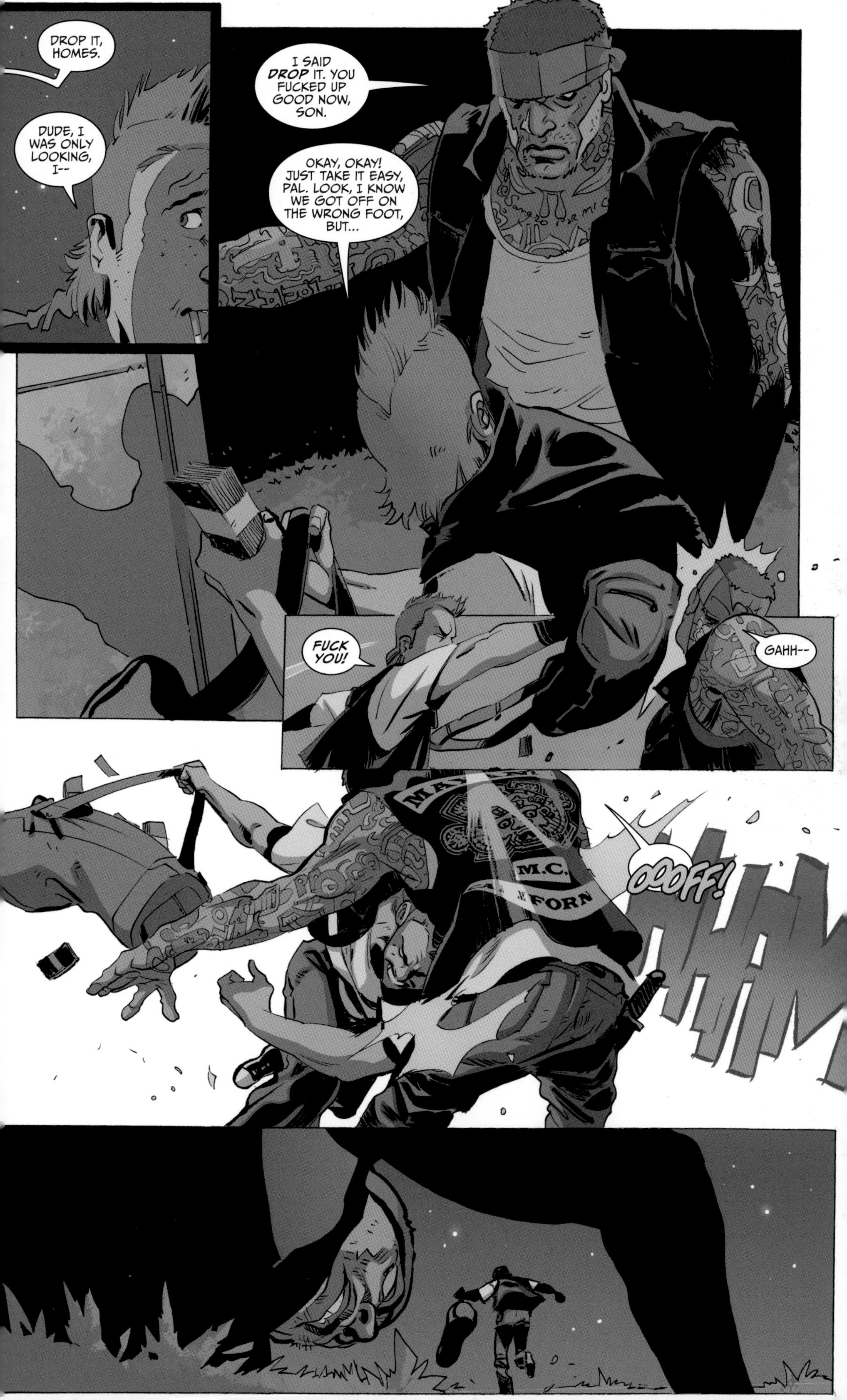
DROP IT, HOMES.
DUDE, I WAS ONLY LOOKING, I--
I SAID DROP IT. YOU FUCKED UP GOOD NOW, SON.
OKAY, OKAY! JUST TAKE IT EASY, PAL. LOOK, I KNOW WE GOT OFF ON THE WRONG FOOT, BUT...
FUCK YOU!
GAHH--
M.C.
FORN
OOOFF!

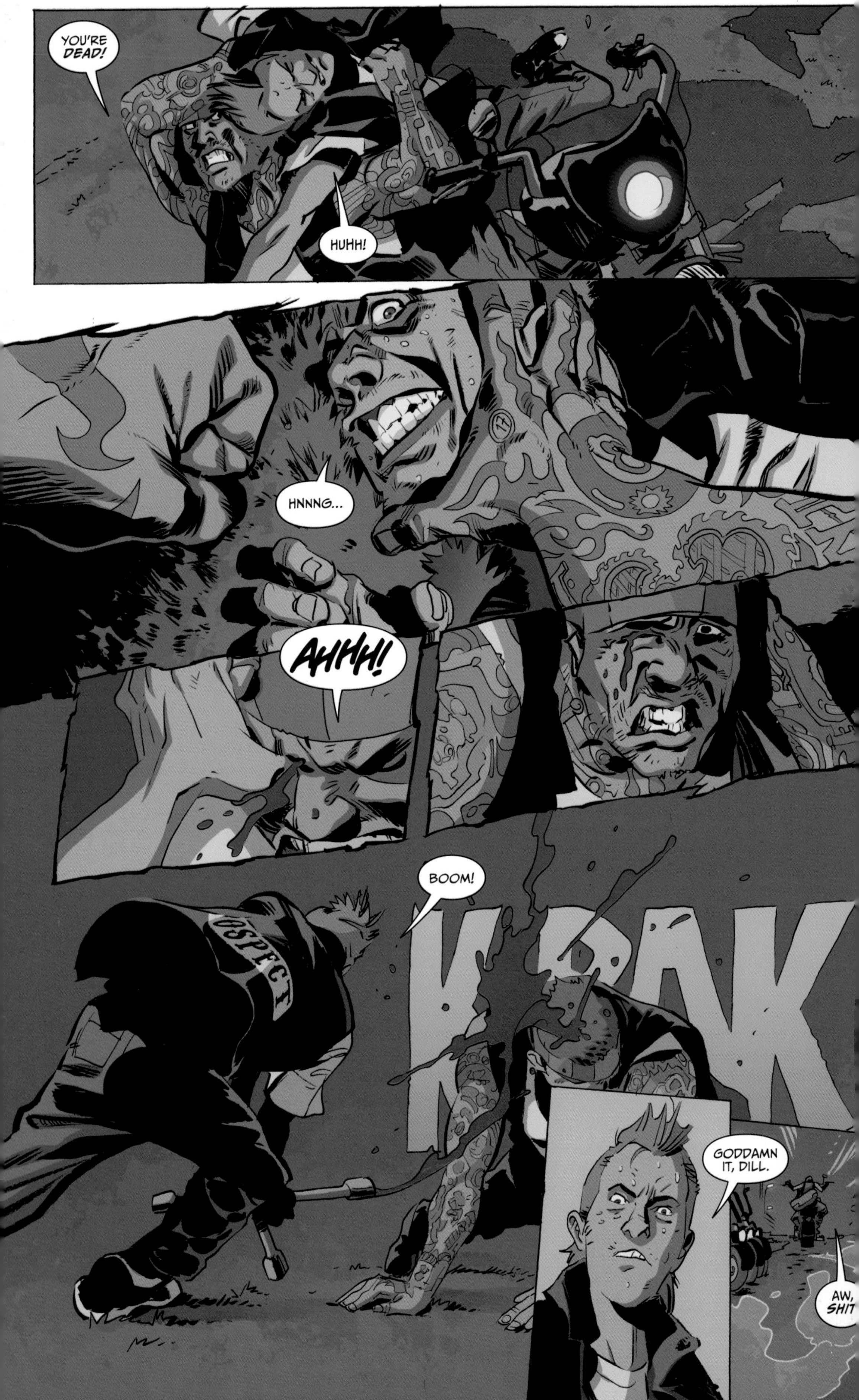
YOU'RE DEAD!
HUHH!
HNNNG...
AHHH!
BOOM!
GODDAMN IT, DILL.
AW, SHIT

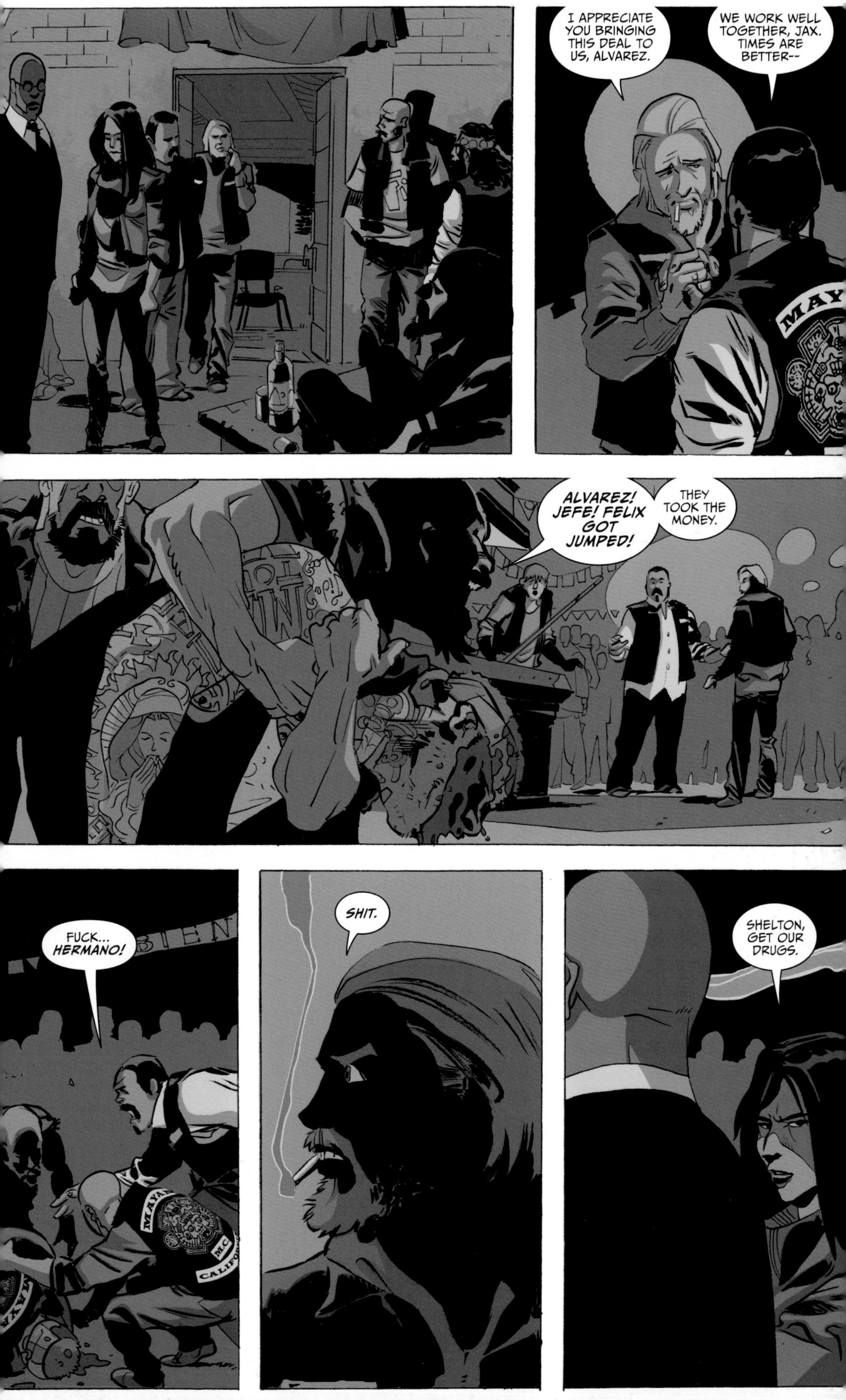
I APPRECIATE YOU BRINGING THIS DEAL TO US, ALVAREZ.
WE WORK WELL TOGETHER, JAX. TIMES ARE BETTER--
ALVAREZ! JEFE! FELIX GOT JUMPED!
THEY TOOK THE MONEY.
FUCK... HERMANO!
SHIT.
SHELTON, GET OUR DRUGS.

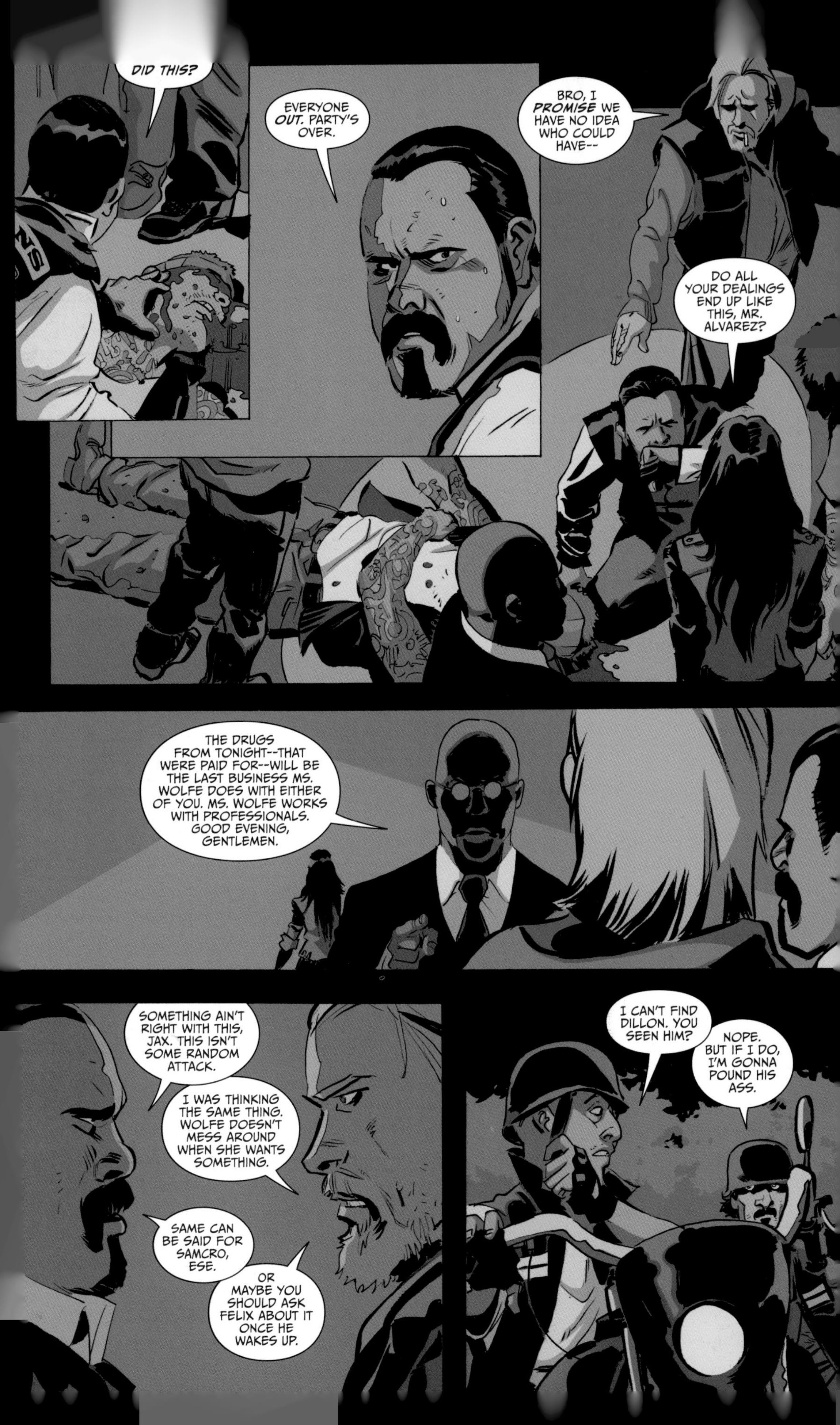

DID THIS?
EVERYONE OUT. PARTY'S OVER.
BRO, I PROMISE WE HAVE NO IDEA WHO COULD HAVE--
DO ALL YOUR DEALINGS END UP LIKE THIS, MR. ALVAREZ?
THE DRUGS FROM TONIGHT--THAT WERE PAID FOR--WILL BE THE LAST BUSINESS MS. WOLFE DOES WITH EITHER OF YOU. MS. WOLFE WORKS WITH PROFESSIONALS. GOOD EVENING, GENTLEMEN.
SOMETHING AIN'T RIGHT WITH THIS, JAX. THIS ISN'T SOME RANDOM ATTACK.
I WAS THINKING THE SAME THING. WOLFE DOESN'T MESS AROUND WHEN SHE WANTS SOMETHING.
SAME CAN BE SAID FOR SAMCRO, ESE.
OR MAYBE YOU SHOULD ASK FELIX ABOUT IT ONCE HE WAKES UP.
I CAN'T FIND DILLON. YOU SEEN HIM?
NOPE. BUT IF I DO, I'M GONNA POUND HIS ASS.

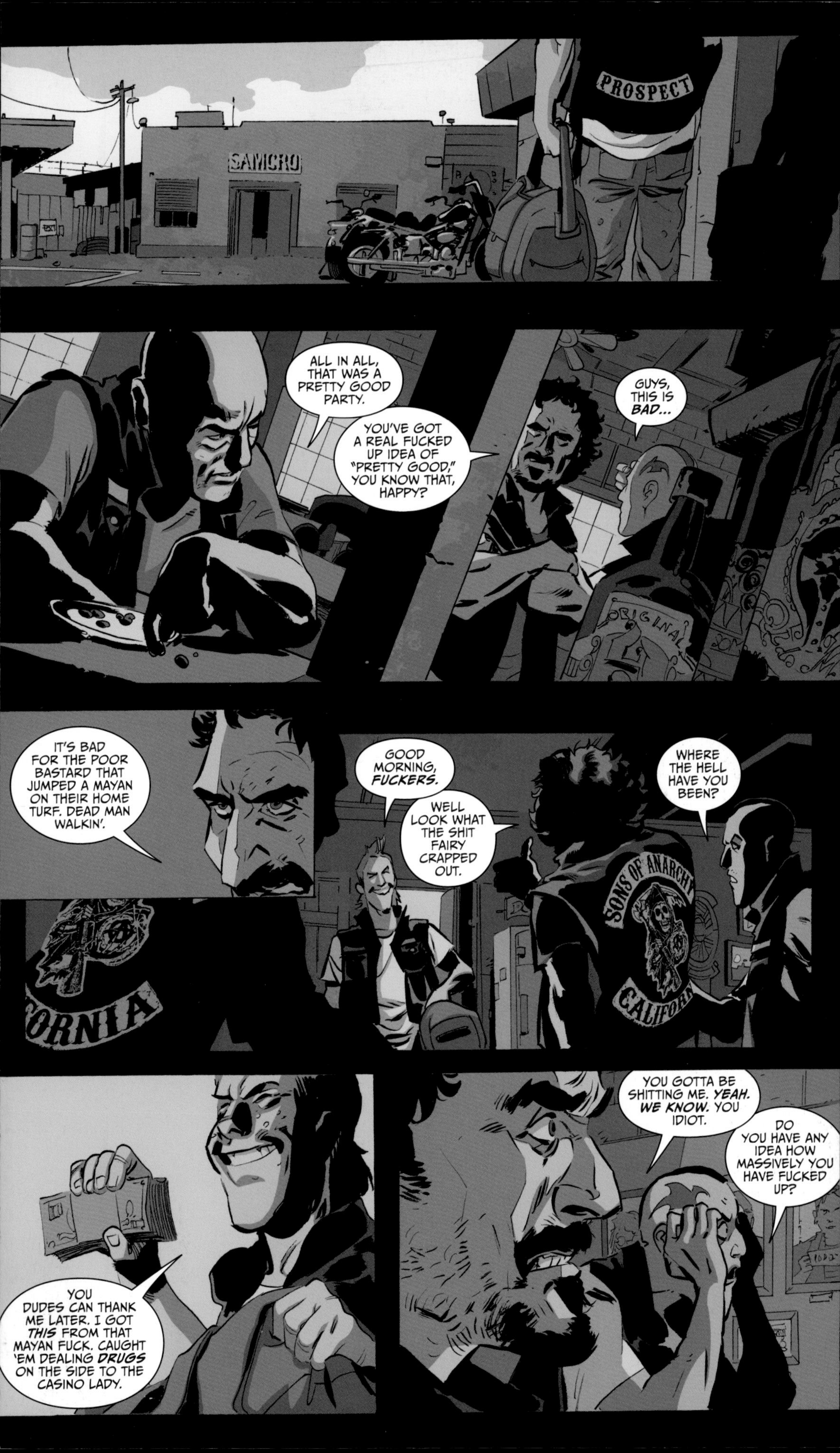
PROSPECT
SAMCRO
ALL IN ALL, THAT WAS A PRETTY GOOD PARTY.
YOU'VE GOT A REAL FUCKED UP IDEA OF "PRETTY GOOD," YOU KNOW THAT, HAPPY?
GUYS, THIS IS **BAD...**
ORIGINAL
IT'S BAD FOR THE POOR BASTARD THAT JUMPED A MAYAN ON THEIR HOME TURF. DEAD MAN WALKIN'.
GOOD MORNING, ***FUCKERS.***
WELL LOOK WHAT THE SHIT FAIRY CRAPPED OUT.
WHERE THE HELL HAVE YOU BEEN?
SONS OF ANARCHY
CALIFORN
ORNIA
YOU DUDES CAN THANK ME LATER. I GOT ***THIS*** FROM THAT MAYAN FUCK. CAUGHT 'EM DEALING ***DRUGS*** ON THE SIDE TO THE CASINO LADY.
YOU GOTTA BE SHITTING ME. ***YEAH. WE KNOW.*** YOU IDIOT.
DO YOU HAVE ANY IDEA HOW MASSIVELY YOU HAVE FUCKED UP?

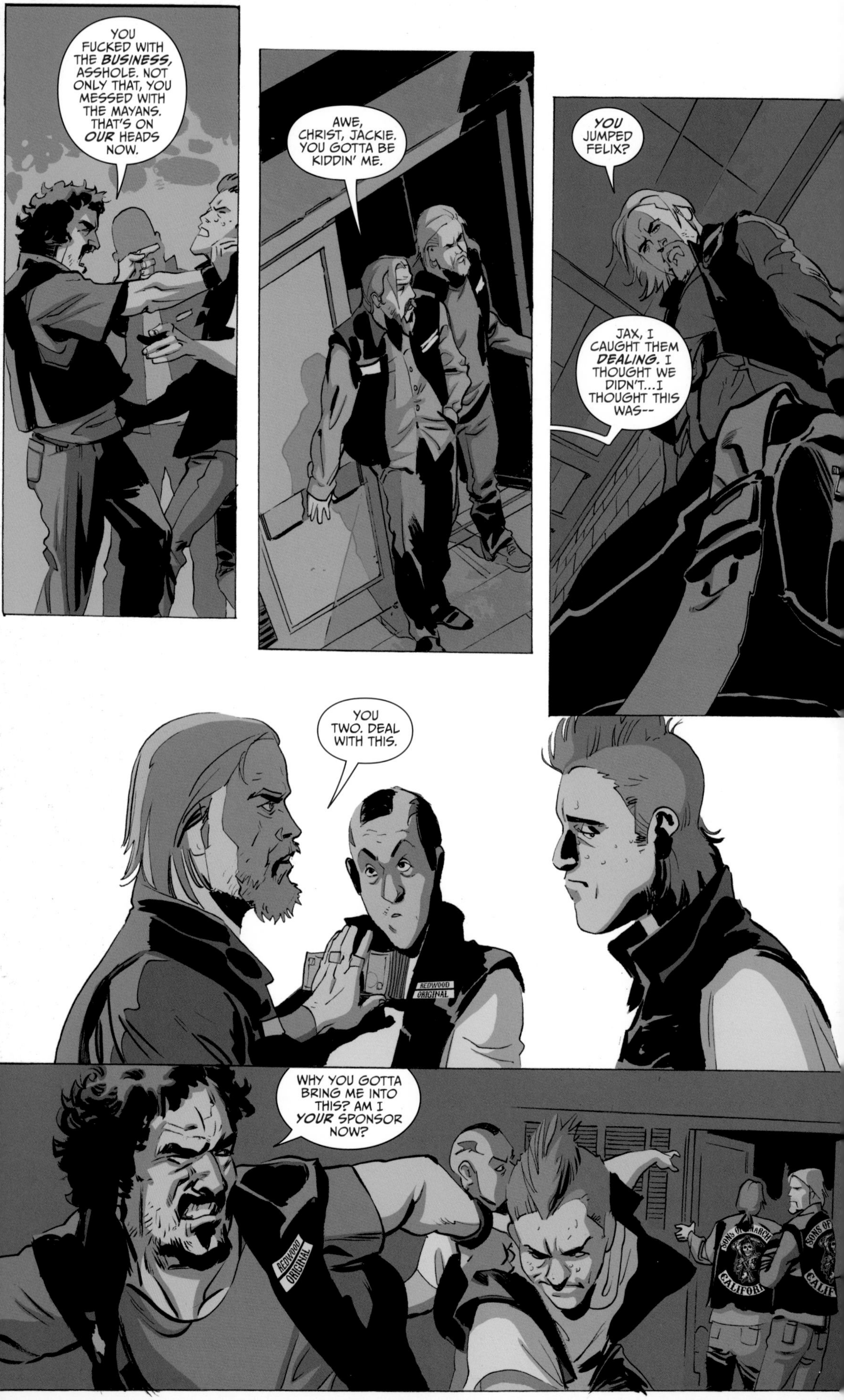

YOU FUCKED WITH THE BUSINESS, ASSHOLE. NOT ONLY THAT, YOU MESSED WITH THE MAYANS. THAT'S ON OUR HEADS NOW.
AWE, CHRIST, JACKIE. YOU GOTTA BE KIDDIN' ME.
YOU JUMPED FELIX?
JAX, I CAUGHT THEM DEALING. I THOUGHT WE DIDN'T...I THOUGHT THIS WAS--
YOU TWO. DEAL WITH THIS.
REDWOOD ORIGINAL
WHY YOU GOTTA BRING ME INTO THIS? AM I YOUR SPONSOR NOW?
REDWOOD ORIGINAL

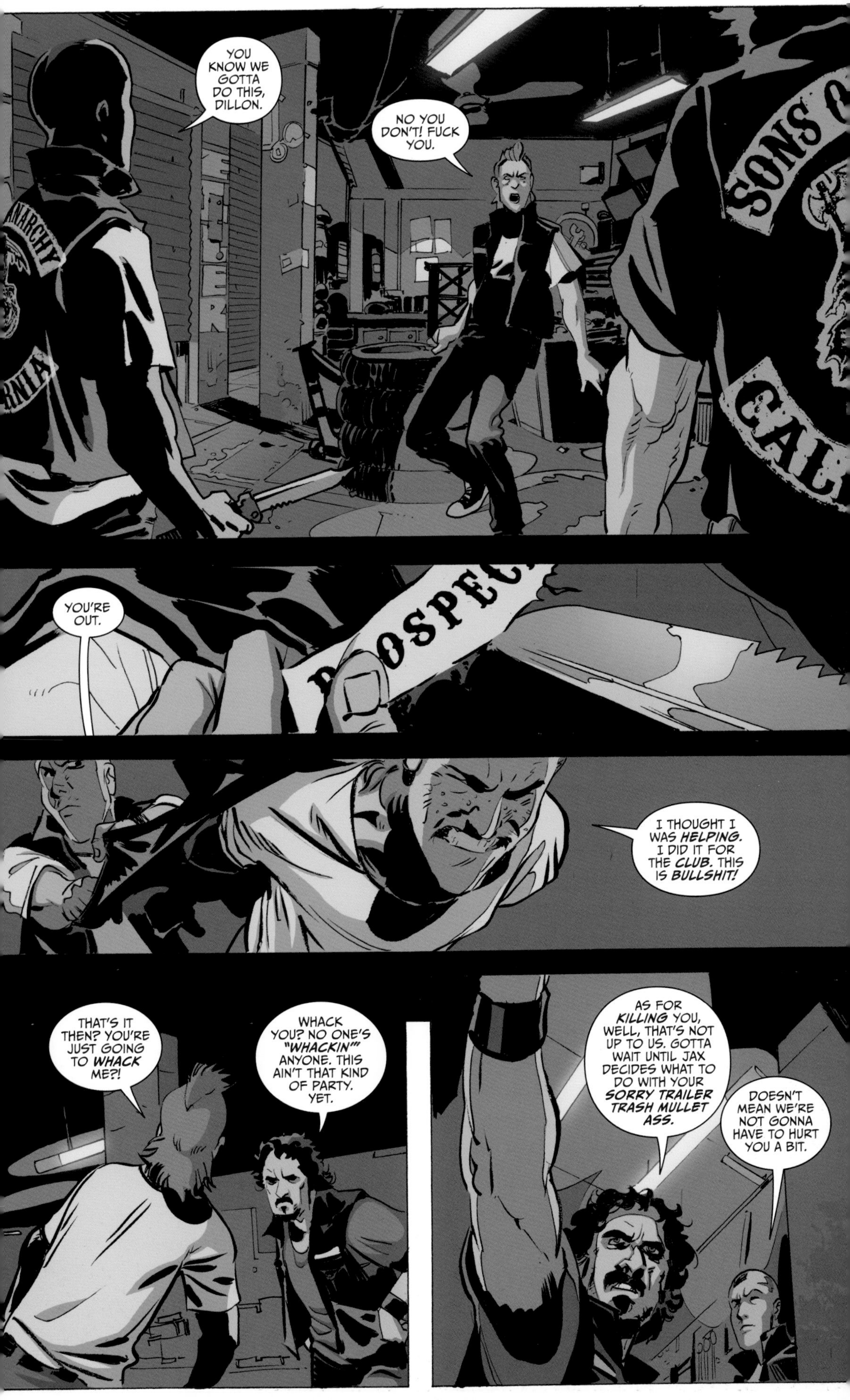
YOU KNOW WE GOTTA DO THIS, DILLON.
NO YOU DON'T! FUCK YOU.
SONS OF
CAL
ANARCHY
RNIA
YOU'RE OUT.
OSPEC
I THOUGHT I WAS *HELPING.* I DID IT FOR THE *CLUB.* THIS IS *BULLSHIT!*
THAT'S IT THEN? YOU'RE JUST GOING TO *WHACK* ME?!
WHACK YOU? NO ONE'S *"WHACKIN'"* ANYONE. THIS AIN'T THAT KIND OF PARTY. YET.
AS FOR *KILLING* YOU, WELL, THAT'S NOT UP TO US. GOTTA WAIT UNTIL JAX DECIDES WHAT TO DO WITH YOUR *SORRY TRAILER TRASH MULLET ASS.*
DOESN'T MEAN WE'RE NOT GONNA HAVE TO HURT YOU A BIT.

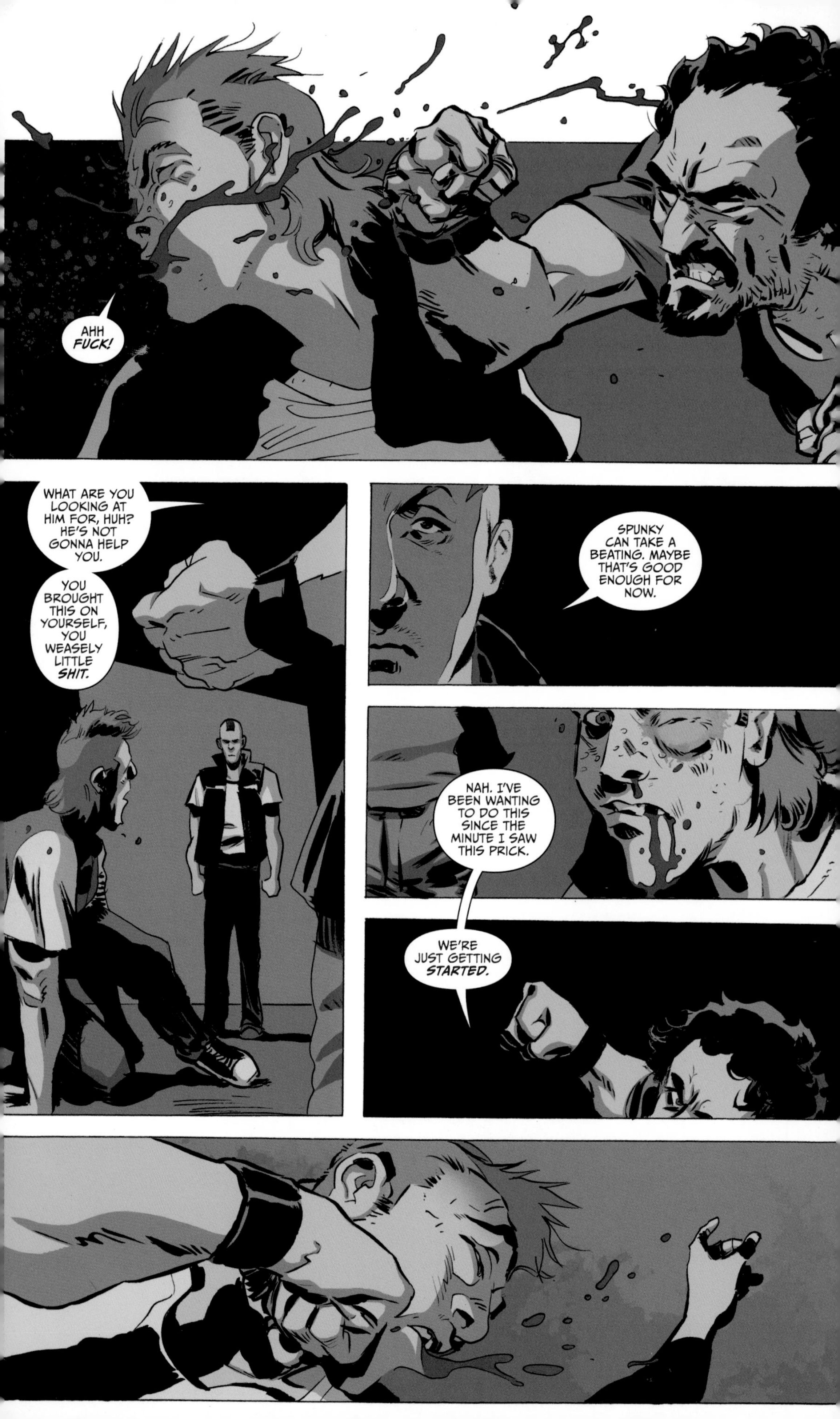
AHH FUCK!
WHAT ARE YOU LOOKING AT HIM FOR, HUH? HE'S NOT GONNA HELP YOU.
YOU BROUGHT THIS ON YOURSELF, YOU WEASELY LITTLE SHIT.
SPUNKY CAN TAKE A BEATING. MAYBE THAT'S GOOD ENOUGH FOR NOW.
NAH. I'VE BEEN WANTING TO DO THIS SINCE THE MINUTE I SAW THIS PRICK.
WE'RE JUST GETTING STARTED.

CHAPTER 20

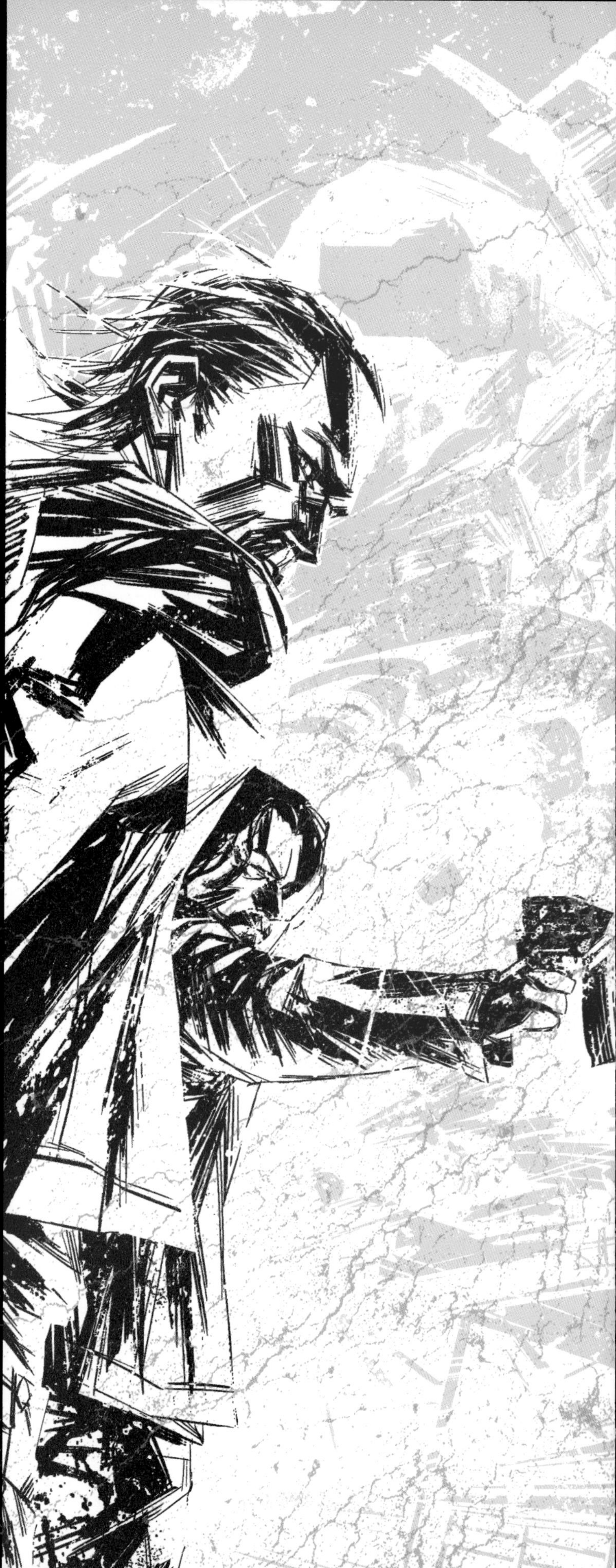

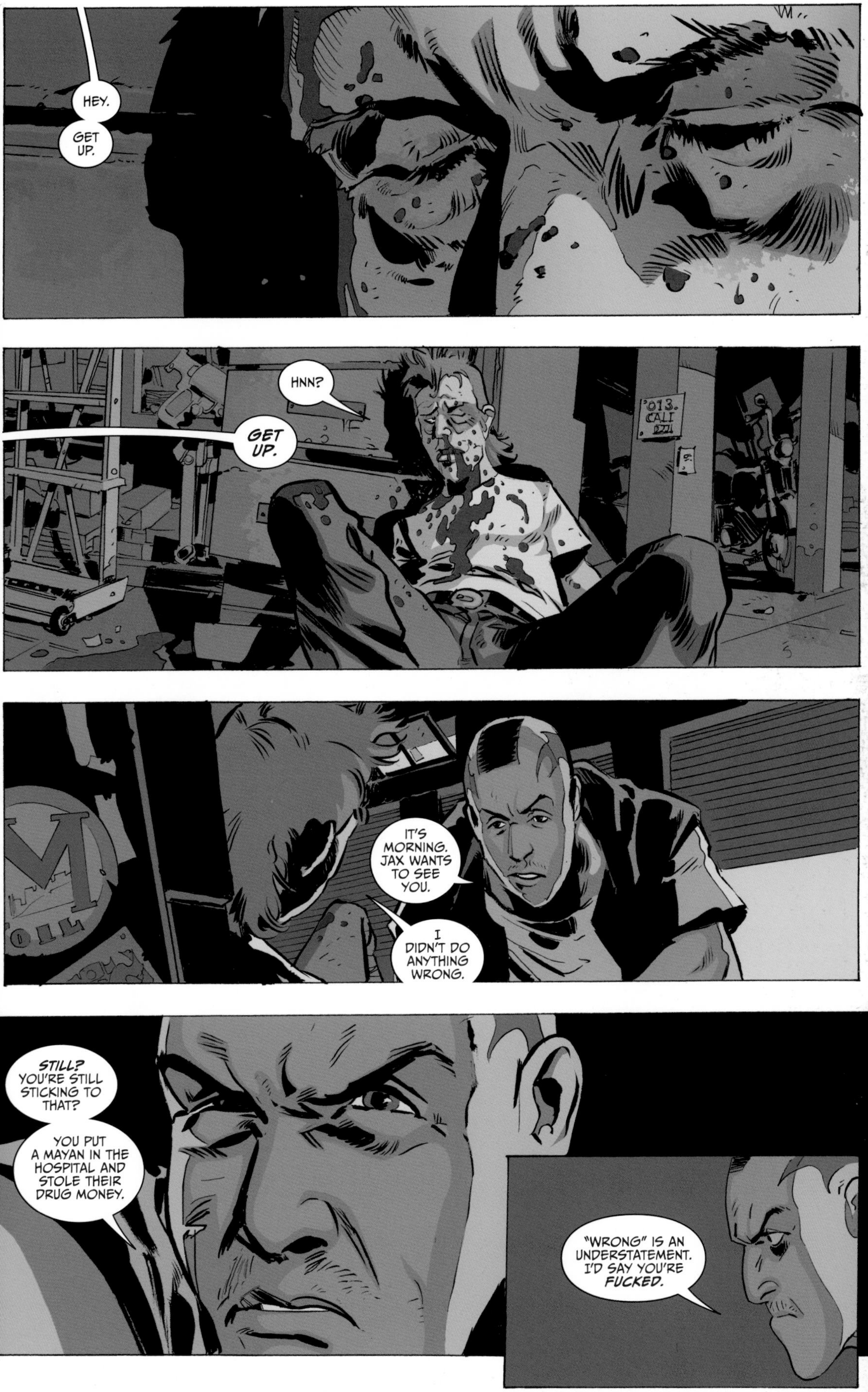

HEY.
GET UP.
HNN?
GET UP.
'013. CALI
IT'S MORNING. JAX WANTS TO SEE YOU.
I DIDN'T DO ANYTHING WRONG.
STILL? YOU'RE STILL STICKING TO THAT?
YOU PUT A MAYAN IN THE HOSPITAL AND STOLE THEIR DRUG MONEY.
"WRONG" IS AN UNDERSTATEMENT. I'D SAY YOU'RE FUCKED.

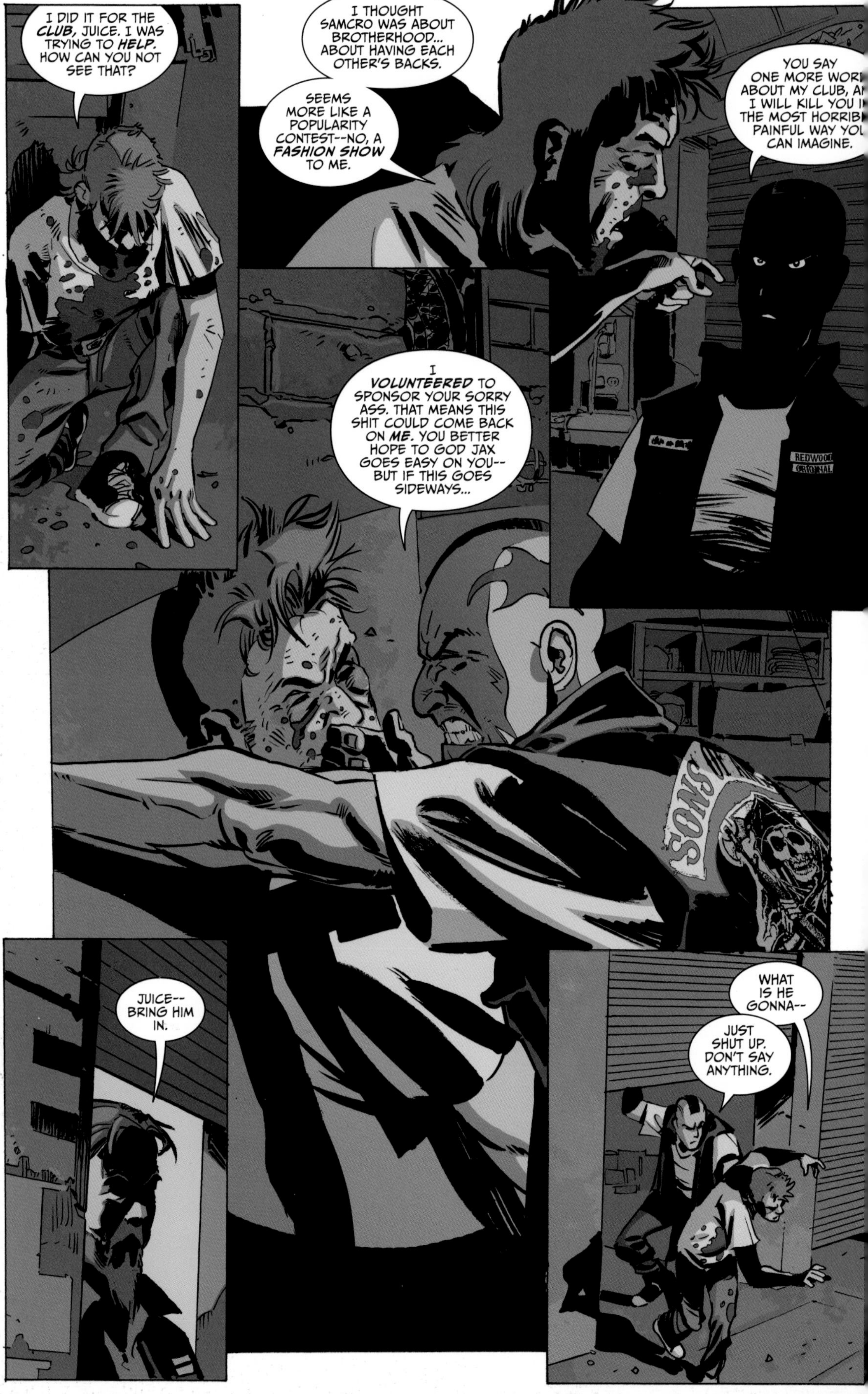
I DID IT FOR THE *CLUB*, JUICE. I WAS TRYING TO *HELP*. HOW CAN YOU NOT SEE THAT?
I THOUGHT SAMCRO WAS ABOUT BROTHERHOOD... ABOUT HAVING EACH OTHER'S BACKS.
SEEMS MORE LIKE A POPULARITY CONTEST--NO, A *FASHION SHOW* TO ME.
YOU SAY ONE MORE WOR ABOUT MY CLUB, A I WILL KILL YOU THE MOST HORRIB PAINFUL WAY YO CAN IMAGINE.
REDWOOD ORIGINAL
I *VOLUNTEERED* TO SPONSOR YOUR SORRY ASS. THAT MEANS THIS SHIT COULD COME BACK ON *ME*. YOU BETTER HOPE TO GOD JAX GOES EASY ON YOU-- BUT IF THIS GOES SIDEWAYS...
SONS
JUICE-- BRING HIM IN.
WHAT IS HE GONNA--
JUST SHUT UP. DON'T SAY ANYTHING.

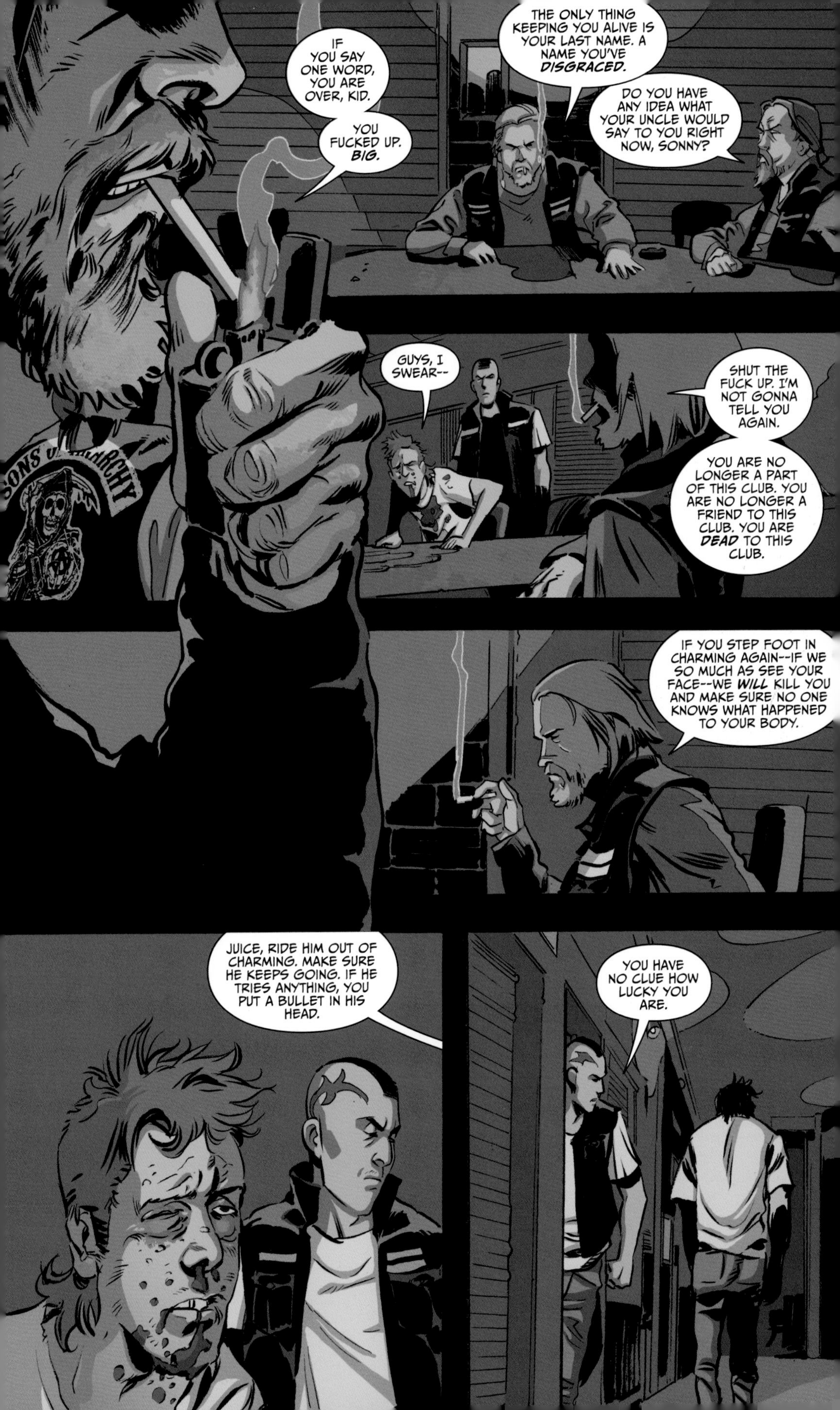
IF YOU SAY ONE WORD, YOU ARE OVER, KID.
YOU FUCKED UP. BIG.
THE ONLY THING KEEPING YOU ALIVE IS YOUR LAST NAME. A NAME YOU'VE DISGRACED.
DO YOU HAVE ANY IDEA WHAT YOUR UNCLE WOULD SAY TO YOU RIGHT NOW, SONNY?
SONS OF ANARCHY
GUYS, I SWEAR--
SHUT THE FUCK UP. I'M NOT GONNA TELL YOU AGAIN.
YOU ARE NO LONGER A PART OF THIS CLUB. YOU ARE NO LONGER A FRIEND TO THIS CLUB. YOU ARE DEAD TO THIS CLUB.
IF YOU STEP FOOT IN CHARMING AGAIN--IF WE SO MUCH AS SEE YOUR FACE--WE WILL KILL YOU AND MAKE SURE NO ONE KNOWS WHAT HAPPENED TO YOUR BODY.
JUICE, RIDE HIM OUT OF CHARMING. MAKE SURE HE KEEPS GOING. IF HE TRIES ANYTHING, YOU PUT A BULLET IN HIS HEAD.
YOU HAVE NO CLUE HOW LUCKY YOU ARE.

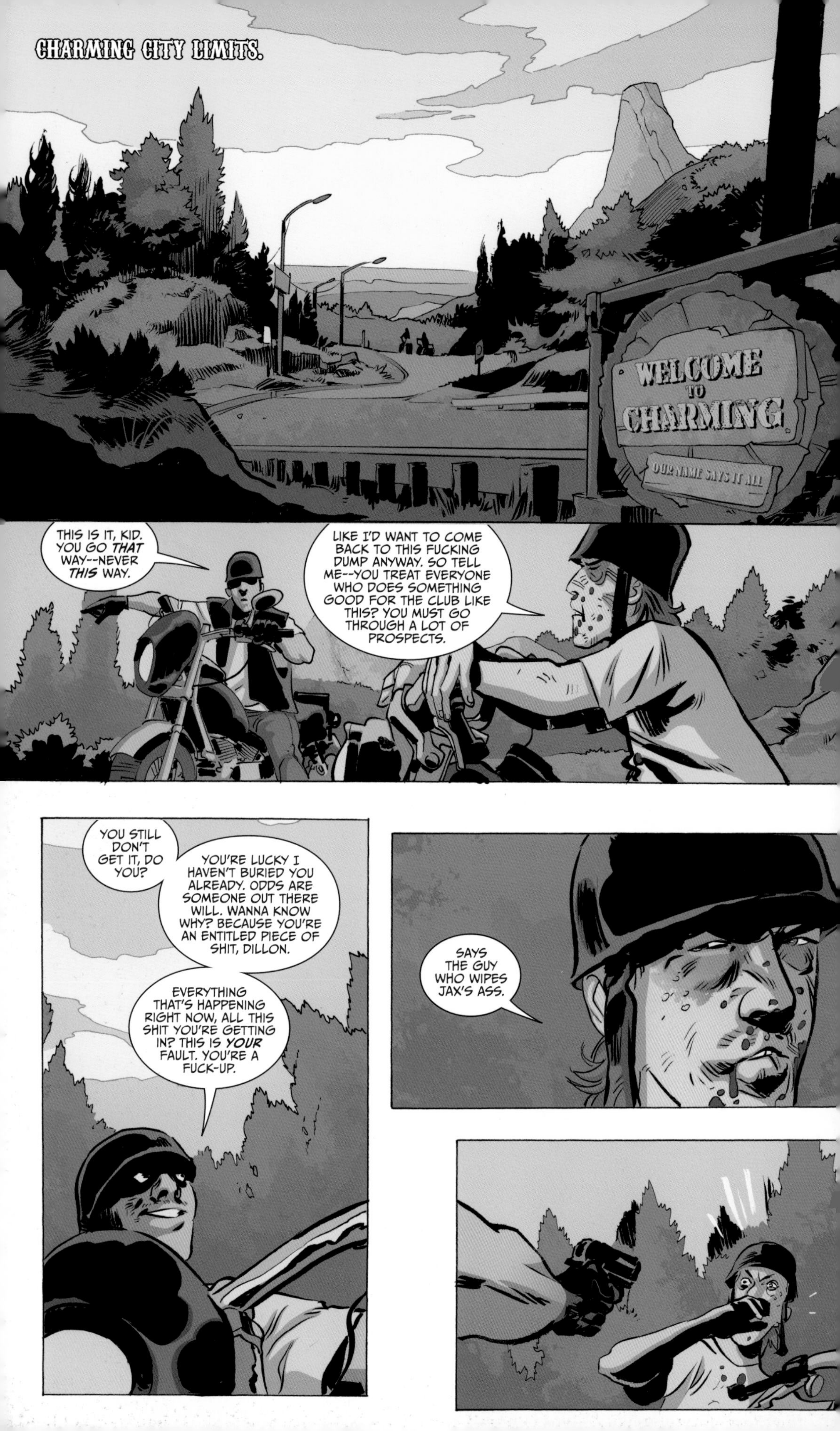
CHARMING CITY LIMITS.
WELCOME TO CHARMING
OUR NAME SAYS IT ALL
THIS IS IT, KID. YOU GO *THAT* WAY--NEVER *THIS* WAY.
LIKE I'D WANT TO COME BACK TO THIS FUCKING DUMP ANYWAY. SO TELL ME--YOU TREAT EVERYONE WHO DOES SOMETHING GOOD FOR THE CLUB LIKE THIS? YOU MUST GO THROUGH A LOT OF PROSPECTS.
YOU STILL DON'T GET IT, DO YOU?
YOU'RE LUCKY I HAVEN'T BURIED YOU ALREADY. ODDS ARE SOMEONE OUT THERE WILL. WANNA KNOW WHY? BECAUSE YOU'RE AN ENTITLED PIECE OF SHIT, DILLON.
EVERYTHING THAT'S HAPPENING RIGHT NOW, ALL THIS SHIT YOU'RE GETTING IN? THIS IS *YOUR* FAULT. YOU'RE A FUCK-UP.
SAYS THE GUY WHO WIPES JAX'S ASS.

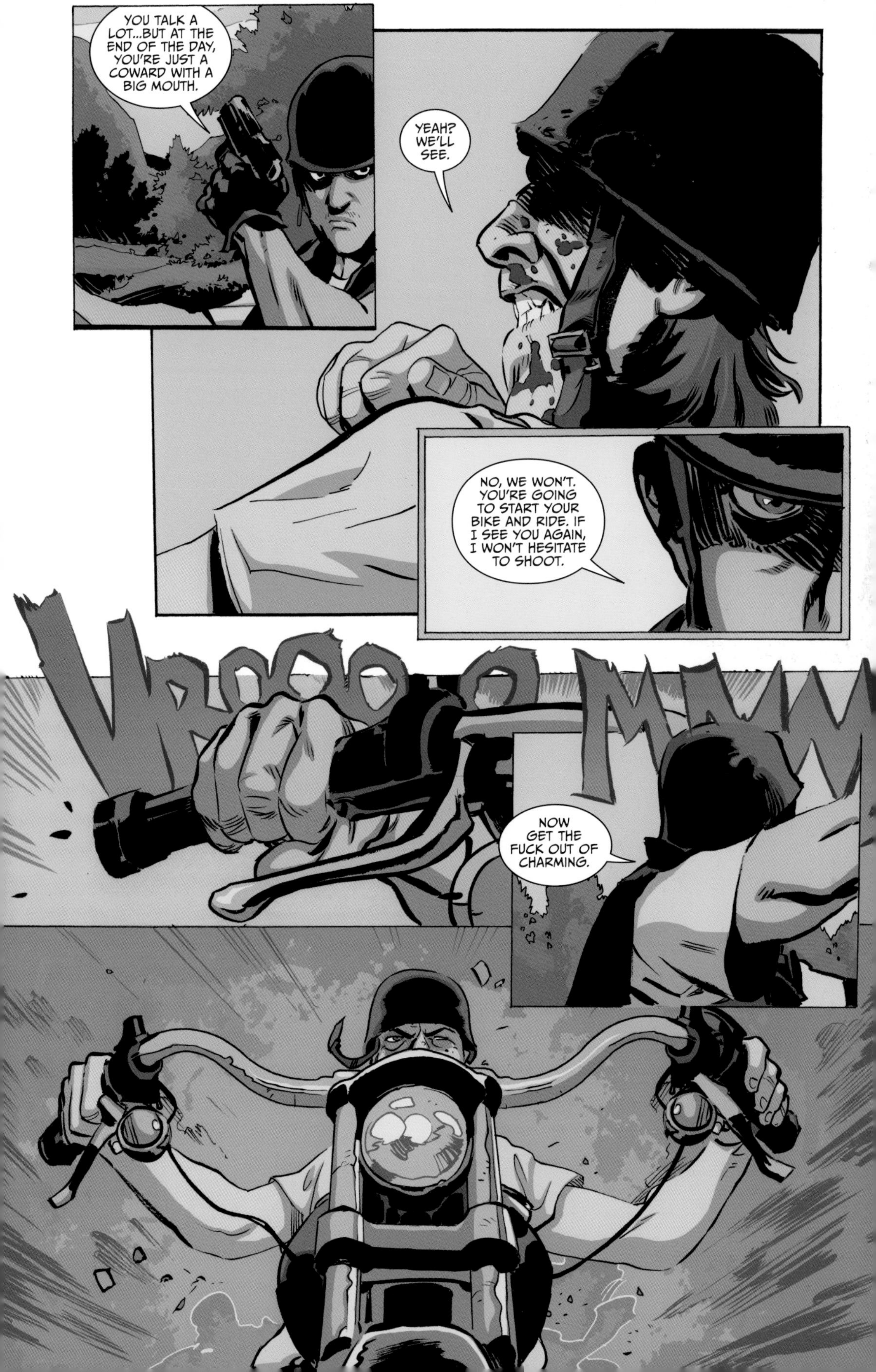
YOU TALK A LOT...BUT AT THE END OF THE DAY, YOU'RE JUST A COWARD WITH A BIG MOUTH.
YEAH? WE'LL SEE.
NO, WE WON'T. YOU'RE GOING TO START YOUR BIKE AND RIDE. IF I SEE YOU AGAIN, I WON'T HESITATE TO SHOOT.
NOW GET THE FUCK OUT OF CHARMING.

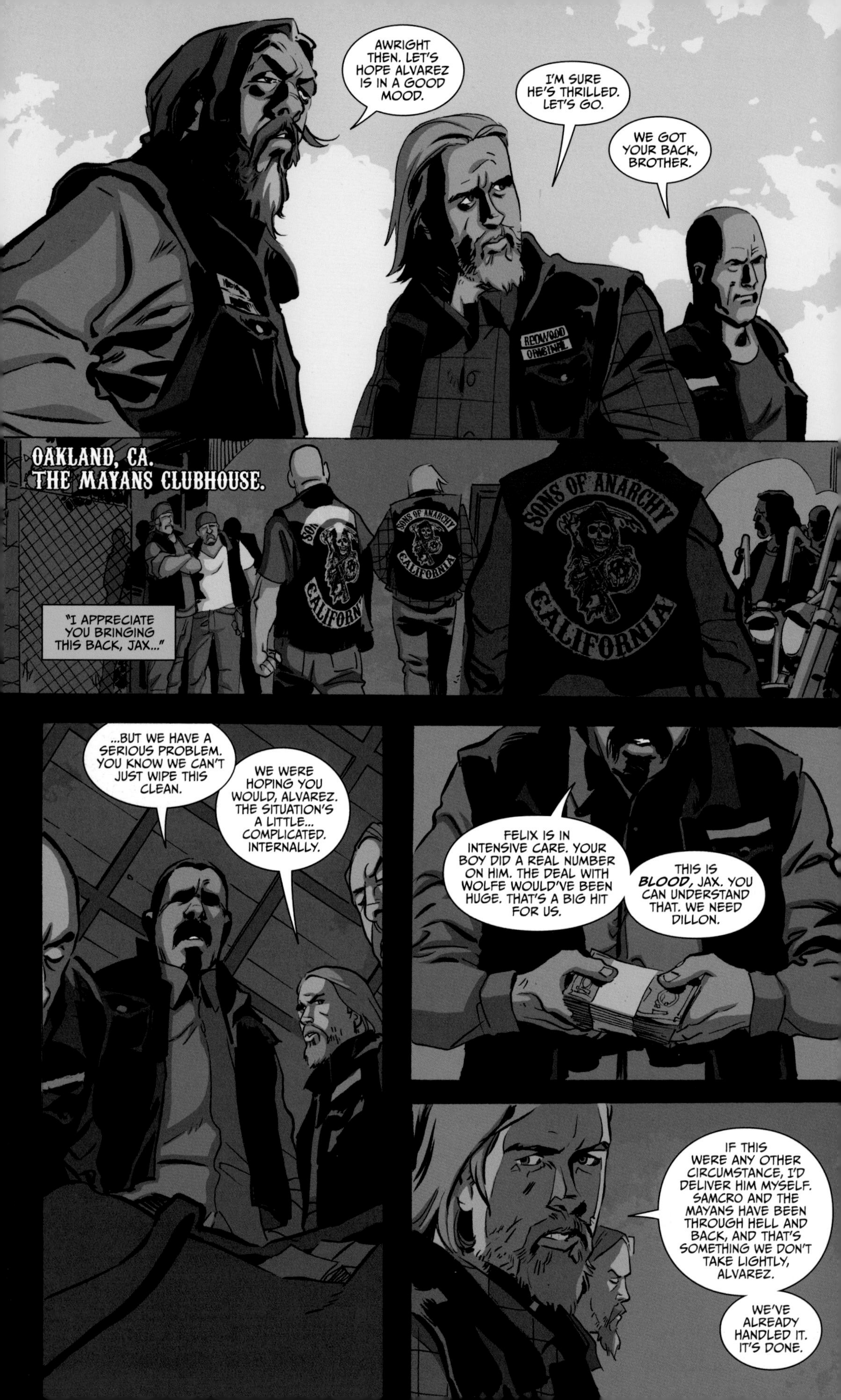
AWRIGHT THEN. LET'S HOPE ALVAREZ IS IN A GOOD MOOD.
I'M SURE HE'S THRILLED. LET'S GO.
WE GOT YOUR BACK, BROTHER.
REDWOOD ORIGINAL
OAKLAND, CA. THE MAYANS CLUBHOUSE.
SONS OF ANARCHY CALIFORNIA
"I APPRECIATE YOU BRINGING THIS BACK, JAX..."
...BUT WE HAVE A SERIOUS PROBLEM. YOU KNOW WE CAN'T JUST WIPE THIS CLEAN.
WE WERE HOPING YOU WOULD, ALVAREZ. THE SITUATION'S A LITTLE... COMPLICATED. INTERNALLY.
FELIX IS IN INTENSIVE CARE. YOUR BOY DID A REAL NUMBER ON HIM. THE DEAL WITH WOLFE WOULD'VE BEEN HUGE. THAT'S A BIG HIT FOR US.
THIS IS ***BLOOD,*** JAX. YOU CAN UNDERSTAND THAT. WE NEED DILLON.
IF THIS WERE ANY OTHER CIRCUMSTANCE, I'D DELIVER HIM MYSELF. SAMCRO AND THE MAYANS HAVE BEEN THROUGH HELL AND BACK, AND THAT'S SOMETHING WE DON'T TAKE LIGHTLY, ALVAREZ.
WE'VE ALREADY HANDLED IT. IT'S DONE.

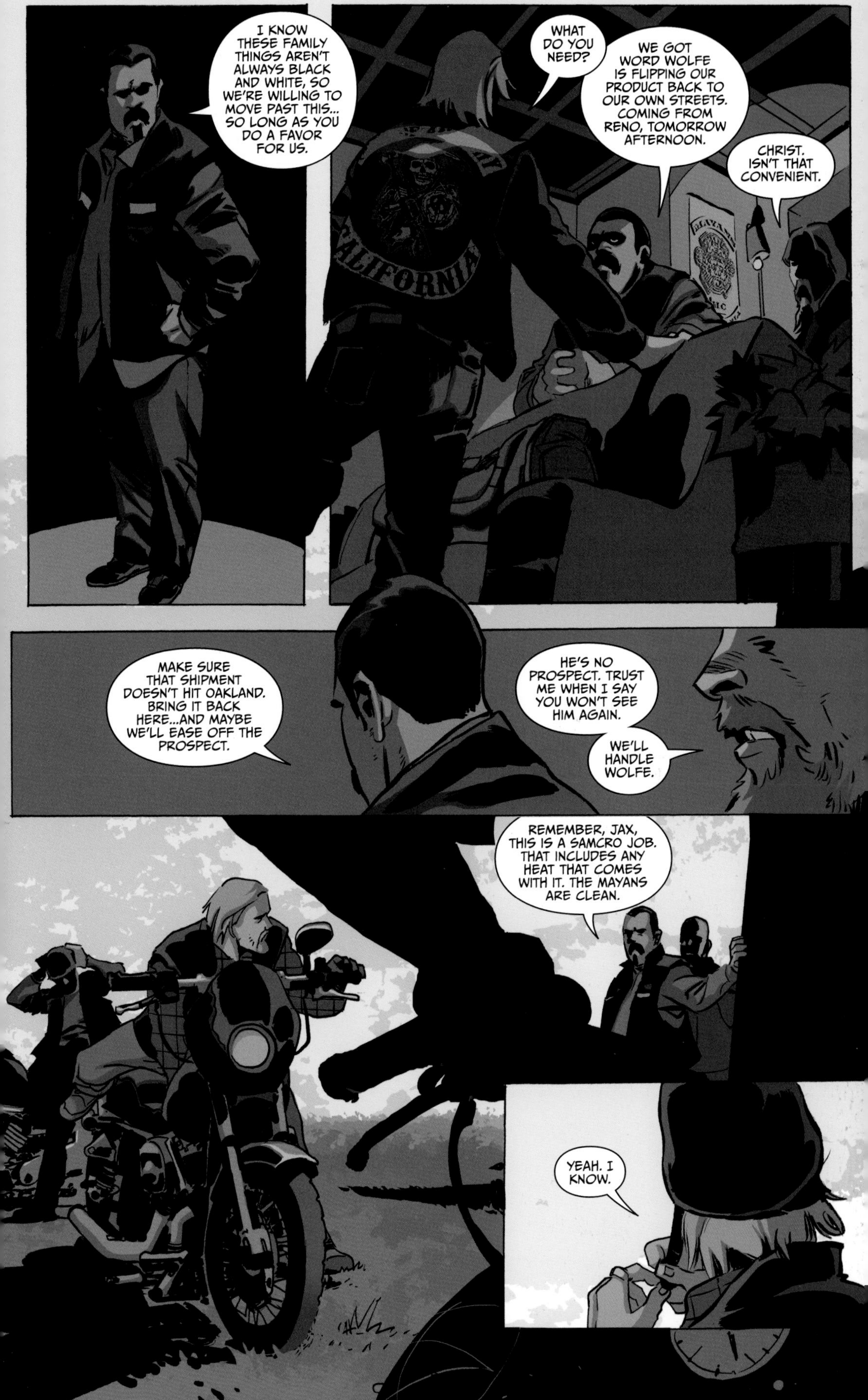
I KNOW THESE FAMILY THINGS AREN'T ALWAYS BLACK AND WHITE, SO WE'RE WILLING TO MOVE PAST THIS... SO LONG AS YOU DO A FAVOR FOR US.
WHAT DO YOU NEED?
WE GOT WORD WOLFE IS FLIPPING OUR PRODUCT BACK TO OUR OWN STREETS. COMING FROM RENO, TOMORROW AFTERNOON.
CHRIST. ISN'T THAT CONVENIENT.
MAKE SURE THAT SHIPMENT DOESN'T HIT OAKLAND. BRING IT BACK HERE...AND MAYBE WE'LL EASE OFF THE PROSPECT.
HE'S NO PROSPECT. TRUST ME WHEN I SAY YOU WON'T SEE HIM AGAIN.
WE'LL HANDLE WOLFE.
REMEMBER, JAX, THIS IS A SAMCRO JOB. THAT INCLUDES ANY HEAT THAT COMES WITH IT. THE MAYANS ARE CLEAN.
YEAH. I KNOW.

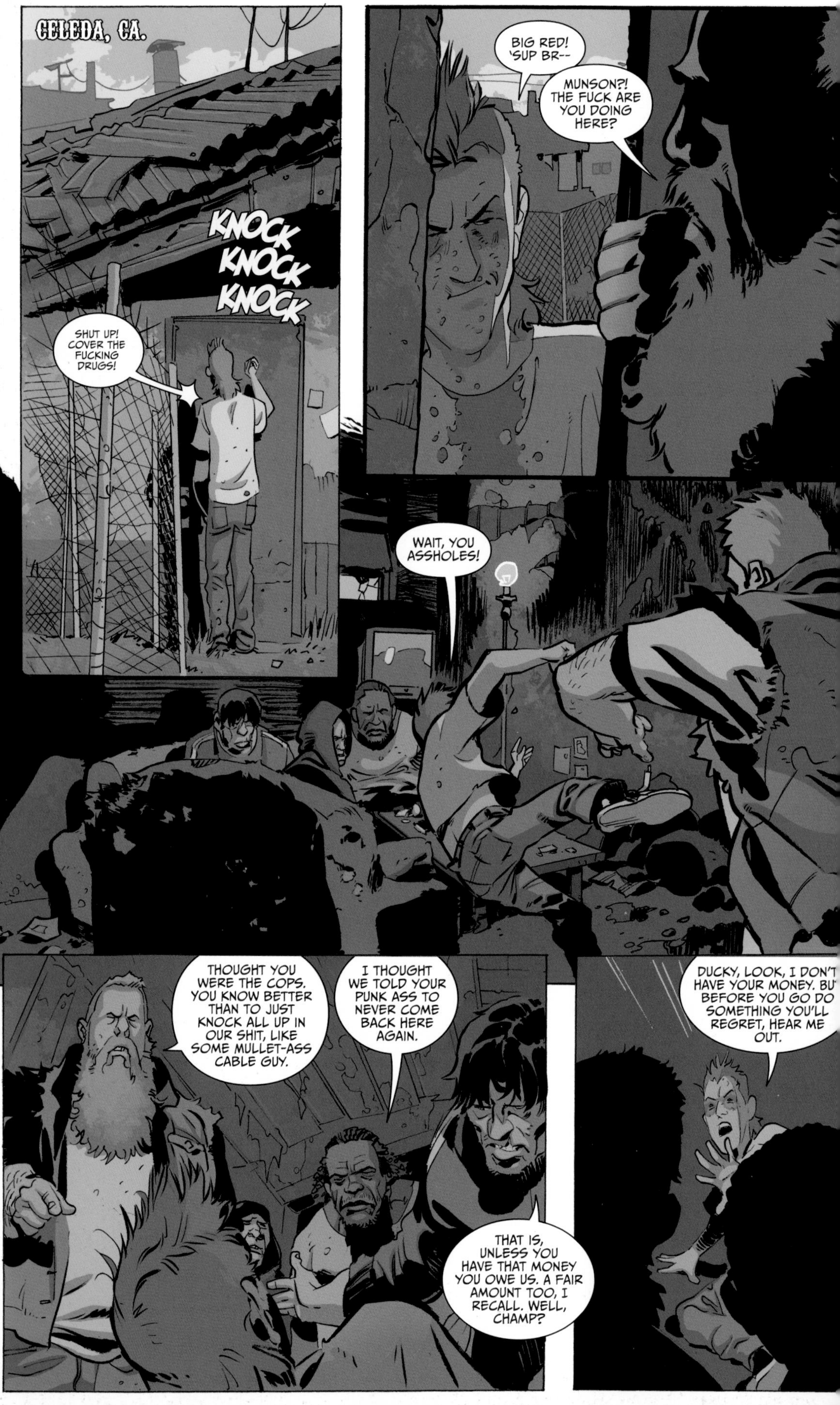
CELEDA, CA.
KNOCK KNOCK KNOCK
SHUT UP! COVER THE FUCKING DRUGS!
BIG RED! 'SUP BR--
MUNSON?! THE FUCK ARE YOU DOING HERE?
WAIT, YOU ASSHOLES!
THOUGHT YOU WERE THE COPS. YOU KNOW BETTER THAN TO JUST KNOCK ALL UP IN OUR SHIT, LIKE SOME MULLET-ASS CABLE GUY.
I THOUGHT WE TOLD YOUR PUNK ASS TO NEVER COME BACK HERE AGAIN.
THAT IS, UNLESS YOU HAVE THAT MONEY YOU OWE US. A FAIR AMOUNT TOO, I RECALL. WELL, CHAMP?
DUCKY, LOOK, I DON'T HAVE YOUR MONEY. BUT BEFORE YOU GO DO SOMETHING YOU'LL REGRET, HEAR ME OUT.

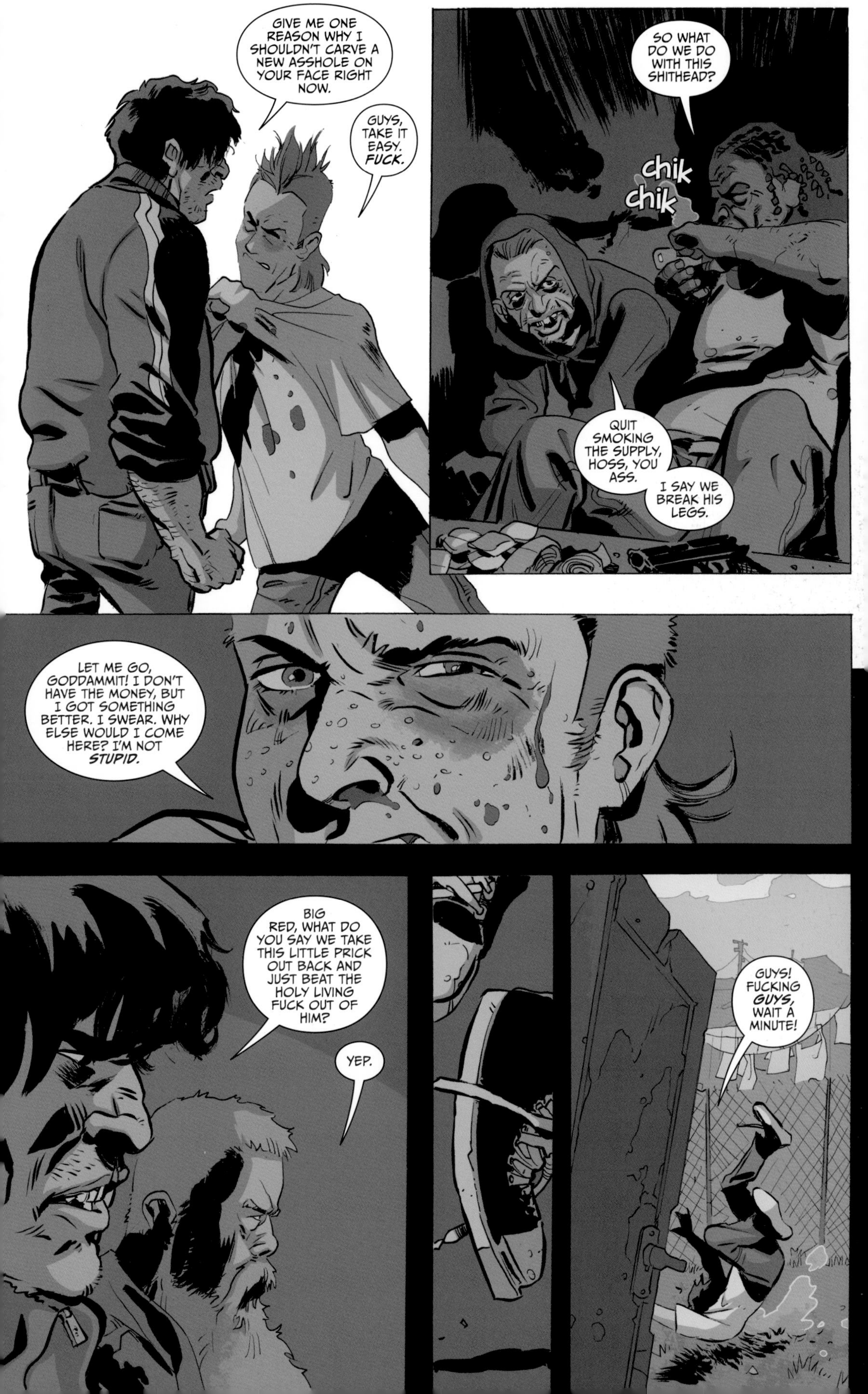
GIVE ME ONE REASON WHY I SHOULDN'T CARVE A NEW ASSHOLE ON YOUR FACE RIGHT NOW.
GUYS, TAKE IT EASY. FUCK.
SO WHAT DO WE DO WITH THIS SHITHEAD?
chik chik
QUIT SMOKING THE SUPPLY, HOSS, YOU ASS.
I SAY WE BREAK HIS LEGS.
LET ME GO, GODDAMMIT! I DON'T HAVE THE MONEY, BUT I GOT SOMETHING BETTER. I SWEAR. WHY ELSE WOULD I COME HERE? I'M NOT STUPID.
BIG RED, WHAT DO YOU SAY WE TAKE THIS LITTLE PRICK OUT BACK AND JUST BEAT THE HOLY LIVING FUCK OUT OF HIM?
YEP.
GUYS! FUCKING GUYS, WAIT A MINUTE!

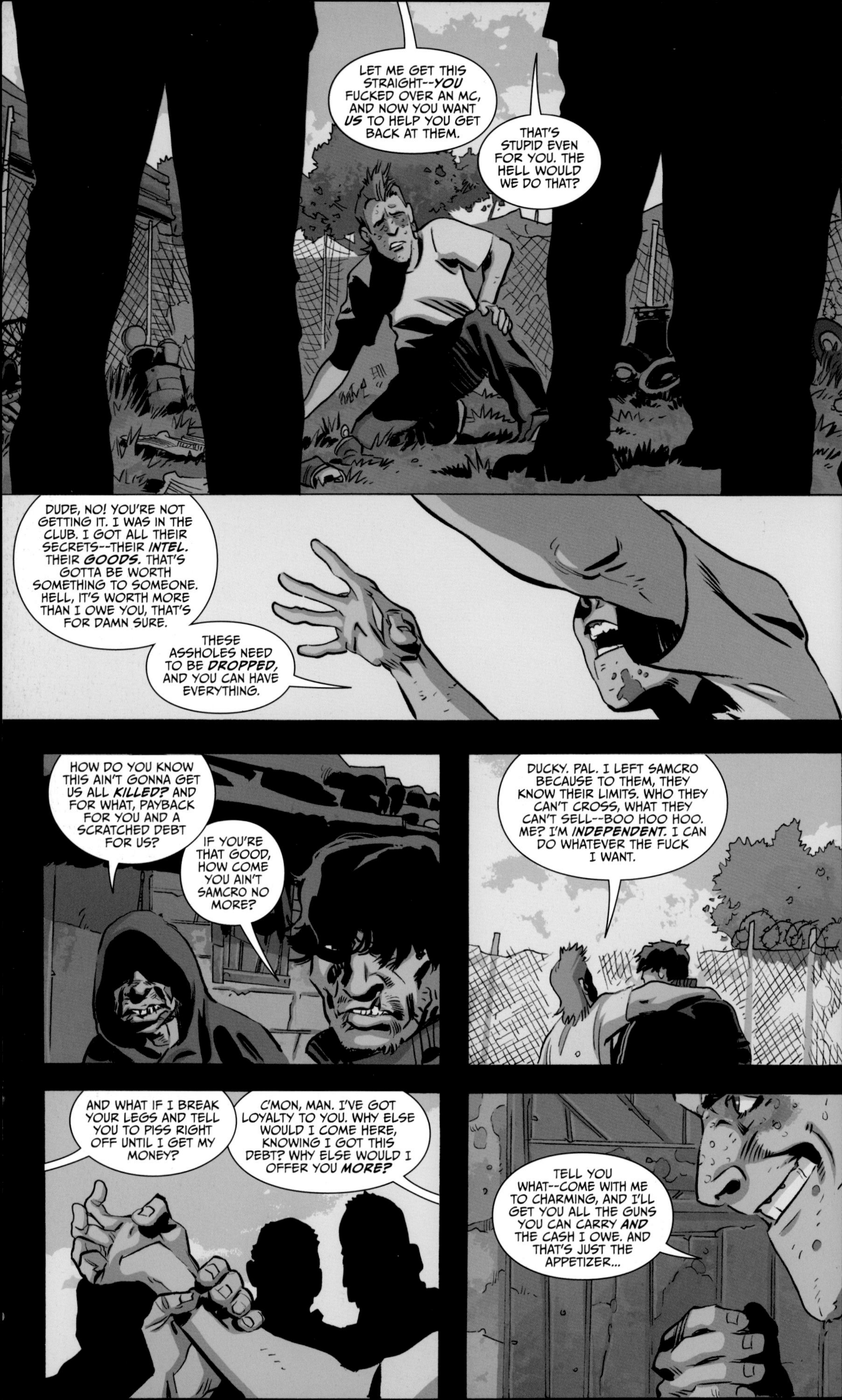

LET ME GET THIS STRAIGHT--YOU FUCKED OVER AN MC, AND NOW YOU WANT US TO HELP YOU GET BACK AT THEM.
THAT'S STUPID EVEN FOR YOU. THE HELL WOULD WE DO THAT?
DUDE, NO! YOU'RE NOT GETTING IT. I WAS IN THE CLUB. I GOT ALL THEIR SECRETS--THEIR INTEL. THEIR GOODS. THAT'S GOTTA BE WORTH SOMETHING TO SOMEONE. HELL, IT'S WORTH MORE THAN I OWE YOU, THAT'S FOR DAMN SURE.
THESE ASSHOLES NEED TO BE DROPPED, AND YOU CAN HAVE EVERYTHING.
HOW DO YOU KNOW THIS AIN'T GONNA GET US ALL KILLED? AND FOR WHAT, PAYBACK FOR YOU AND A SCRATCHED DEBT FOR US?
IF YOU'RE THAT GOOD, HOW COME YOU AIN'T SAMCRO NO MORE?
DUCKY. PAL. I LEFT SAMCRO BECAUSE TO THEM, THEY KNOW THEIR LIMITS. WHO THEY CAN'T CROSS, WHAT THEY CAN'T SELL--BOO HOO HOO. ME? I'M INDEPENDENT. I CAN DO WHATEVER THE FUCK I WANT.
AND WHAT IF I BREAK YOUR LEGS AND TELL YOU TO PISS RIGHT OFF UNTIL I GET MY MONEY?
C'MON, MAN. I'VE GOT LOYALTY TO YOU. WHY ELSE WOULD I COME HERE, KNOWING I GOT THIS DEBT? WHY ELSE WOULD I OFFER YOU MORE?
TELL YOU WHAT--COME WITH ME TO CHARMING, AND I'LL GET YOU ALL THE GUNS YOU CAN CARRY AND THE CASH I OWE. AND THAT'S JUST THE APPETIZER...

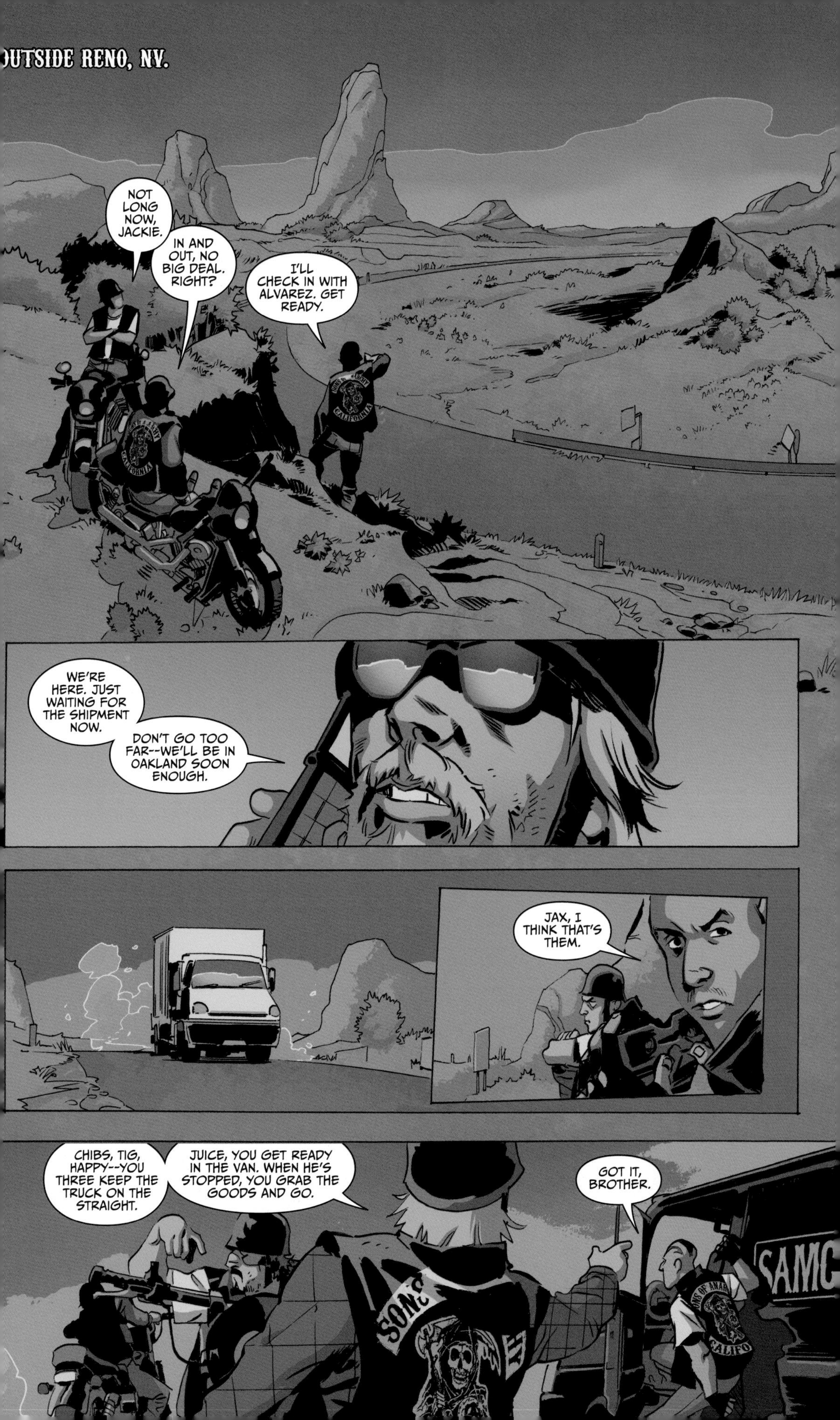
OUTSIDE RENO, NV.
NOT LONG NOW, JACKIE.
IN AND OUT, NO BIG DEAL. RIGHT?
I'LL CHECK IN WITH ALVAREZ. GET READY.
WE'RE HERE. JUST WAITING FOR THE SHIPMENT NOW.
DON'T GO TOO FAR--WE'LL BE IN OAKLAND SOON ENOUGH.
JAX, I THINK THAT'S THEM.
CHIBS, TIG, HAPPY--YOU THREE KEEP THE TRUCK ON THE STRAIGHT.
JUICE, YOU GET READY IN THE VAN. WHEN HE'S STOPPED, YOU GRAB THE GOODS AND GO.
GOT IT, BROTHER.

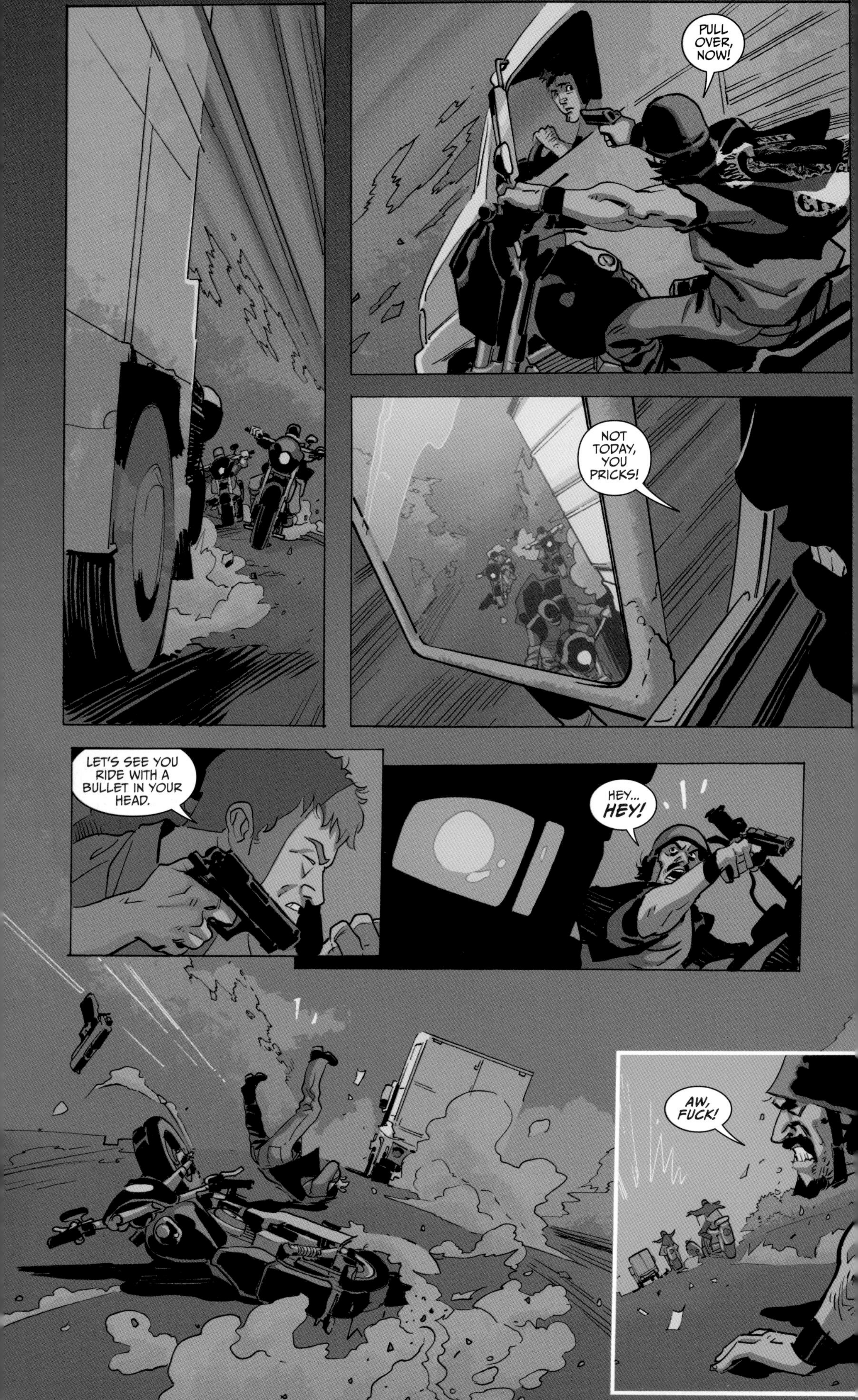
PULL OVER, NOW!
NOT TODAY, YOU PRICKS!
LET'S SEE YOU RIDE WITH A BULLET IN YOUR HEAD.
HEY... HEY!
AW, FUCK!

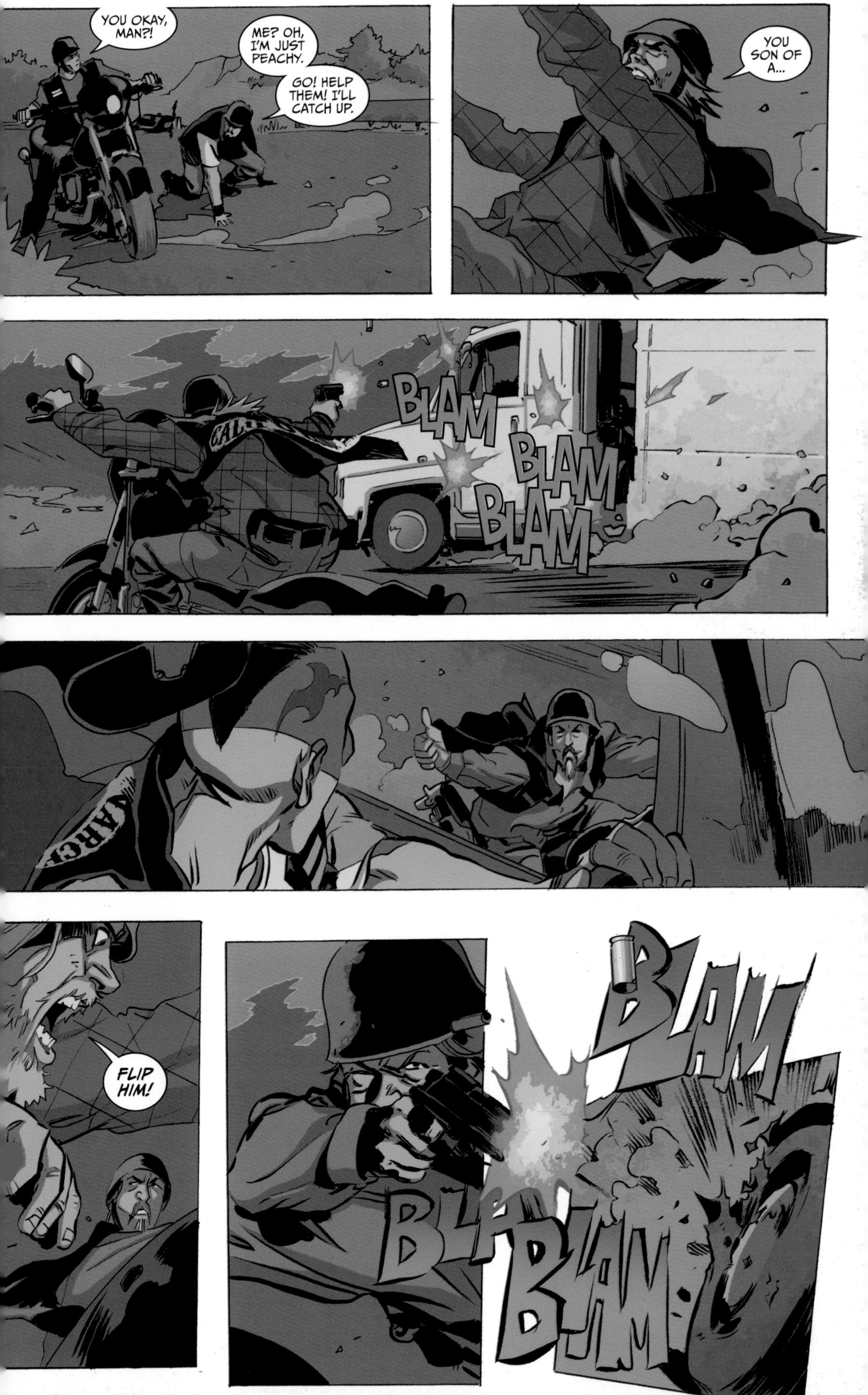
YOU OKAY, MAN?!
ME? OH, I'M JUST PEACHY.
GO! HELP THEM! I'LL CATCH UP.
YOU SON OF A...
BLAM
BLAM
BLAM
FLIP HIM!
BLAM
BLAM
BLAM

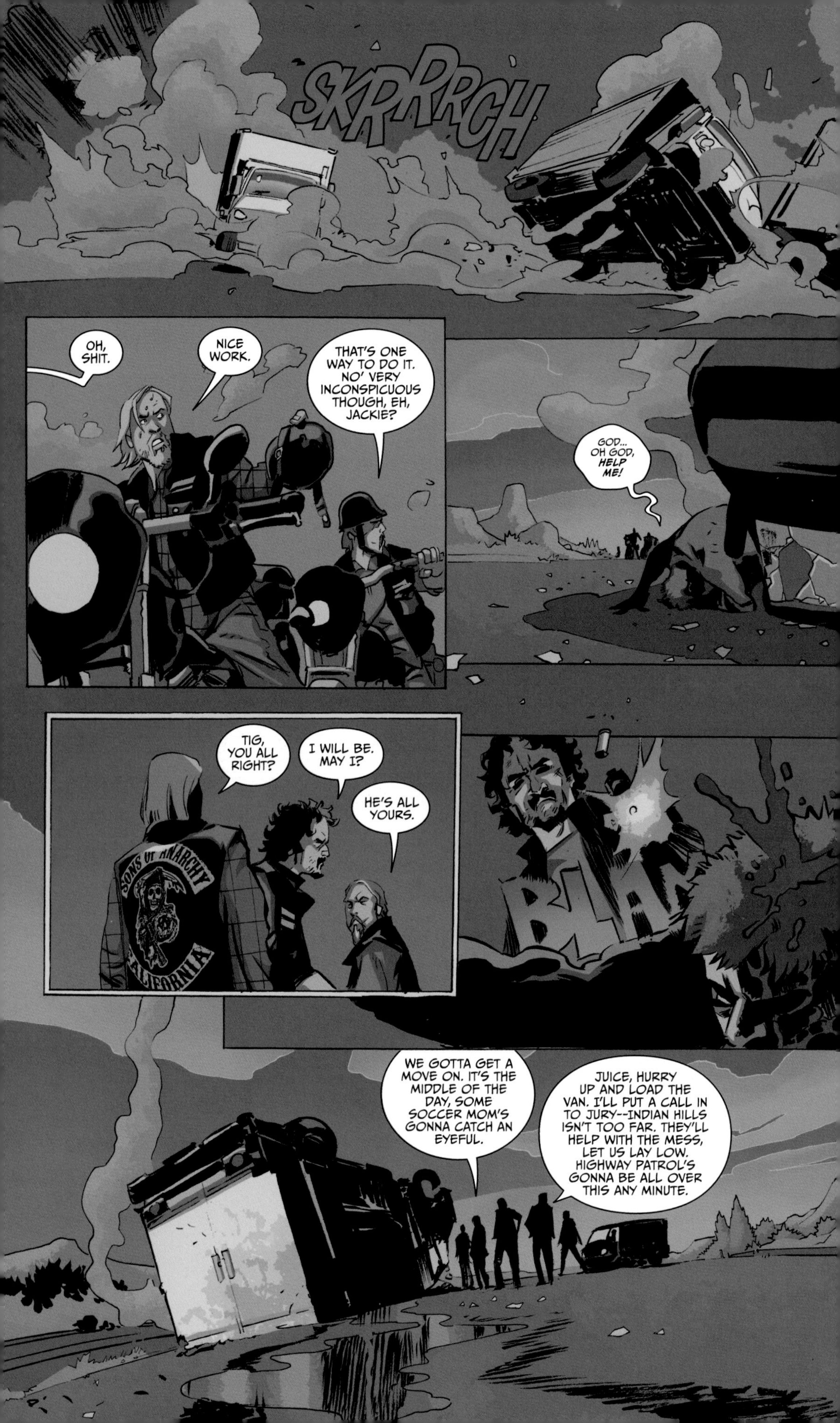
SKRRRCH
OH, SHIT.
NICE WORK.
THAT'S ONE WAY TO DO IT. NO' VERY INCONSPICUOUS THOUGH, EH, JACKIE?
GOD... OH GOD, HELP ME!
TIG, YOU ALL RIGHT?
I WILL BE. MAY I?
HE'S ALL YOURS.
SONS OF ANARCHY
CALIFORNIA
WE GOTTA GET A MOVE ON. IT'S THE MIDDLE OF THE DAY, SOME SOCCER MOM'S GONNA CATCH AN EYEFUL.
JUICE, HURRY UP AND LOAD THE VAN. I'LL PUT A CALL IN TO JURY--INDIAN HILLS ISN'T TOO FAR. THEY'LL HELP WITH THE MESS, LET US LAY LOW. HIGHWAY PATROL'S GONNA BE ALL OVER THIS ANY MINUTE.

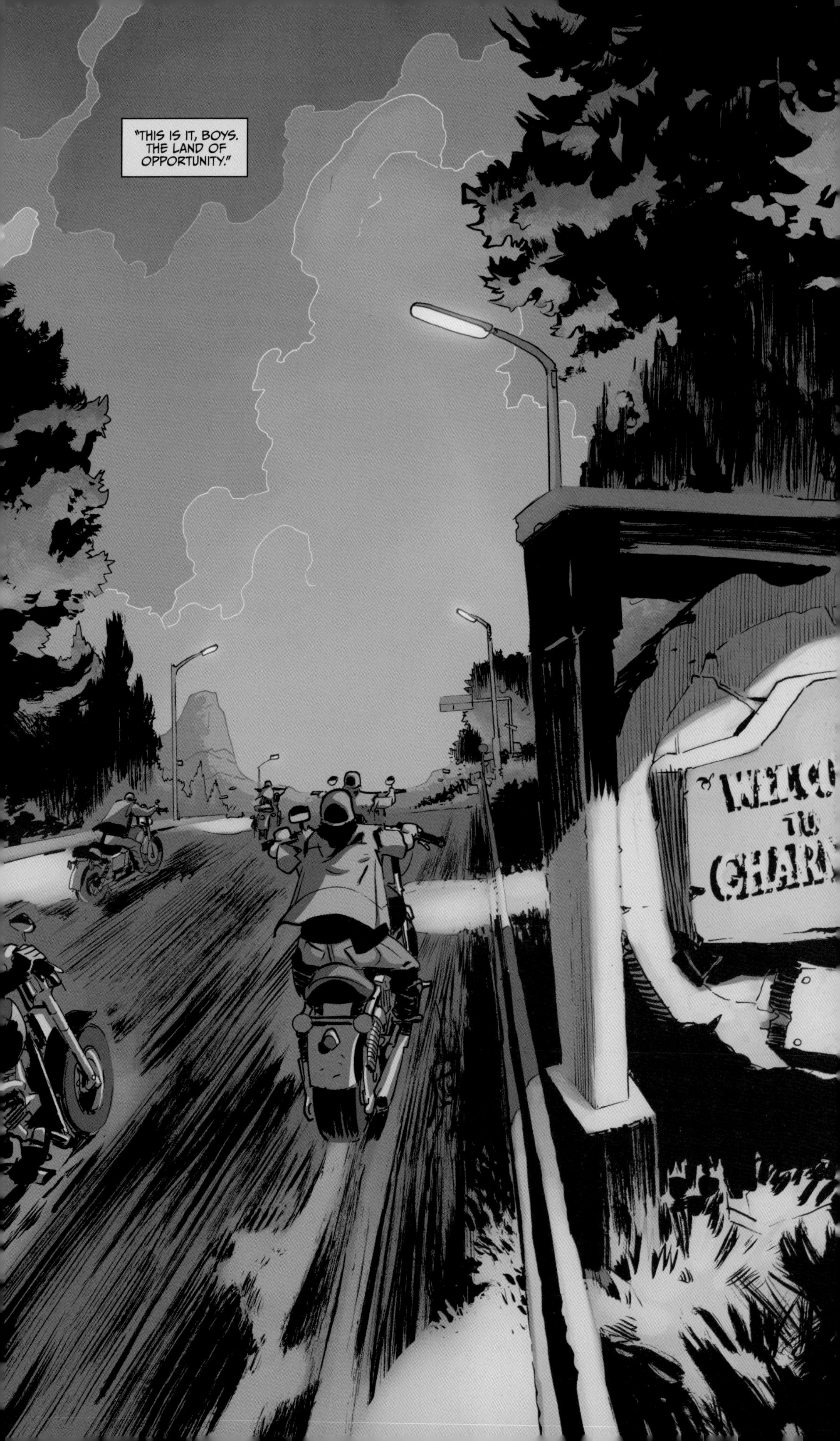
"THIS IS IT, BOYS. THE LAND OF OPPORTUNITY."

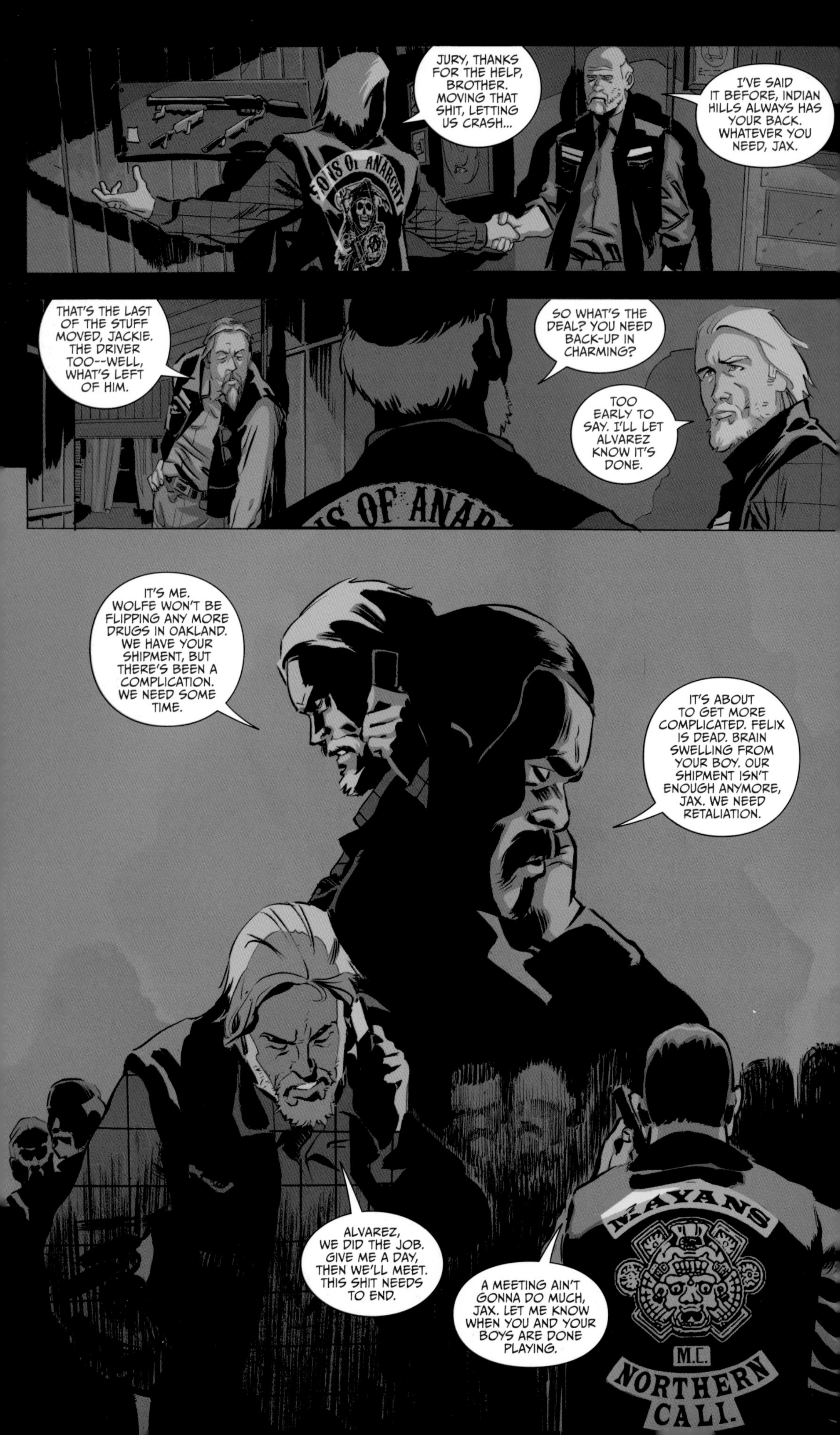

JURY, THANKS FOR THE HELP, BROTHER. MOVING THAT SHIT, LETTING US CRASH...
I'VE SAID IT BEFORE, INDIAN HILLS ALWAYS HAS YOUR BACK. WHATEVER YOU NEED, JAX.
SONS OF ANARCHY
THAT'S THE LAST OF THE STUFF MOVED, JACKIE. THE DRIVER TOO--WELL, WHAT'S LEFT OF HIM.
SO WHAT'S THE DEAL? YOU NEED BACK-UP IN CHARMING?
TOO EARLY TO SAY. I'LL LET ALVAREZ KNOW IT'S DONE.
IT'S ME. WOLFE WON'T BE FLIPPING ANY MORE DRUGS IN OAKLAND. WE HAVE YOUR SHIPMENT, BUT THERE'S BEEN A COMPLICATION. WE NEED SOME TIME.
IT'S ABOUT TO GET MORE COMPLICATED. FELIX IS DEAD. BRAIN SWELLING FROM YOUR BOY. OUR SHIPMENT ISN'T ENOUGH ANYMORE, JAX. WE NEED RETALIATION.
ALVAREZ, WE DID THE JOB. GIVE ME A DAY, THEN WE'LL MEET. THIS SHIT NEEDS TO END.
A MEETING AIN'T GONNA DO MUCH, JAX. LET ME KNOW WHEN YOU AND YOUR BOYS ARE DONE PLAYING.
MAYANS
M.C.
NORTHERN
CALI.

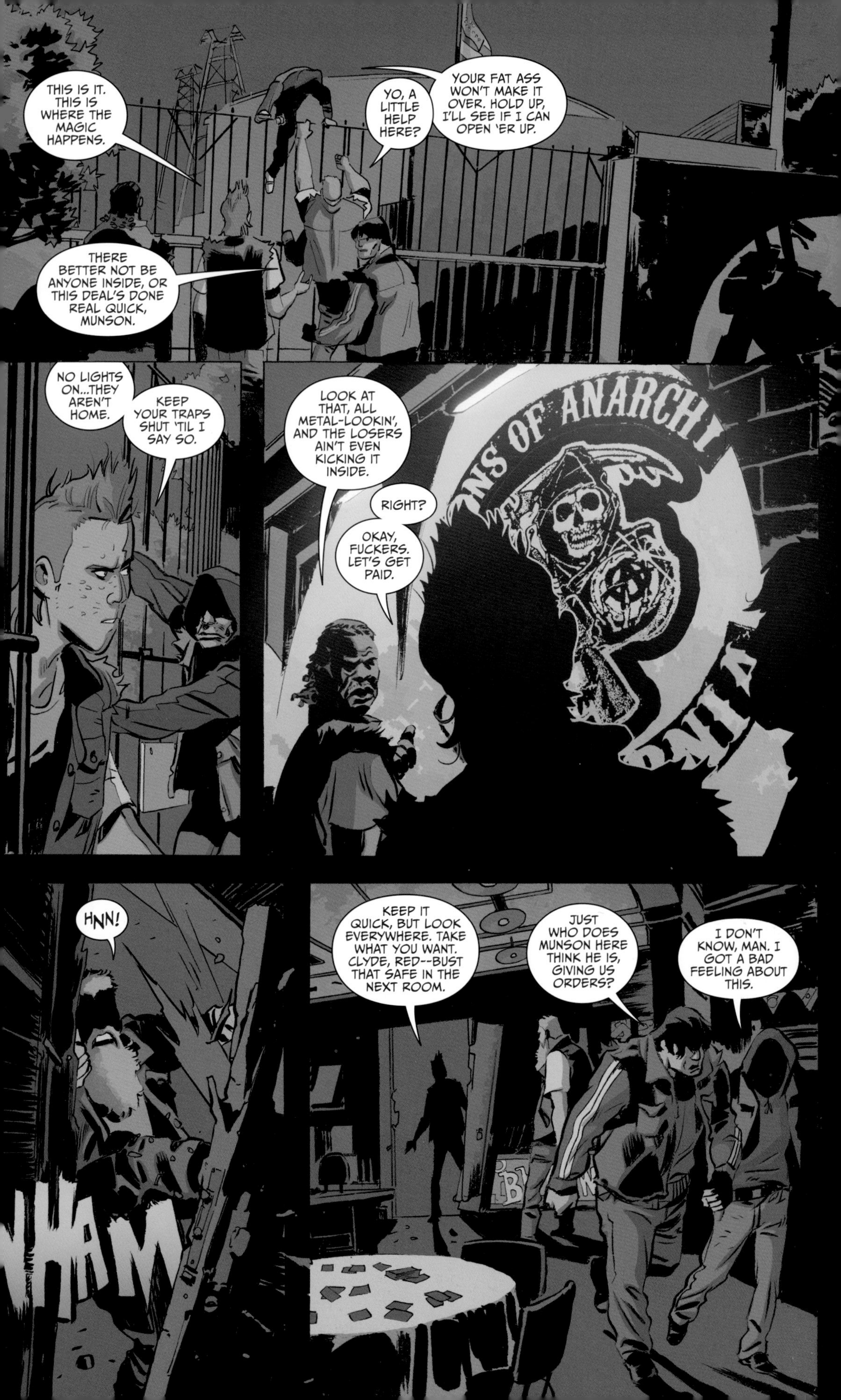
THIS IS IT. THIS IS WHERE THE MAGIC HAPPENS.
YO, A LITTLE HELP HERE?
YOUR FAT ASS WON'T MAKE IT OVER. HOLD UP, I'LL SEE IF I CAN OPEN 'ER UP.
THERE BETTER NOT BE ANYONE INSIDE, OR THIS DEAL'S DONE REAL QUICK, MUNSON.
NO LIGHTS ON...THEY AREN'T HOME.
KEEP YOUR TRAPS SHUT 'TIL I SAY SO.
LOOK AT THAT, ALL METAL-LOOKIN', AND THE LOSERS AIN'T EVEN KICKING IT INSIDE.
RIGHT?
OKAY, FUCKERS. LET'S GET PAID.
SONS OF ANARCHY
HNN!
HAM
KEEP IT QUICK, BUT LOOK EVERYWHERE. TAKE WHAT YOU WANT. CLYDE, RED--BUST THAT SAFE IN THE NEXT ROOM.
JUST WHO DOES MUNSON HERE THINK HE IS, GIVING US ORDERS?
I DON'T KNOW, MAN. I GOT A BAD FEELING ABOUT THIS.

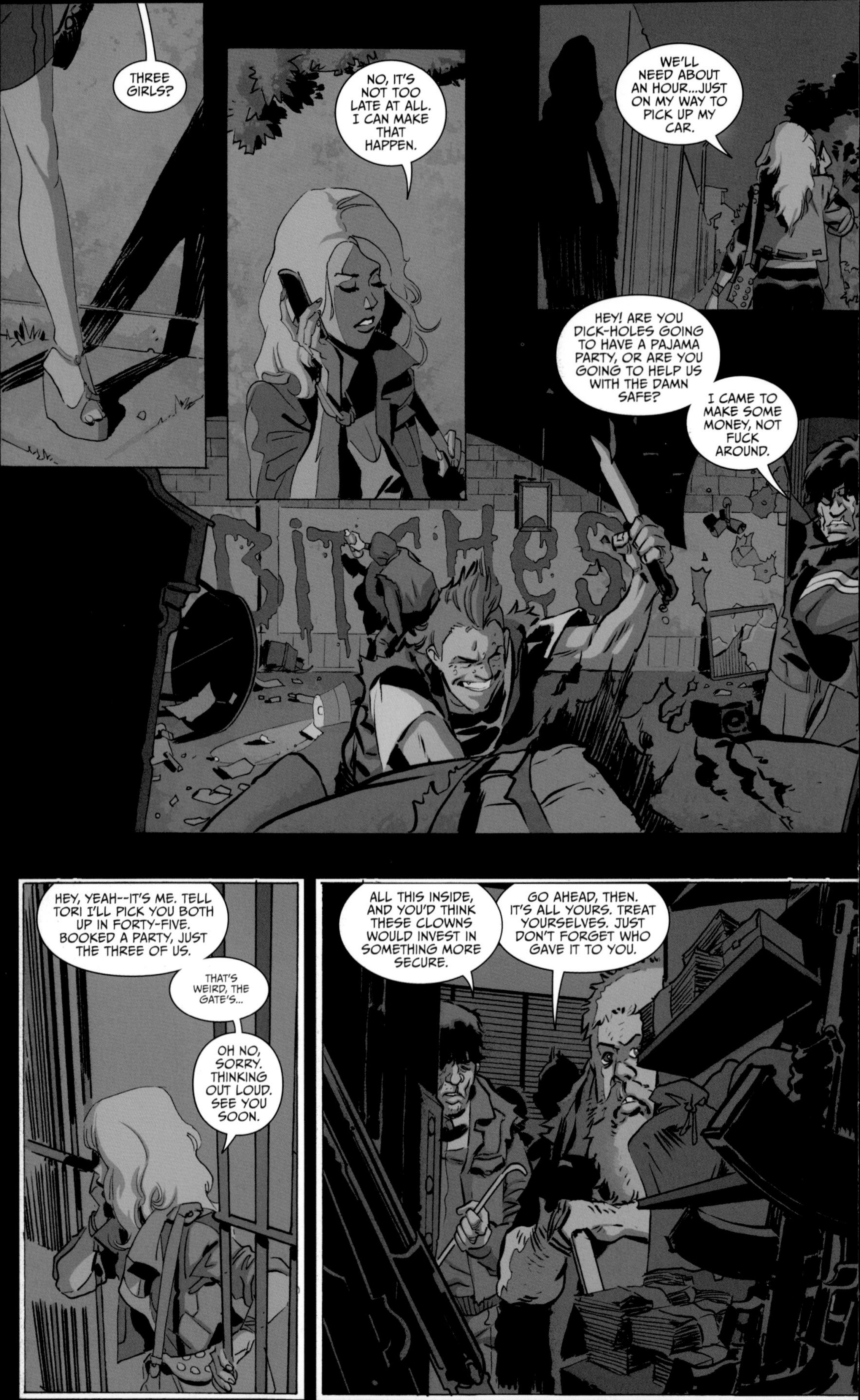
THREE GIRLS?
NO, IT'S NOT TOO LATE AT ALL. I CAN MAKE THAT HAPPEN.
WE'LL NEED ABOUT AN HOUR...JUST ON MY WAY TO PICK UP MY CAR.
HEY! ARE YOU DICK-HOLES GOING TO HAVE A PAJAMA PARTY, OR ARE YOU GOING TO HELP US WITH THE DAMN SAFE?
I CAME TO MAKE SOME MONEY, NOT FUCK AROUND.
HEY, YEAH--IT'S ME. TELL TORI I'LL PICK YOU BOTH UP IN FORTY-FIVE. BOOKED A PARTY, JUST THE THREE OF US.
THAT'S WEIRD, THE GATE'S...
OH NO, SORRY. THINKING OUT LOUD. SEE YOU SOON.
ALL THIS INSIDE, AND YOU'D THINK THESE CLOWNS WOULD INVEST IN SOMETHING MORE SECURE.
GO AHEAD, THEN. IT'S ALL YOURS. TREAT YOURSELVES. JUST DON'T FORGET WHO GAVE IT TO YOU.

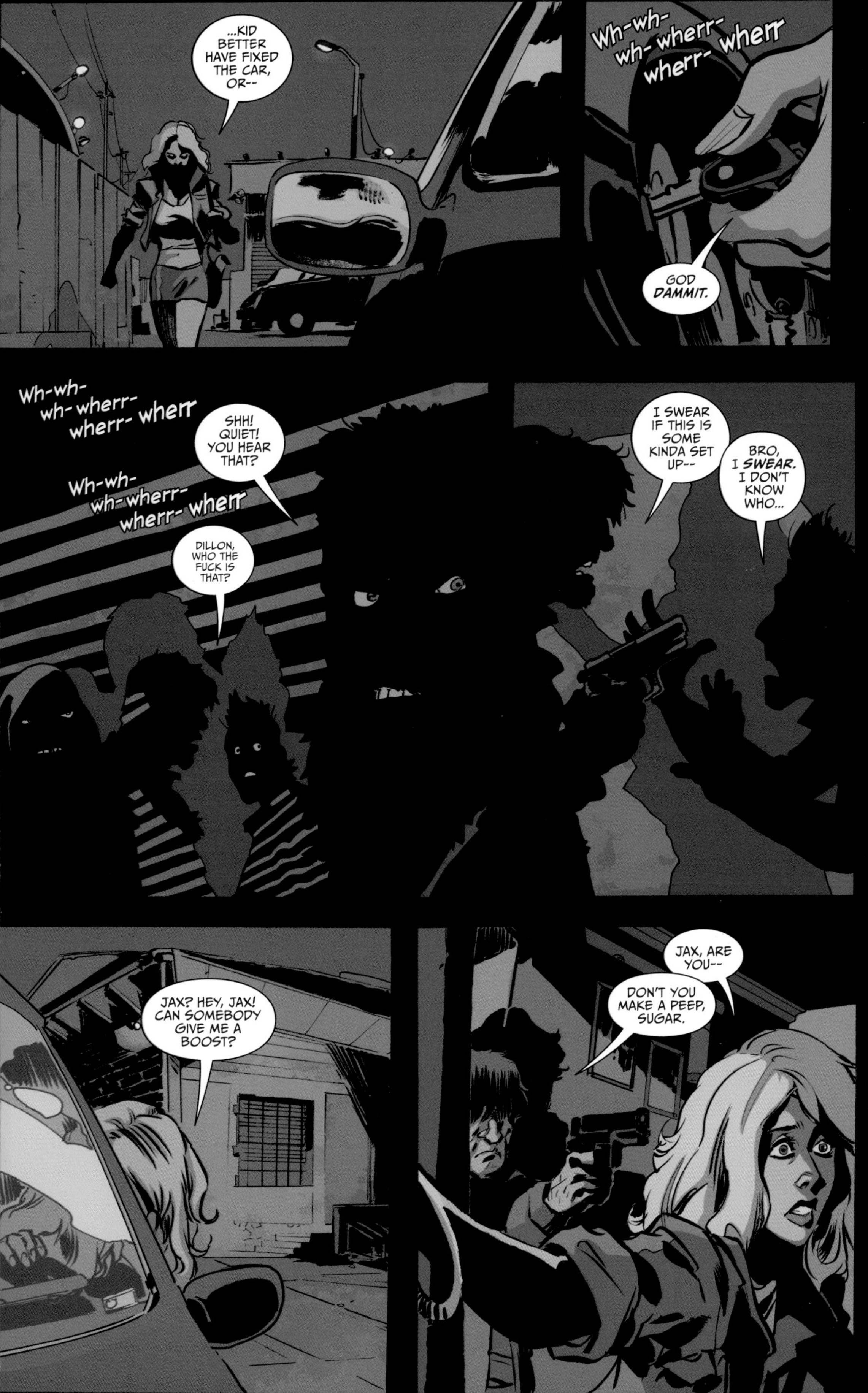
...KID BETTER HAVE FIXED THE CAR, OR--
Wh-wh- wh- wherr- wherr- wherr
GOD DAMMIT.
Wh-wh- wh- wherr- wherr- wherr
SHH! QUIET! YOU HEAR THAT?
Wh-wh- wh- wherr- wherr- wherr
DILLON, WHO THE FUCK IS THAT?
I SWEAR IF THIS IS SOME KINDA SET UP--
BRO, I SWEAR. I DON'T KNOW WHO...
JAX? HEY, JAX! CAN SOMEBODY GIVE ME A BOOST?
JAX, ARE YOU--
DON'T YOU MAKE A PEEP, SUGAR.

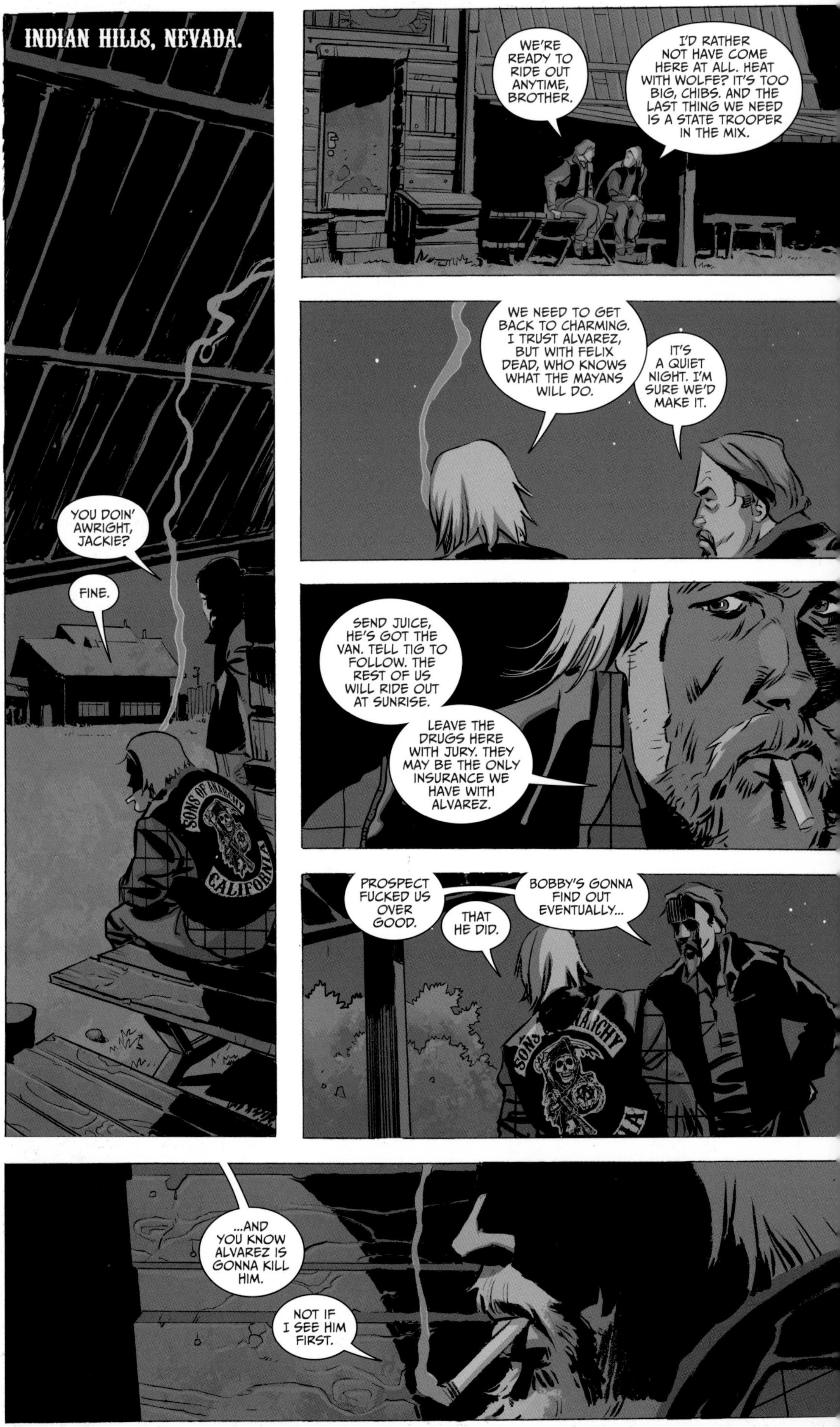
INDIAN HILLS, NEVADA.
YOU DOIN' AWRIGHT, JACKIE?
FINE.
WE'RE READY TO RIDE OUT ANYTIME, BROTHER.
I'D RATHER NOT HAVE COME HERE AT ALL. HEAT WITH WOLFE? IT'S TOO BIG, CHIBS. AND THE LAST THING WE NEED IS A STATE TROOPER IN THE MIX.
WE NEED TO GET BACK TO CHARMING. I TRUST ALVAREZ, BUT WITH FELIX DEAD, WHO KNOWS WHAT THE MAYANS WILL DO.
IT'S A QUIET NIGHT. I'M SURE WE'D MAKE IT.
SEND JUICE, HE'S GOT THE VAN. TELL TIG TO FOLLOW. THE REST OF US WILL RIDE OUT AT SUNRISE.
LEAVE THE DRUGS HERE WITH JURY. THEY MAY BE THE ONLY INSURANCE WE HAVE WITH ALVAREZ.
PROSPECT FUCKED US OVER GOOD.
THAT HE DID.
BOBBY'S GONNA FIND OUT EVENTUALLY...
...AND YOU KNOW ALVAREZ IS GONNA KILL HIM.
NOT IF I SEE HIM FIRST.

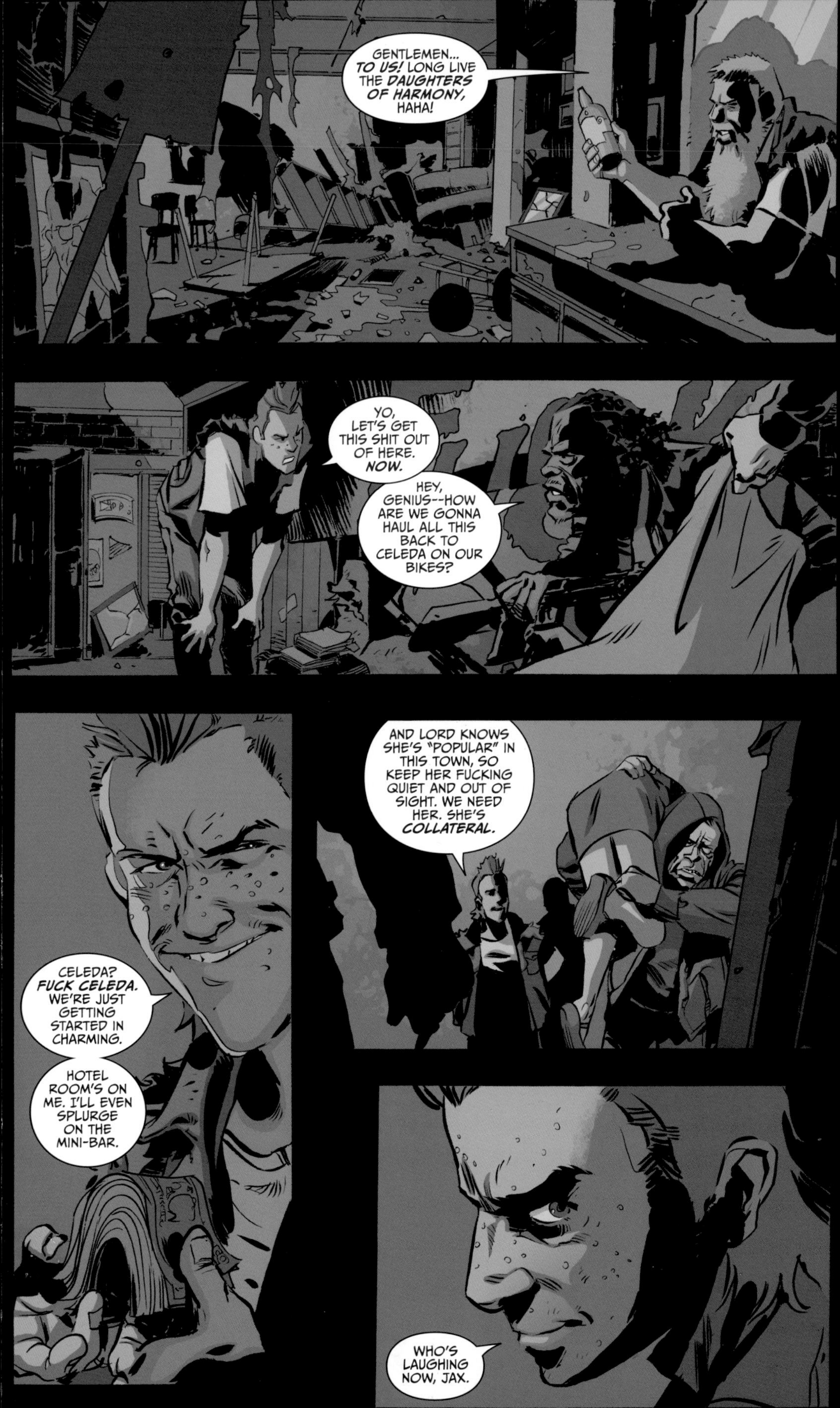
GENTLEMEN... TO US! LONG LIVE THE DAUGHTERS OF HARMONY, HAHA!
YO, LET'S GET THIS SHIT OUT OF HERE. NOW.
HEY, GENIUS--HOW ARE WE GONNA HAUL ALL THIS BACK TO CELEDA ON OUR BIKES?
CELEDA? FUCK CELEDA. WE'RE JUST GETTING STARTED IN CHARMING.
HOTEL ROOM'S ON ME. I'LL EVEN SPLURGE ON THE MINI-BAR.
AND LORD KNOWS SHE'S "POPULAR" IN THIS TOWN, SO KEEP HER FUCKING QUIET AND OUT OF SIGHT. WE NEED HER. SHE'S COLLATERAL.
WHO'S LAUGHING NOW, JAX.

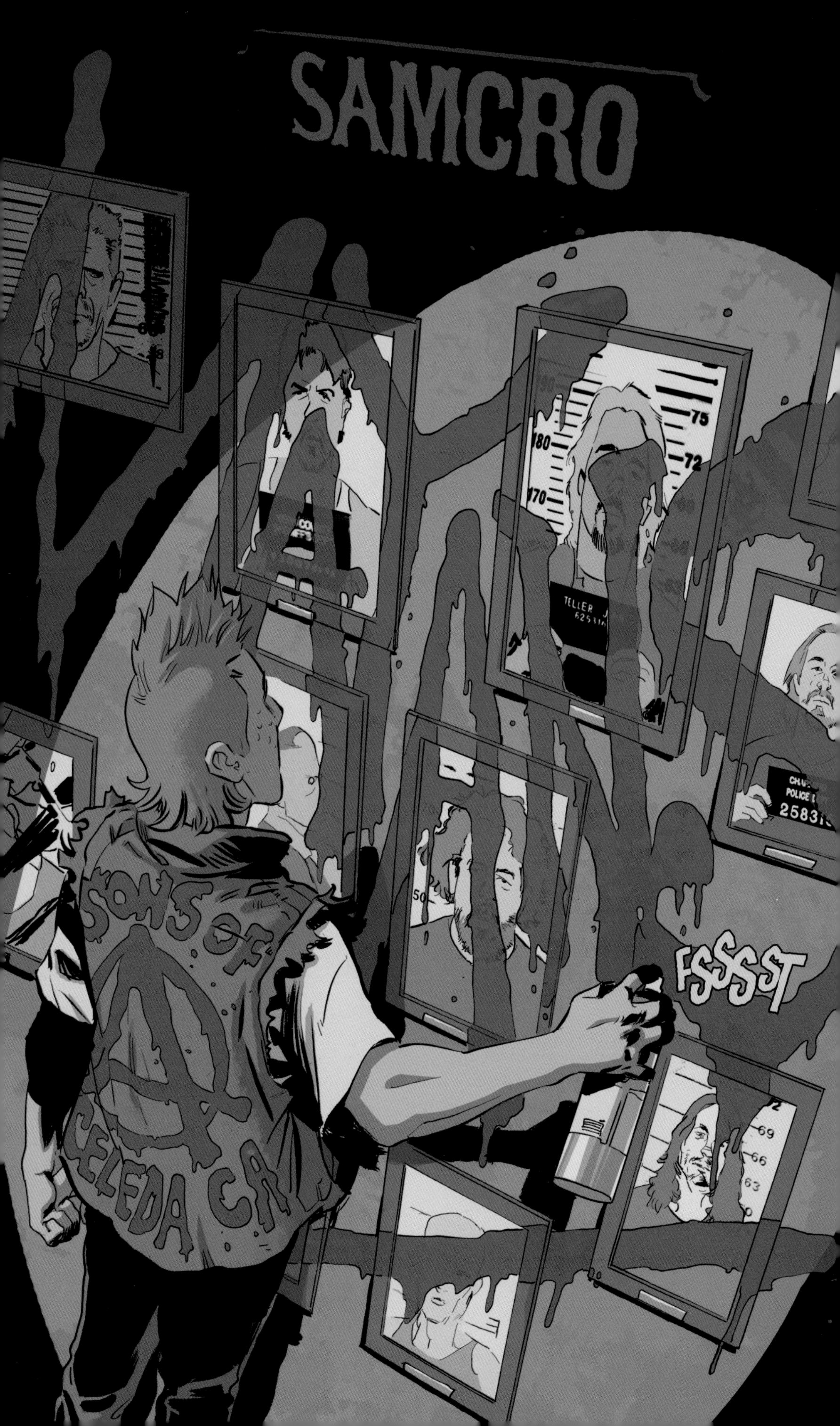
SAMCRO
SONS OF
CELEDA CA
FSSSST

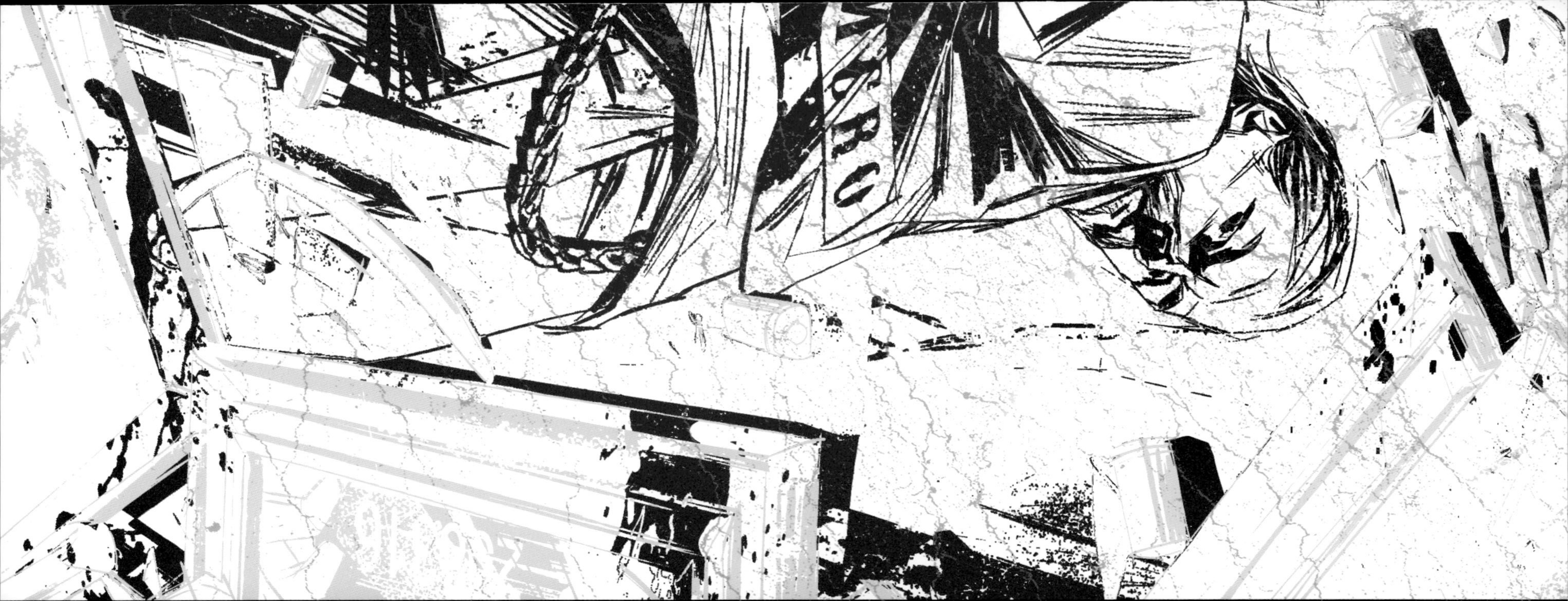

CHAPTER 21

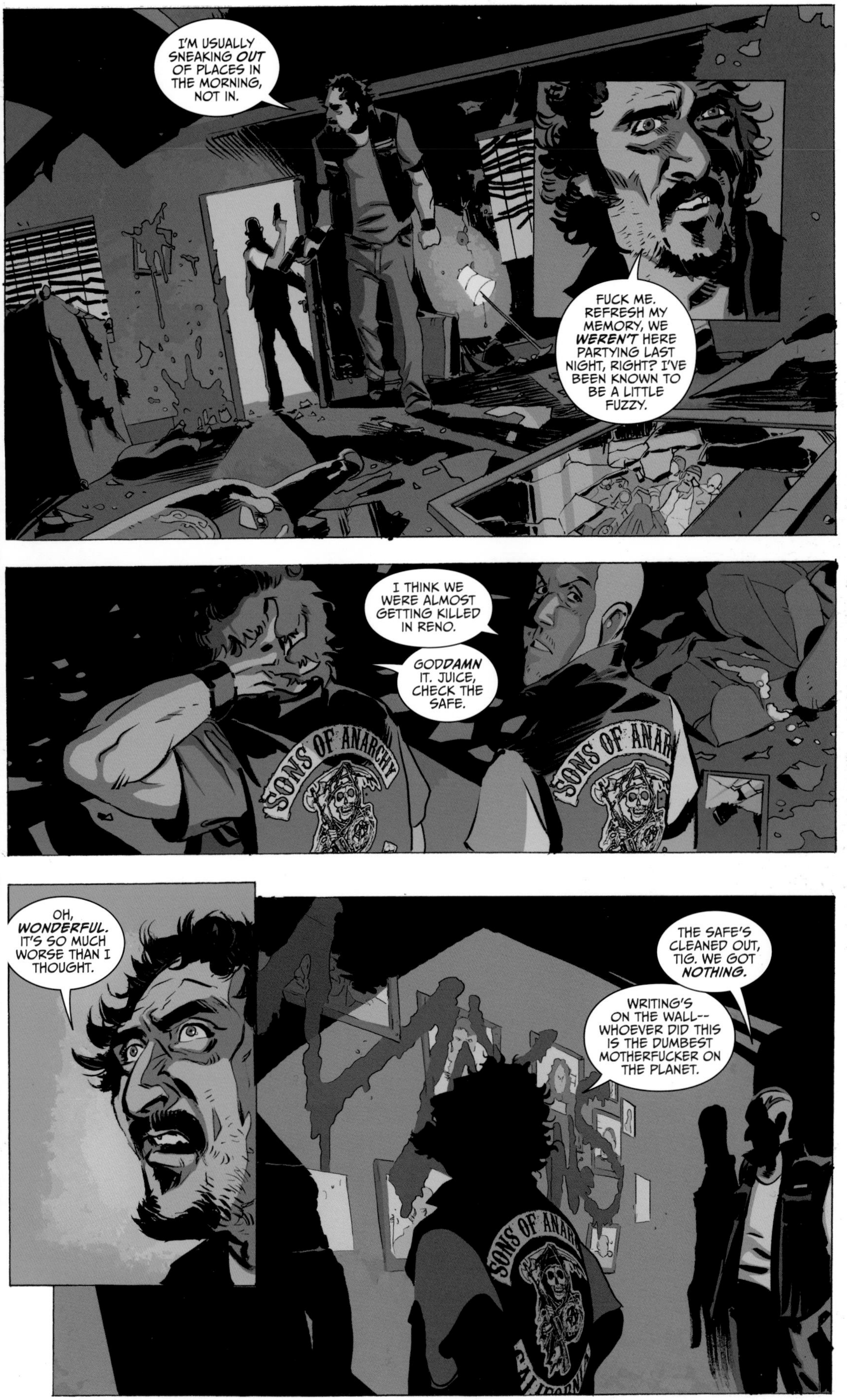
I'M USUALLY SNEAKING OUT OF PLACES IN THE MORNING, NOT IN.
FUCK ME. REFRESH MY MEMORY, WE WEREN'T HERE PARTYING LAST NIGHT, RIGHT? I'VE BEEN KNOWN TO BE A LITTLE FUZZY.
I THINK WE WERE ALMOST GETTING KILLED IN RENO.
GODDAMN IT. JUICE, CHECK THE SAFE.
SONS OF ANARCHY
SONS OF ANARCHY
OH, WONDERFUL. IT'S SO MUCH WORSE THAN I THOUGHT.
THE SAFE'S CLEANED OUT, TIG. WE GOT NOTHING.
WRITING'S ON THE WALL-- WHOEVER DID THIS IS THE DUMBEST MOTHERFUCKER ON THE PLANET.

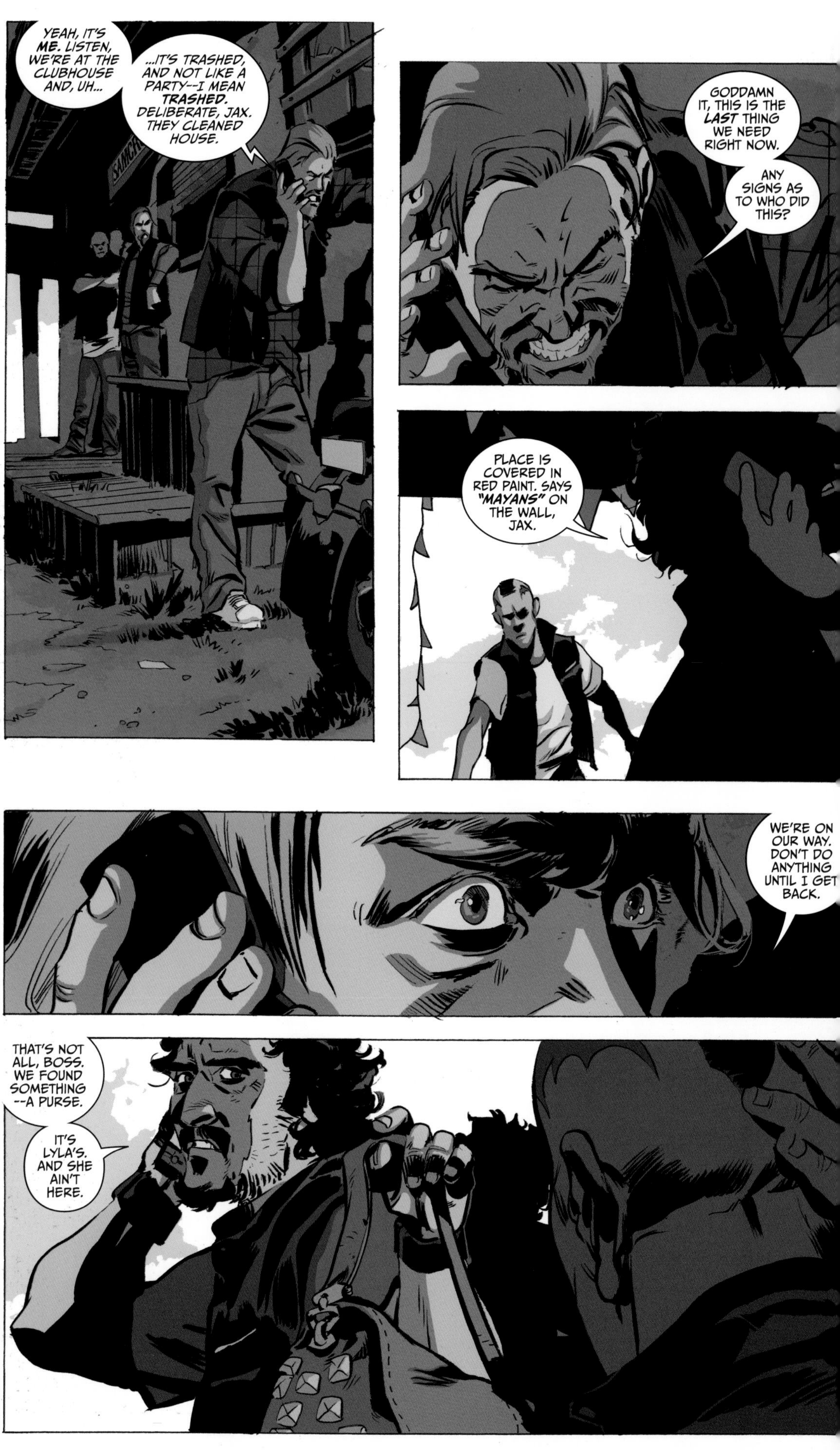
YEAH, IT'S ME. LISTEN, WE'RE AT THE CLUBHOUSE AND, UH...
...IT'S TRASHED, AND NOT LIKE A PARTY--I MEAN TRASHED. DELIBERATE, JAX. THEY CLEANED HOUSE.
GODDAMN IT, THIS IS THE LAST THING WE NEED RIGHT NOW.
ANY SIGNS AS TO WHO DID THIS?
PLACE IS COVERED IN RED PAINT. SAYS "MAYANS" ON THE WALL, JAX.
WE'RE ON OUR WAY. DON'T DO ANYTHING UNTIL I GET BACK.
THAT'S NOT ALL, BOSS. WE FOUND SOMETHING --A PURSE.
IT'S LYLA'S. AND SHE AIN'T HERE.

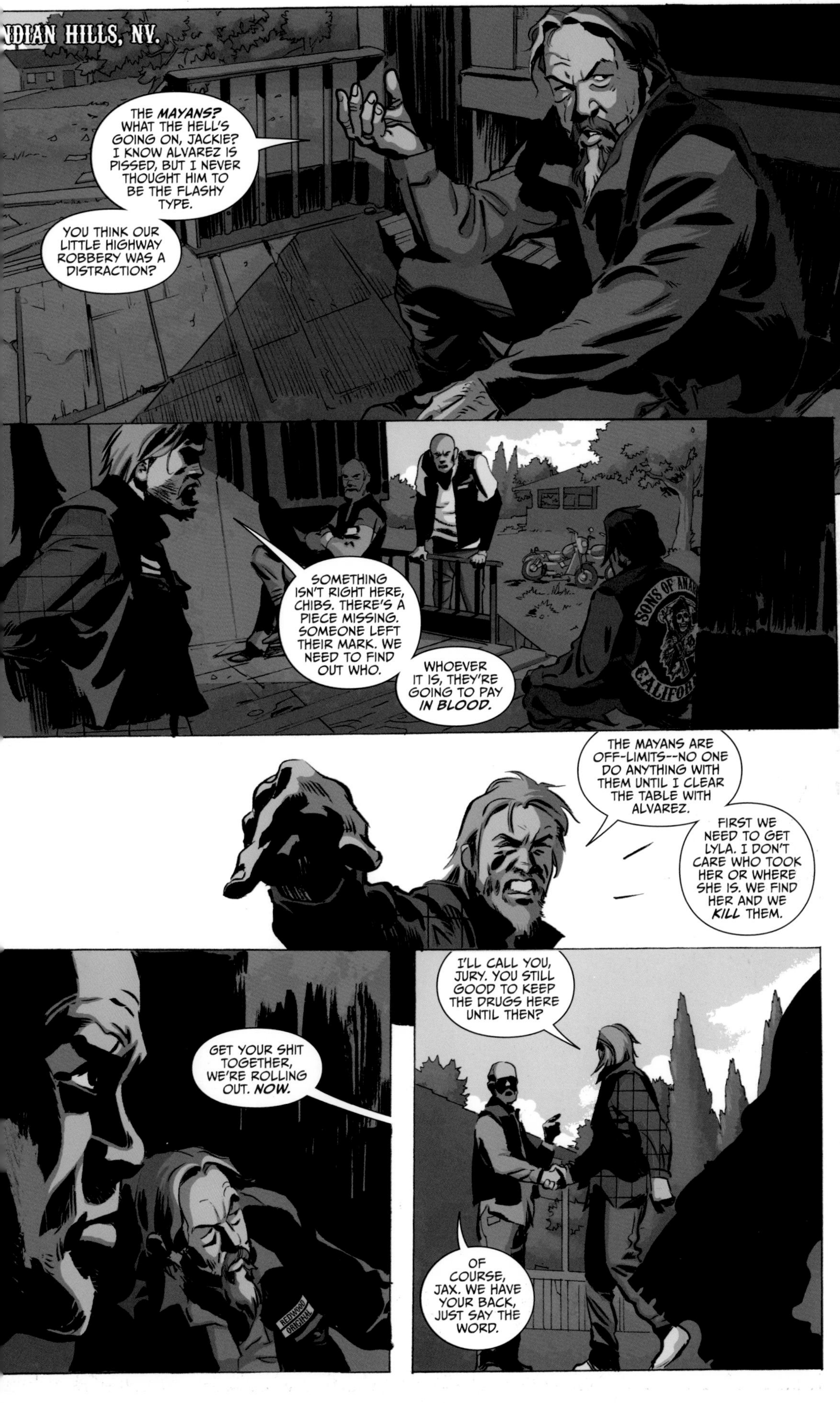

IDIAN HILLS, NV.
THE MAYANS? WHAT THE HELL'S GOING ON, JACKIE? I KNOW ALVAREZ IS PISSED, BUT I NEVER THOUGHT HIM TO BE THE FLASHY TYPE.
YOU THINK OUR LITTLE HIGHWAY ROBBERY WAS A DISTRACTION?
SOMETHING ISN'T RIGHT HERE, CHIBS. THERE'S A PIECE MISSING. SOMEONE LEFT THEIR MARK. WE NEED TO FIND OUT WHO.
WHOEVER IT IS, THEY'RE GOING TO PAY IN BLOOD.
THE MAYANS ARE OFF-LIMITS--NO ONE DO ANYTHING WITH THEM UNTIL I CLEAR THE TABLE WITH ALVAREZ.
FIRST WE NEED TO GET LYLA. I DON'T CARE WHO TOOK HER OR WHERE SHE IS. WE FIND HER AND WE KILL THEM.
GET YOUR SHIT TOGETHER, WE'RE ROLLING OUT. NOW.
I'LL CALL YOU, JURY. YOU STILL GOOD TO KEEP THE DRUGS HERE UNTIL THEN?
OF COURSE, JAX. WE HAVE YOUR BACK, JUST SAY THE WORD.

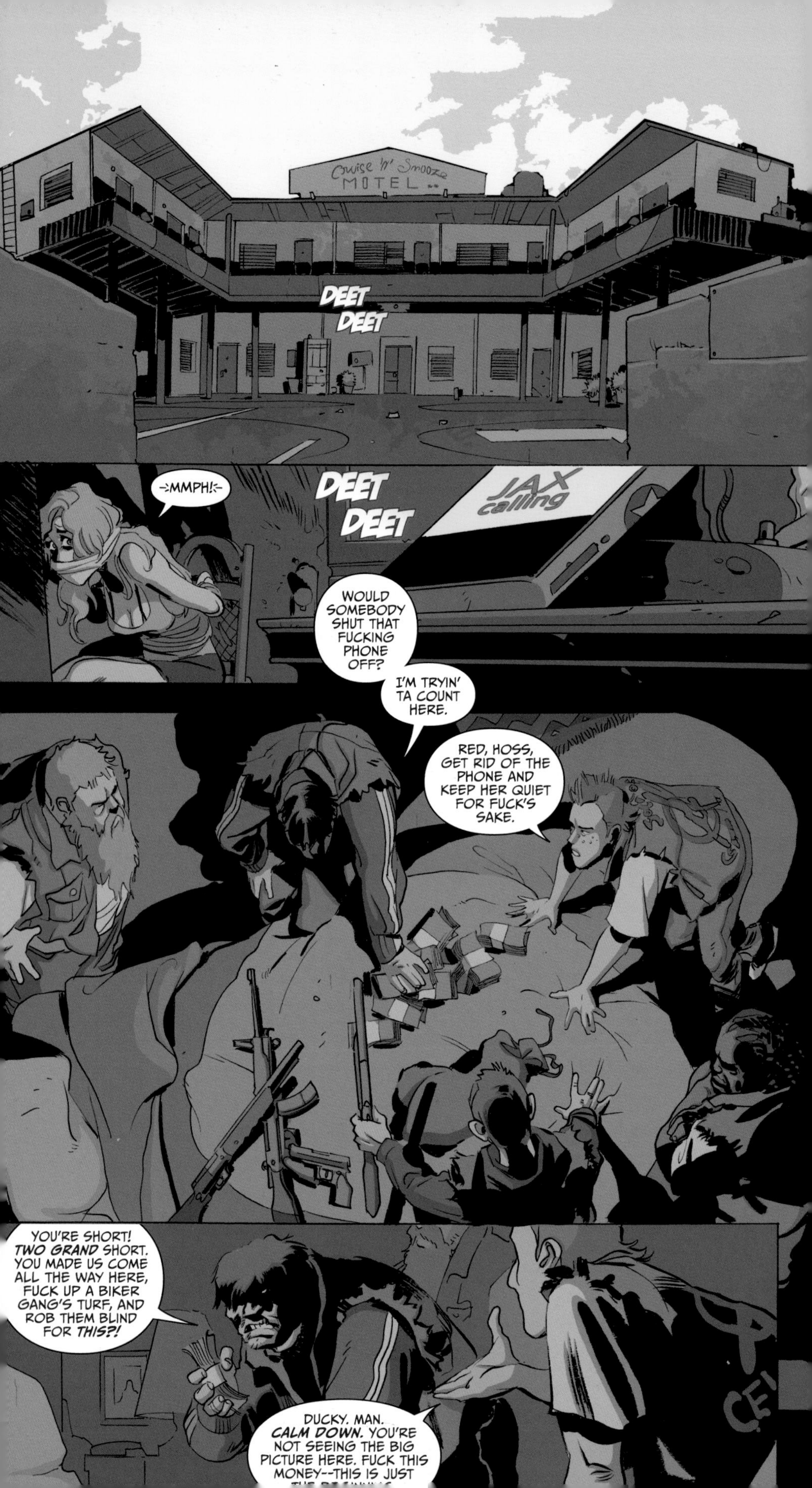
Cruise 'n' Snooze
MOTEL
DEET DEET
-MMPH!-
DEET DEET
JAX calling
WOULD SOMEBODY SHUT THAT FUCKING PHONE OFF?
I'M TRYIN' TA COUNT HERE.
RED, HOSS, GET RID OF THE PHONE AND KEEP HER QUIET FOR FUCK'S SAKE.
YOU'RE SHORT! *TWO GRAND* SHORT. YOU MADE US COME ALL THE WAY HERE, FUCK UP A BIKER GANG'S TURF, AND ROB THEM BLIND FOR *THIS?!*
DUCKY. MAN. *CALM DOWN.* YOU'RE NOT SEEING THE BIG PICTURE HERE. FUCK THIS MONEY--THIS IS JUST

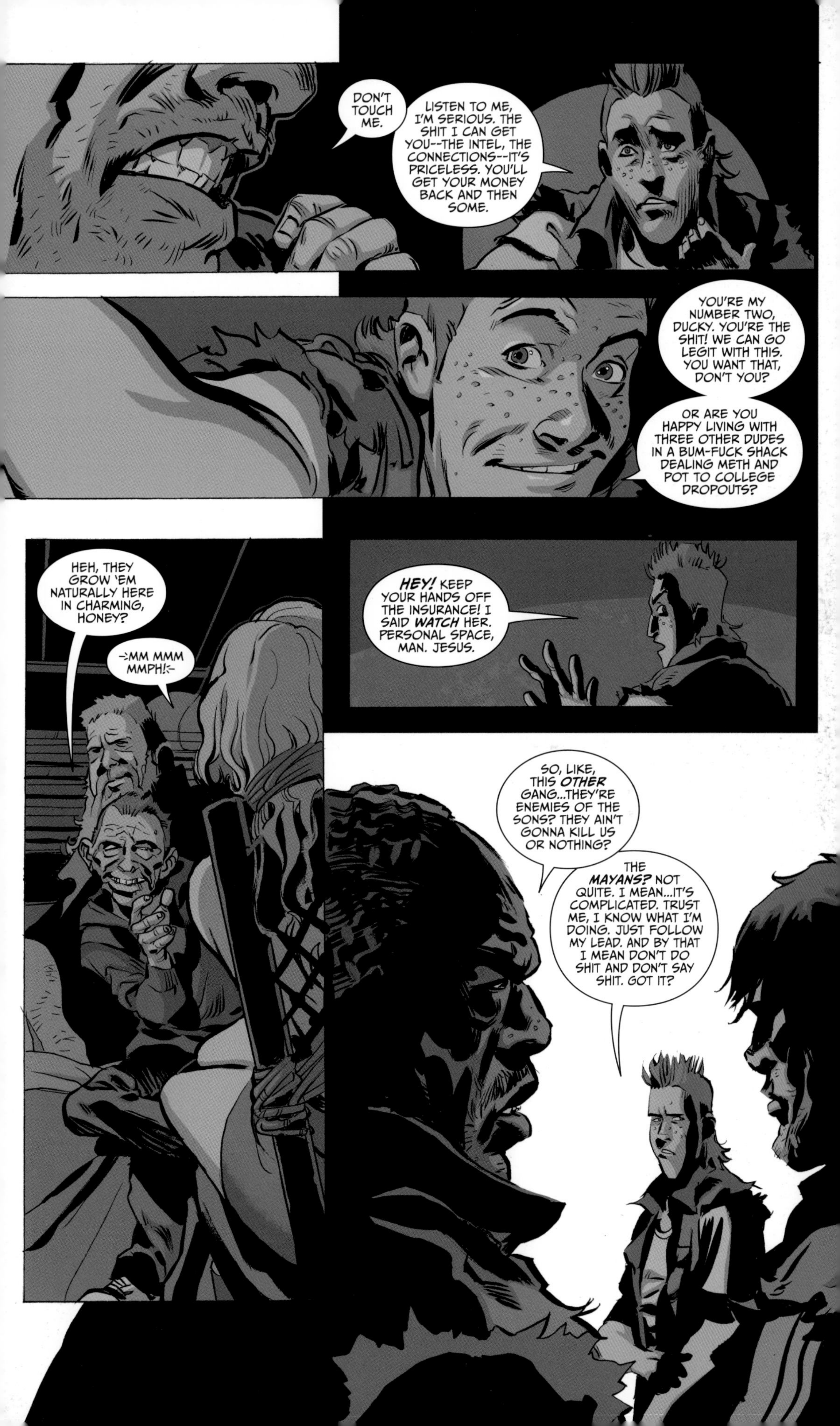
DON'T TOUCH ME.
LISTEN TO ME, I'M SERIOUS. THE SHIT I CAN GET YOU--THE INTEL, THE CONNECTIONS--IT'S PRICELESS. YOU'LL GET YOUR MONEY BACK AND THEN SOME.
YOU'RE MY NUMBER TWO, DUCKY. YOU'RE THE SHIT! WE CAN GO LEGIT WITH THIS. YOU WANT THAT, DON'T YOU?
OR ARE YOU HAPPY LIVING WITH THREE OTHER DUDES IN A BUM-FUCK SHACK DEALING METH AND POT TO COLLEGE DROPOUTS?
HEH, THEY GROW 'EM NATURALLY HERE IN CHARMING, HONEY?
MM MMM MMPH!
HEY! KEEP YOUR HANDS OFF THE INSURANCE! I SAID WATCH HER. PERSONAL SPACE, MAN. JESUS.
SO, LIKE, THIS OTHER GANG...THEY'RE ENEMIES OF THE SONS? THEY AIN'T GONNA KILL US OR NOTHING?
THE MAYANS? NOT QUITE. I MEAN...IT'S COMPLICATED. TRUST ME, I KNOW WHAT I'M DOING. JUST FOLLOW MY LEAD. AND BY THAT I MEAN DON'T DO SHIT AND DON'T SAY SHIT. GOT IT?

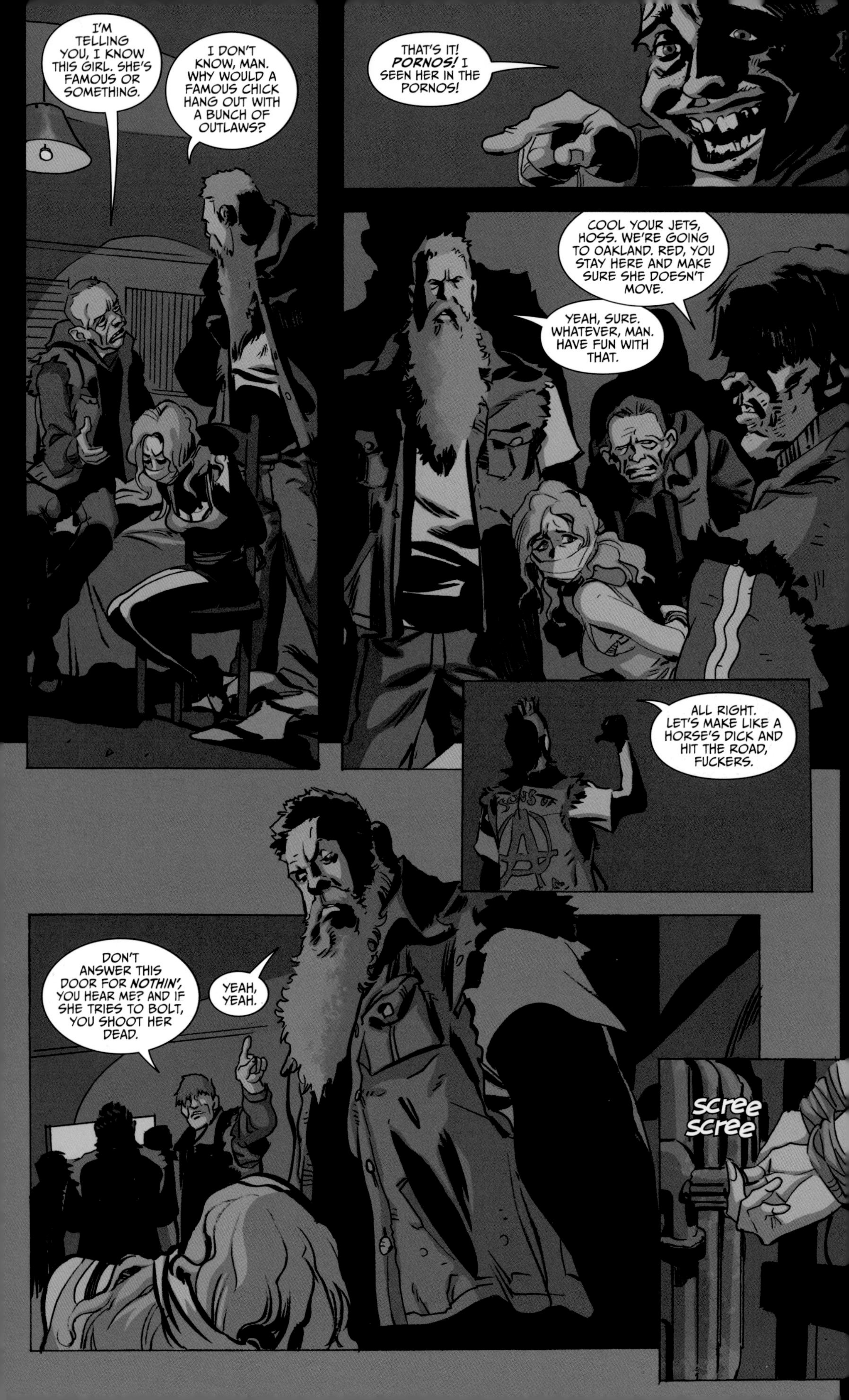
I'M TELLING YOU, I KNOW THIS GIRL. SHE'S FAMOUS OR SOMETHING.
I DON'T KNOW, MAN. WHY WOULD A FAMOUS CHICK HANG OUT WITH A BUNCH OF OUTLAWS?
THAT'S IT! PORNOS! I SEEN HER IN THE PORNOS!
COOL YOUR JETS, HOSS. WE'RE GOING TO OAKLAND. RED, YOU STAY HERE AND MAKE SURE SHE DOESN'T MOVE.
YEAH, SURE. WHATEVER, MAN. HAVE FUN WITH THAT.
ALL RIGHT. LET'S MAKE LIKE A HORSE'S DICK AND HIT THE ROAD, FUCKERS.
SONS OF
DON'T ANSWER THIS DOOR FOR NOTHIN', YOU HEAR ME? AND IF SHE TRIES TO BOLT, YOU SHOOT HER DEAD.
YEAH, YEAH.
scree
scree

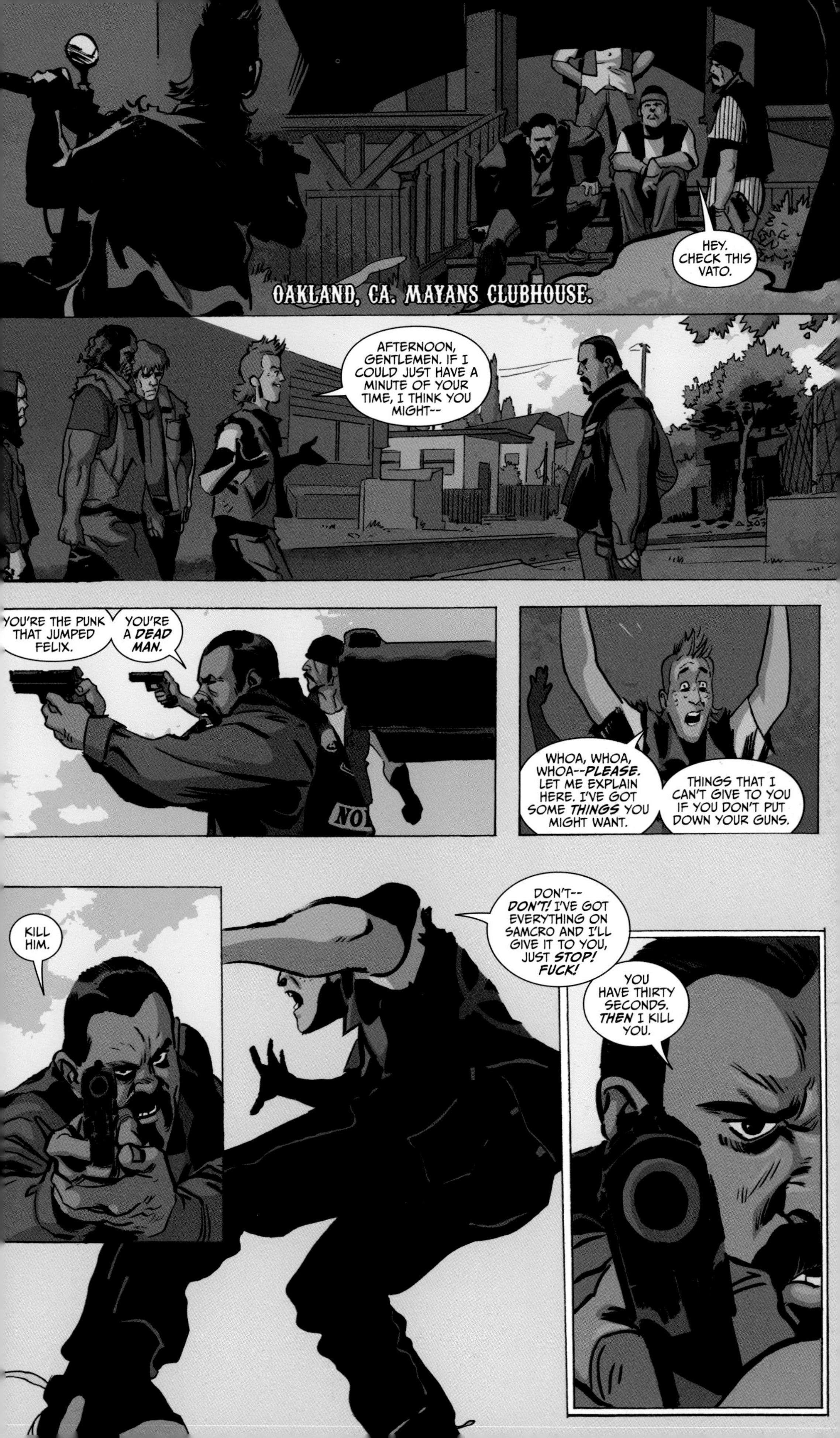
OAKLAND, CA. MAYANS CLUBHOUSE.
HEY. CHECK THIS VATO.
AFTERNOON, GENTLEMEN. IF I COULD JUST HAVE A MINUTE OF YOUR TIME, I THINK YOU MIGHT--
YOU'RE THE PUNK THAT JUMPED FELIX.
YOU'RE A *DEAD MAN.*
WHOA, WHOA, WHOA--*PLEASE.* LET ME EXPLAIN HERE. I'VE GOT SOME *THINGS* YOU MIGHT WANT.
THINGS THAT I CAN'T GIVE TO YOU IF YOU DON'T PUT DOWN YOUR GUNS.
KILL HIM.
DON'T-- *DON'T!* I'VE GOT EVERYTHING ON SAMCRO AND I'LL GIVE IT TO YOU, JUST *STOP! FUCK!*
YOU HAVE THIRTY SECONDS. *THEN* I KILL YOU.

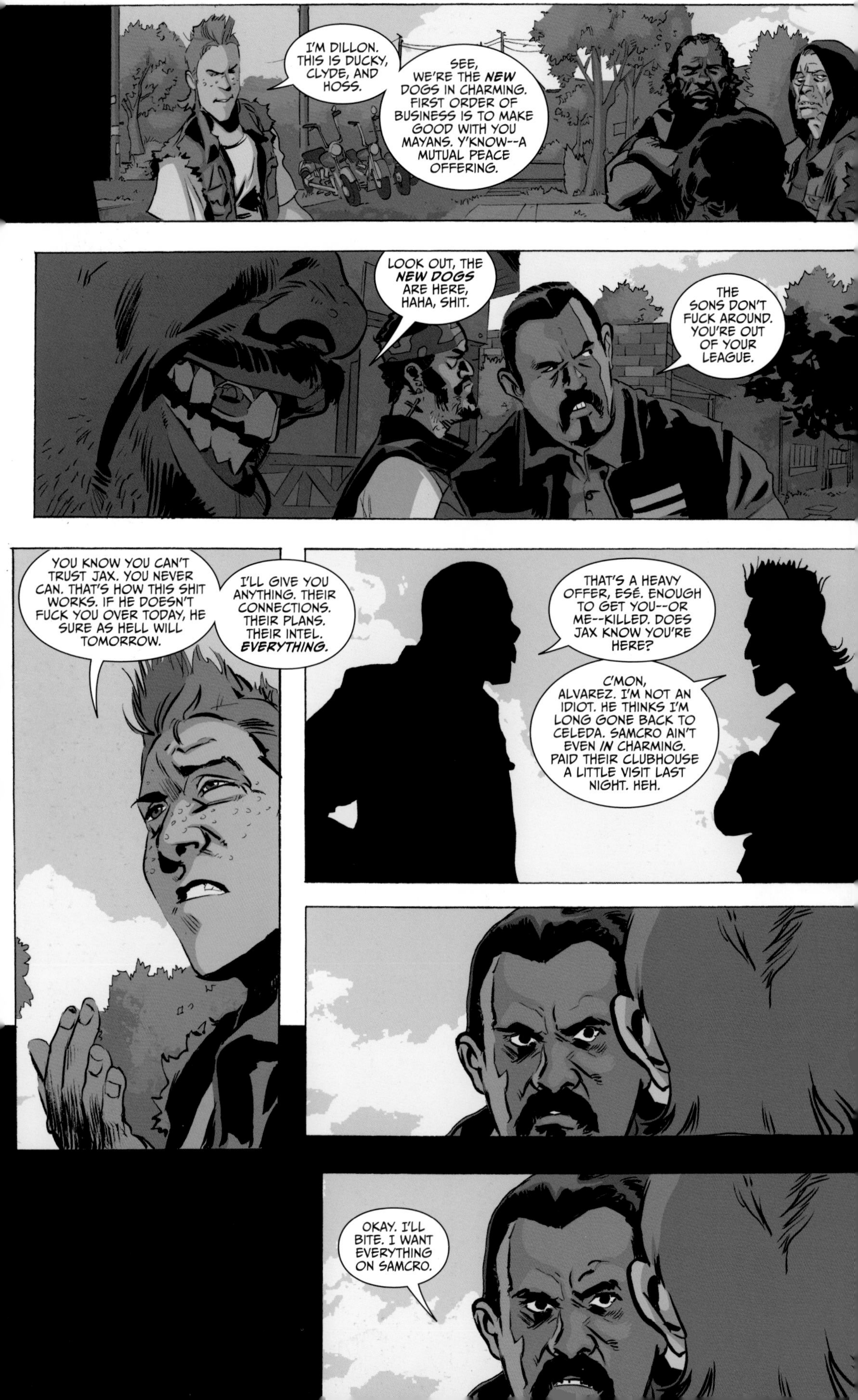
I'M DILLON. THIS IS DUCKY, CLYDE, AND HOSS.
SEE, WE'RE THE NEW DOGS IN CHARMING. FIRST ORDER OF BUSINESS IS TO MAKE GOOD WITH YOU MAYANS. Y'KNOW--A MUTUAL PEACE OFFERING.
LOOK OUT, THE NEW DOGS ARE HERE, HAHA, SHIT.
THE SONS DON'T FUCK AROUND. YOU'RE OUT OF YOUR LEAGUE.
YOU KNOW YOU CAN'T TRUST JAX. YOU NEVER CAN. THAT'S HOW THIS SHIT WORKS. IF HE DOESN'T FUCK YOU OVER TODAY, HE SURE AS HELL WILL TOMORROW.
I'LL GIVE YOU ANYTHING. THEIR CONNECTIONS. THEIR PLANS. THEIR INTEL. EVERYTHING.
THAT'S A HEAVY OFFER, ESÉ. ENOUGH TO GET YOU--OR ME--KILLED. DOES JAX KNOW YOU'RE HERE?
C'MON, ALVAREZ. I'M NOT AN IDIOT. HE THINKS I'M LONG GONE BACK TO CELEDA. SAMCRO AIN'T EVEN IN CHARMING. PAID THEIR CLUBHOUSE A LITTLE VISIT LAST NIGHT. HEH.
OKAY. I'LL BITE. I WANT EVERYTHING ON SAMCRO.

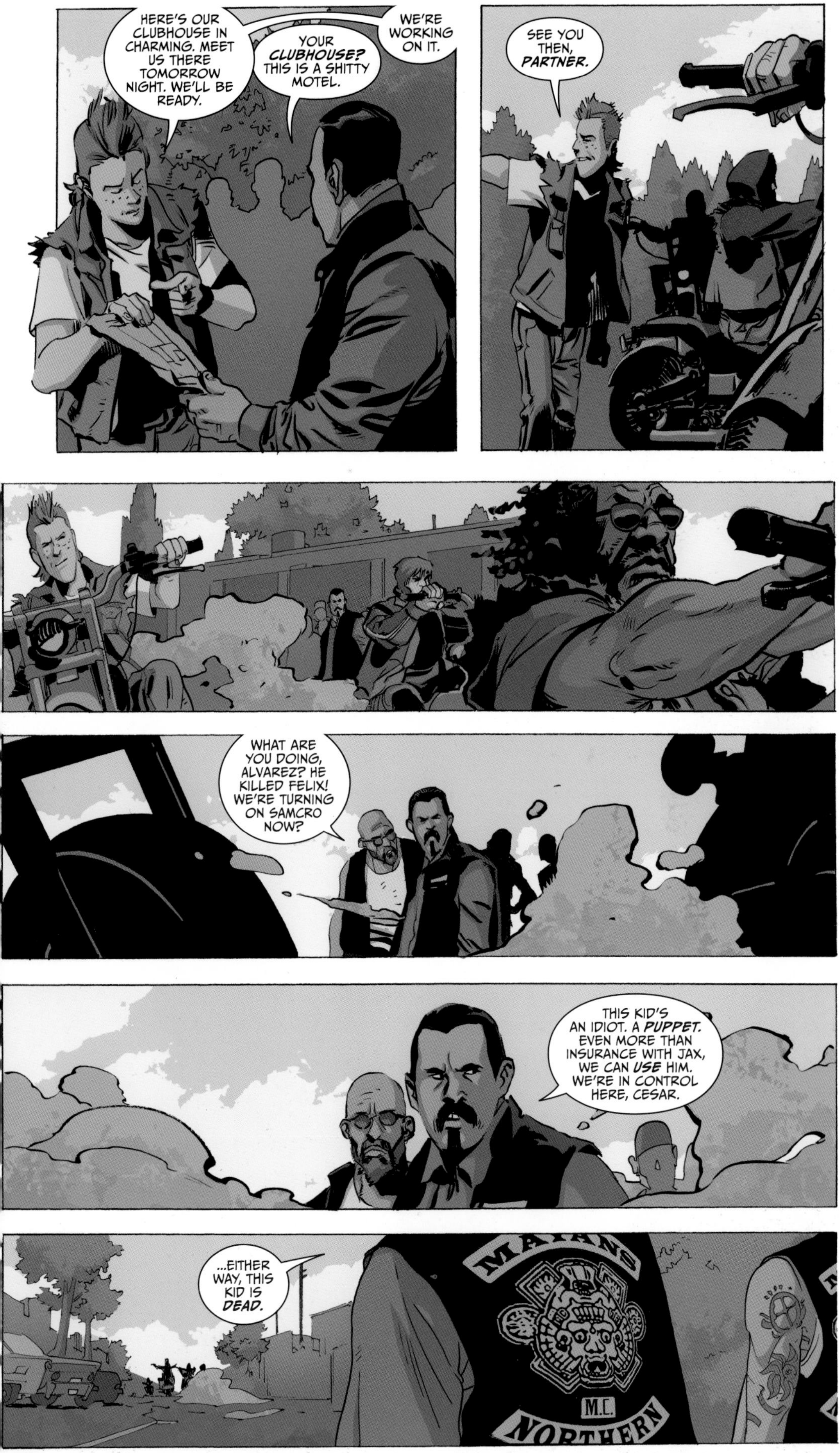

HERE'S OUR CLUBHOUSE IN CHARMING. MEET US THERE TOMORROW NIGHT. WE'LL BE READY.
YOUR CLUBHOUSE? THIS IS A SHITTY MOTEL.
WE'RE WORKING ON IT.
SEE YOU THEN, PARTNER.
WHAT ARE YOU DOING, ALVAREZ? HE KILLED FELIX! WE'RE TURNING ON SAMCRO NOW?
THIS KID'S AN IDIOT. A PUPPET. EVEN MORE THAN INSURANCE WITH JAX, WE CAN USE HIM. WE'RE IN CONTROL HERE, CESAR.
...EITHER WAY, THIS KID IS DEAD.
MAYANS
M.C.
NORTHERN

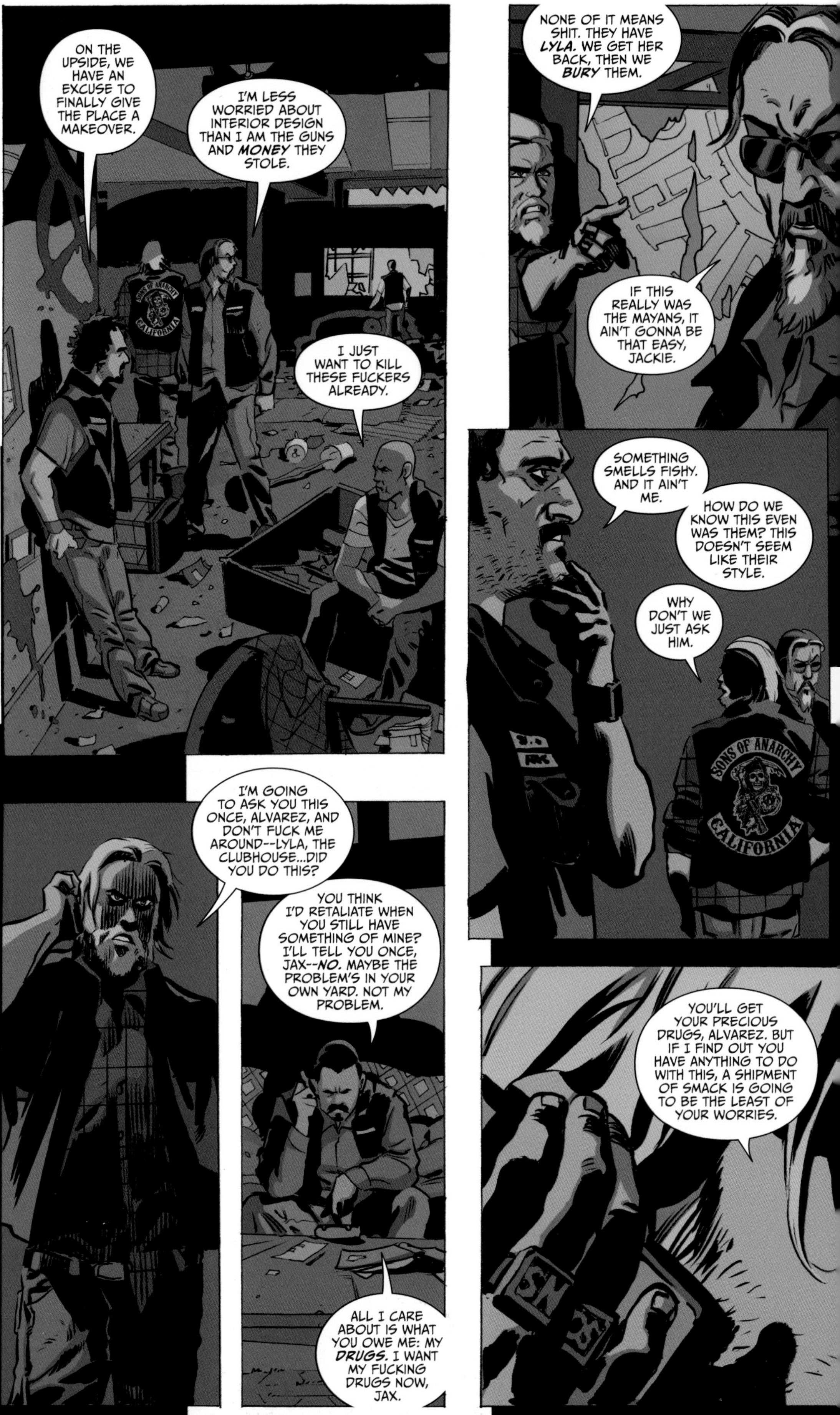
ON THE UPSIDE, WE HAVE AN EXCUSE TO FINALLY GIVE THE PLACE A MAKEOVER.
I'M LESS WORRIED ABOUT INTERIOR DESIGN THAN I AM THE GUNS AND MONEY THEY STOLE.
SONS OF ANARCHY
CALIFORNIA
I JUST WANT TO KILL THESE FUCKERS ALREADY.
NONE OF IT MEANS SHIT. THEY HAVE LYLA. WE GET HER BACK, THEN WE BURY THEM.
IF THIS REALLY WAS THE MAYANS, IT AIN'T GONNA BE THAT EASY, JACKIE.
SOMETHING SMELLS FISHY. AND IT AIN'T ME.
HOW DO WE KNOW THIS EVEN WAS THEM? THIS DOESN'T SEEM LIKE THEIR STYLE.
WHY DON'T WE JUST ASK HIM.
SONS OF ANARCHY
CALIFORNIA
I'M GOING TO ASK YOU THIS ONCE, ALVAREZ, AND DON'T FUCK ME AROUND--LYLA, THE CLUBHOUSE...DID YOU DO THIS?
YOU THINK I'D RETALIATE WHEN YOU STILL HAVE SOMETHING OF MINE? I'LL TELL YOU ONCE, JAX--NO. MAYBE THE PROBLEM'S IN YOUR OWN YARD. NOT MY PROBLEM.
ALL I CARE ABOUT IS WHAT YOU OWE ME: MY DRUGS. I WANT MY FUCKING DRUGS NOW, JAX.
YOU'LL GET YOUR PRECIOUS DRUGS, ALVAREZ. BUT IF I FIND OUT YOU HAVE ANYTHING TO DO WITH THIS, A SHIPMENT OF SMACK IS GOING TO BE THE LEAST OF YOUR WORRIES.

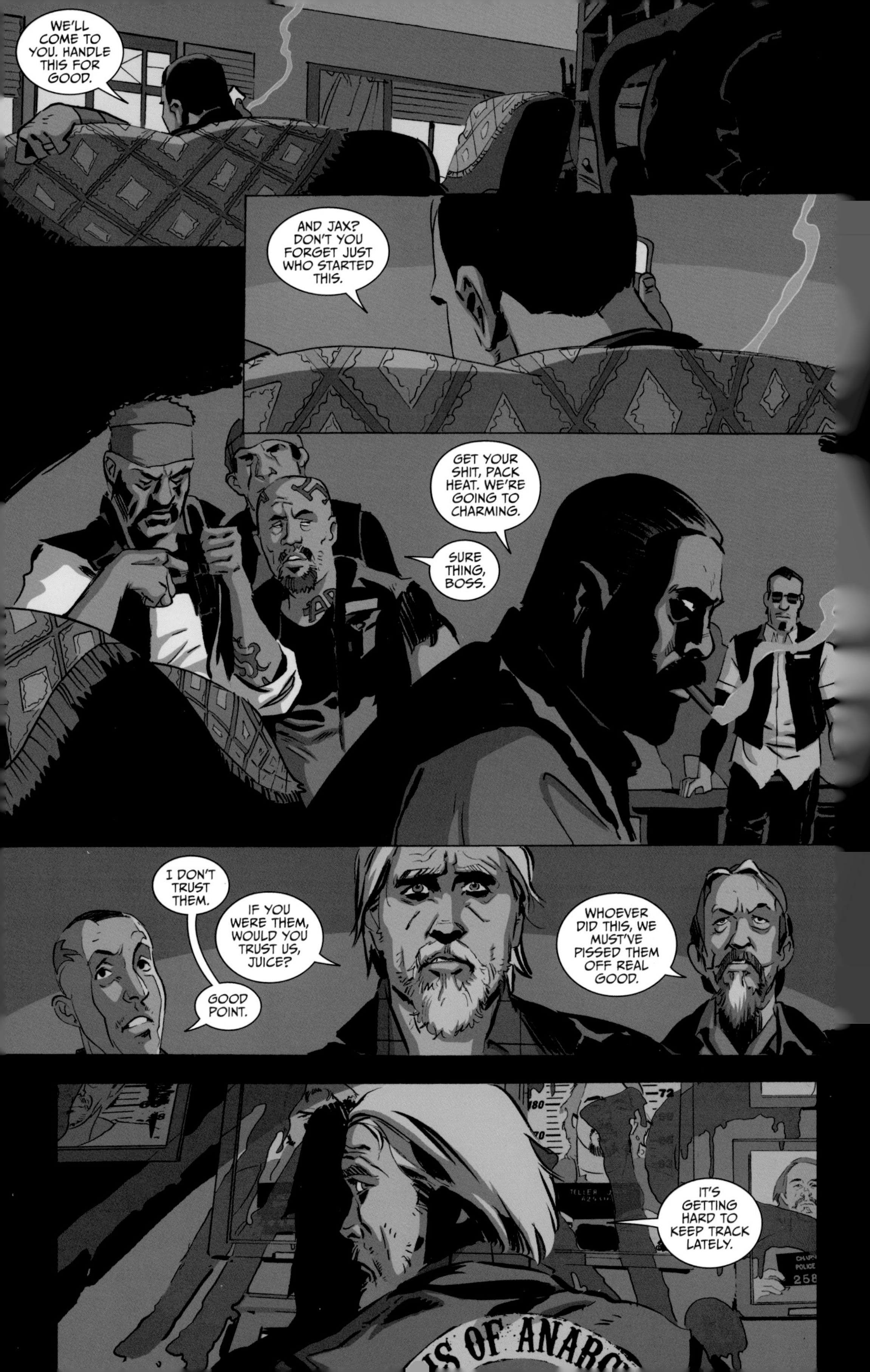
WE'LL COME TO YOU. HANDLE THIS FOR GOOD.
AND JAX? DON'T YOU FORGET JUST WHO STARTED THIS.
GET YOUR SHIT, PACK HEAT. WE'RE GOING TO CHARMING.
SURE THING, BOSS.
I DON'T TRUST THEM.
IF YOU WERE THEM, WOULD YOU TRUST US, JUICE?
GOOD POINT.
WHOEVER DID THIS, WE MUST'VE PISSED THEM OFF REAL GOOD.
IT'S GETTING HARD TO KEEP TRACK LATELY.

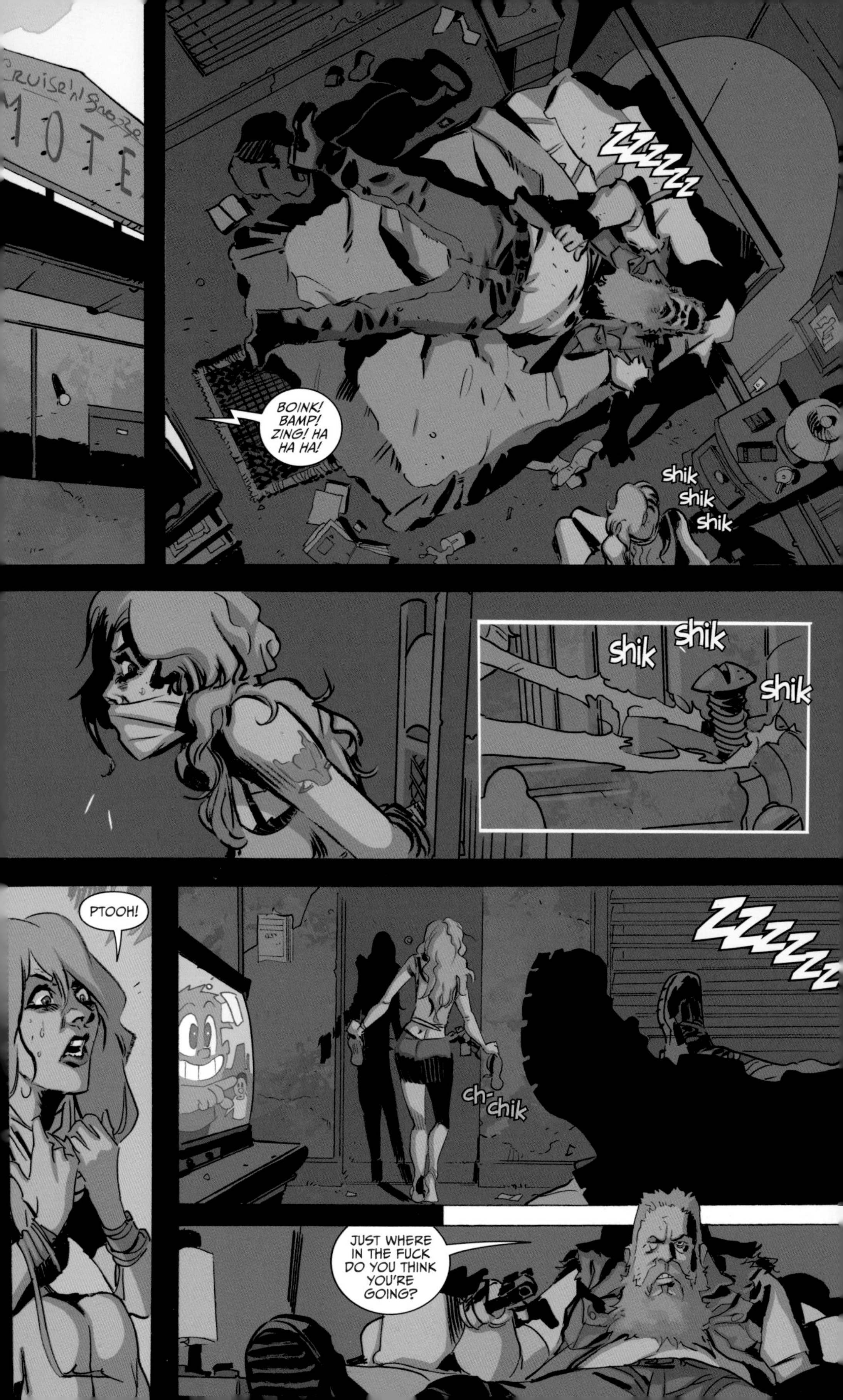
CRUISE'N'BOOZE
MOTE
ZZZZZZ
BOINK! BAMP! ZING! HA HA HA!
shik shik shik
shik shik shik
PTOOH!
ZZZZZZ
ch-chik
JUST WHERE IN THE FUCK DO YOU THINK YOU'RE GOING?

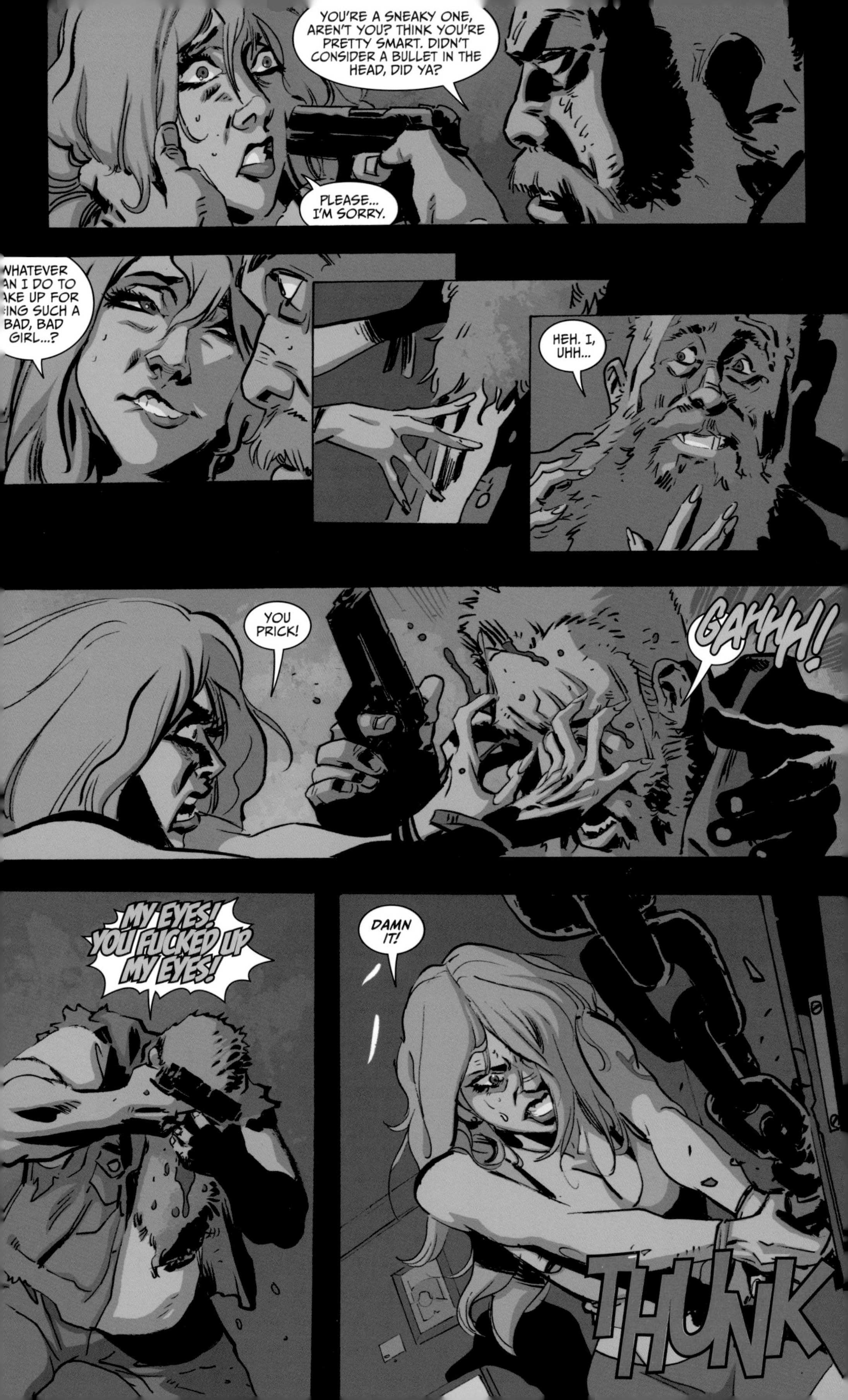
YOU'RE A SNEAKY ONE, AREN'T YOU? THINK YOU'RE PRETTY SMART. DIDN'T CONSIDER A BULLET IN THE HEAD, DID YA?
PLEASE... I'M SORRY.
WHATEVER AN I DO TO AKE UP FOR ING SUCH A BAD, BAD GIRL...?
HEH. I, UHH...
YOU PRICK!
GAHHH!
MY EYES! YOU FUCKED UP MY EYES!
DAMN IT!
THUNK

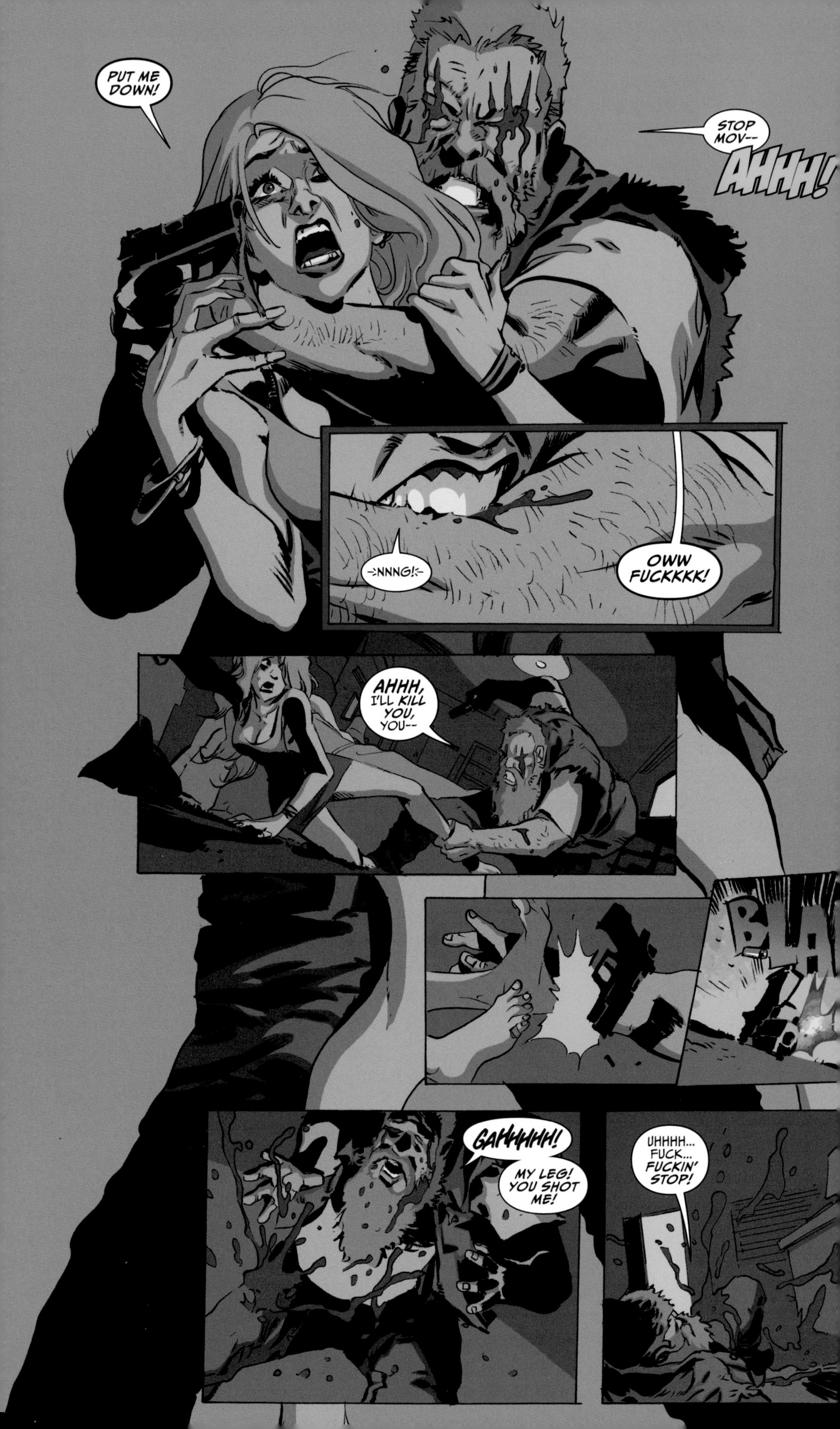
PUT ME DOWN!
STOP MOV--
AHHH!
-NNNG!-
OWW FUCKKKK!
AHHH, I'LL KILL YOU, YOU--
GAHHHHH!
MY LEG! YOU SHOT ME!
UHHHH... FUCK... FUCKIN' STOP!

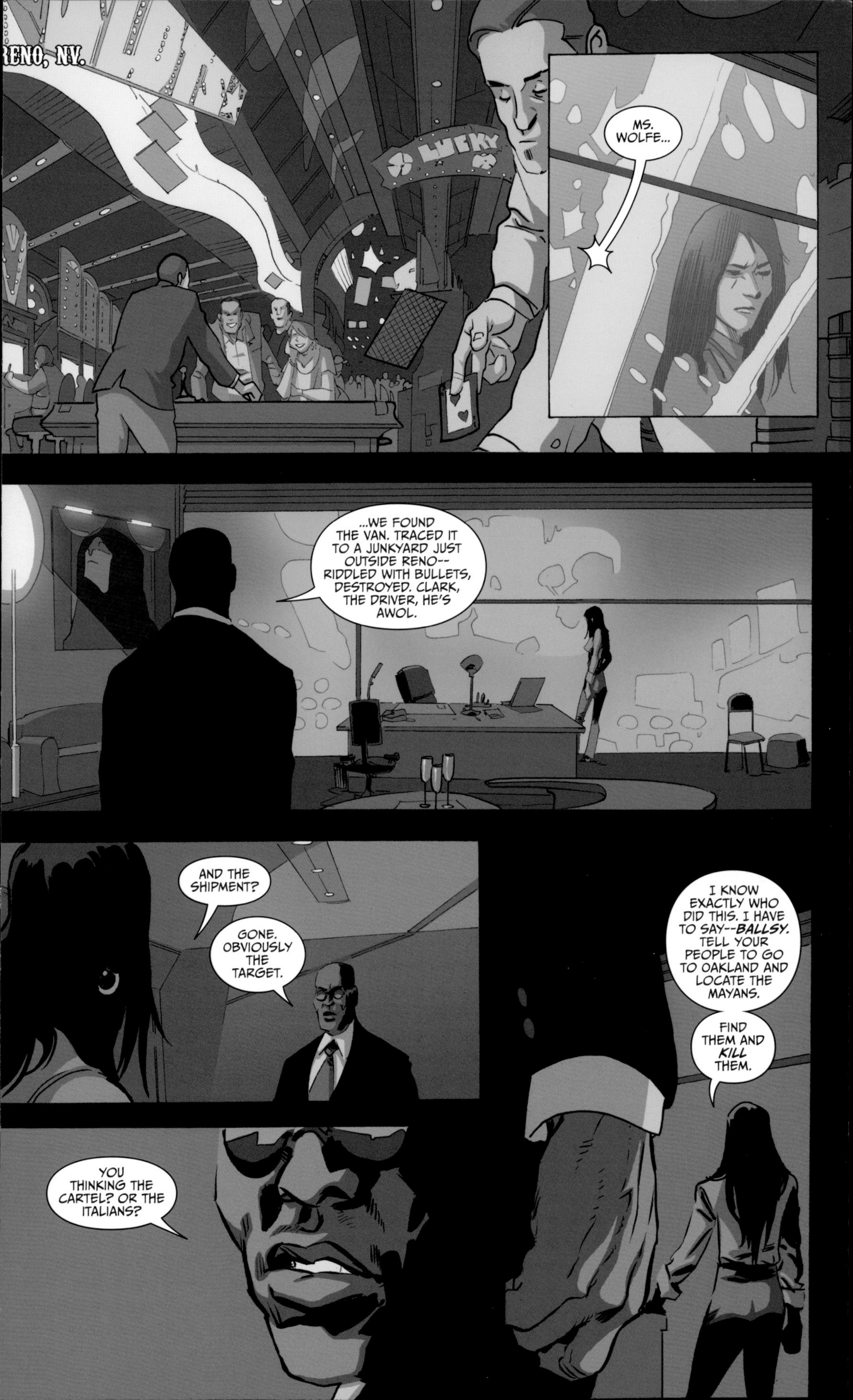
RENO, NV.
LUCKY
MS. WOLFE...
...WE FOUND THE VAN. TRACED IT TO A JUNKYARD JUST OUTSIDE RENO--RIDDLED WITH BULLETS, DESTROYED. CLARK, THE DRIVER, HE'S AWOL.
AND THE SHIPMENT?
GONE. OBVIOUSLY THE TARGET.
I KNOW EXACTLY WHO DID THIS. I HAVE TO SAY--***BALLSY.*** TELL YOUR PEOPLE TO GO TO OAKLAND AND LOCATE THE MAYANS.
FIND THEM AND ***KILL*** THEM.
YOU THINKING THE CARTEL? OR THE ITALIANS?

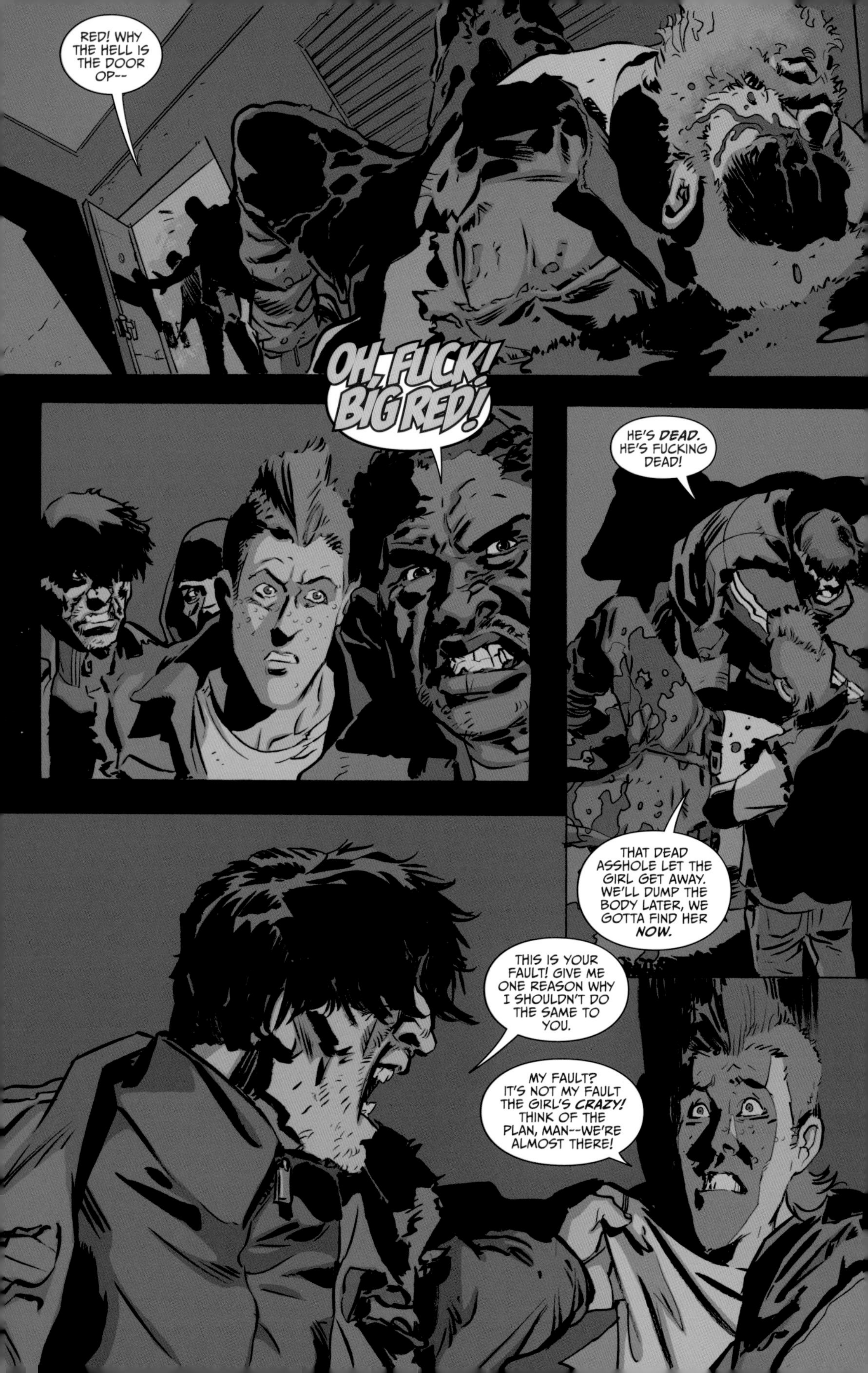
RED! WHY THE HELL IS THE DOOR OP--
OH, FUCK! BIG RED!
HE'S **DEAD.** HE'S FUCKING DEAD!
THAT DEAD ASSHOLE LET THE GIRL GET AWAY. WE'LL DUMP THE BODY LATER, WE GOTTA FIND HER **NOW.**
THIS IS YOUR FAULT! GIVE ME ONE REASON WHY I SHOULDN'T DO THE SAME TO YOU.
MY FAULT? IT'S NOT MY FAULT THE GIRL'S **CRAZY!** THINK OF THE PLAN, MAN--WE'RE ALMOST THERE!

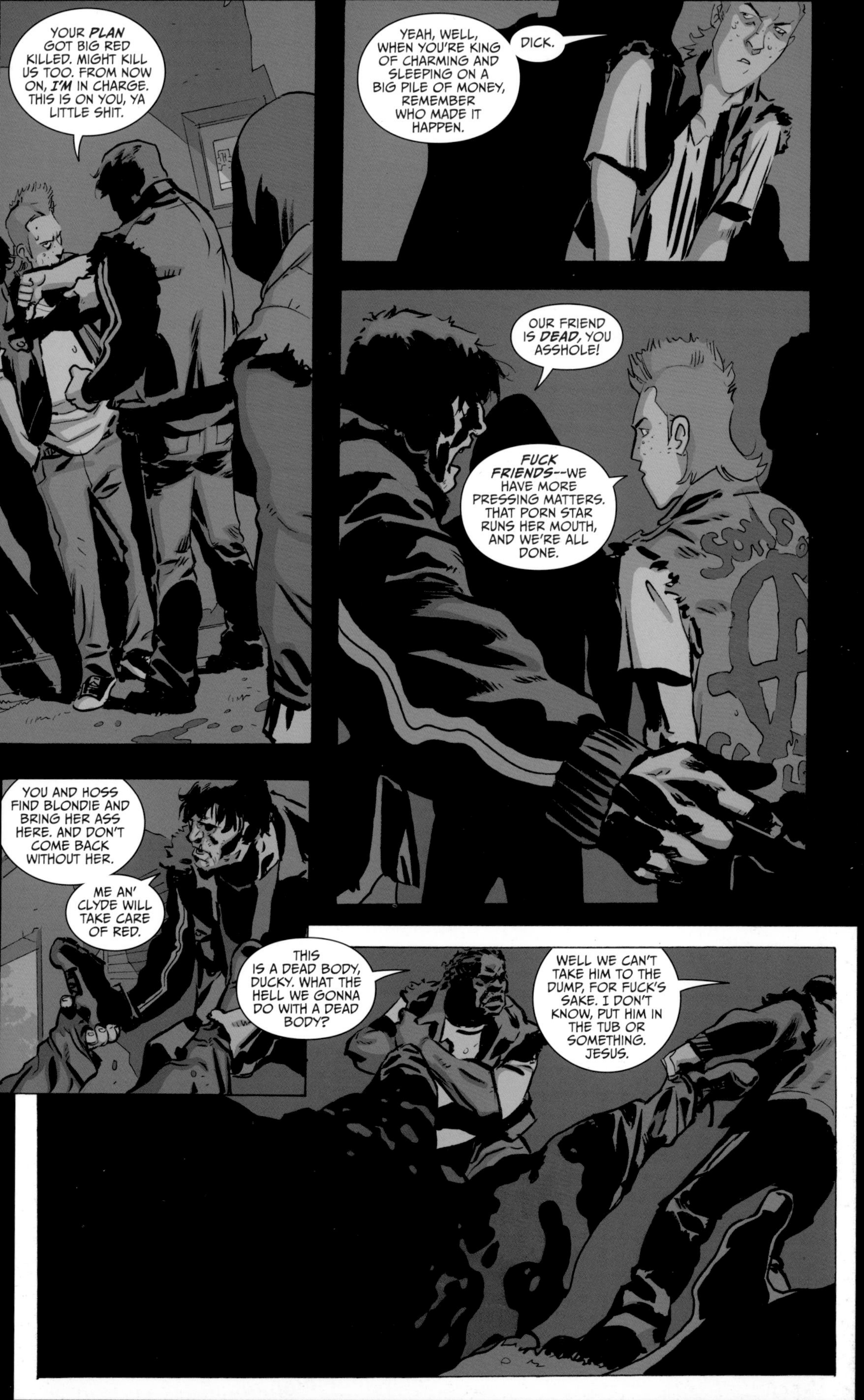
YOUR PLAN GOT BIG RED KILLED. MIGHT KILL US TOO. FROM NOW ON, I'M IN CHARGE. THIS IS ON YOU, YA LITTLE SHIT.
YEAH, WELL, WHEN YOU'RE KING OF CHARMING AND SLEEPING ON A BIG PILE OF MONEY, REMEMBER WHO MADE IT HAPPEN.
DICK.
OUR FRIEND IS DEAD, YOU ASSHOLE!
FUCK FRIENDS--WE HAVE MORE PRESSING MATTERS. THAT PORN STAR RUNS HER MOUTH, AND WE'RE ALL DONE.
YOU AND HOSS FIND BLONDIE AND BRING HER ASS HERE. AND DON'T COME BACK WITHOUT HER.
ME AN' CLYDE WILL TAKE CARE OF RED.
THIS IS A DEAD BODY, DUCKY. WHAT THE HELL WE GONNA DO WITH A DEAD BODY?
WELL WE CAN'T TAKE HIM TO THE DUMP, FOR FUCK'S SAKE. I DON'T KNOW, PUT HIM IN THE TUB OR SOMETHING. JESUS.

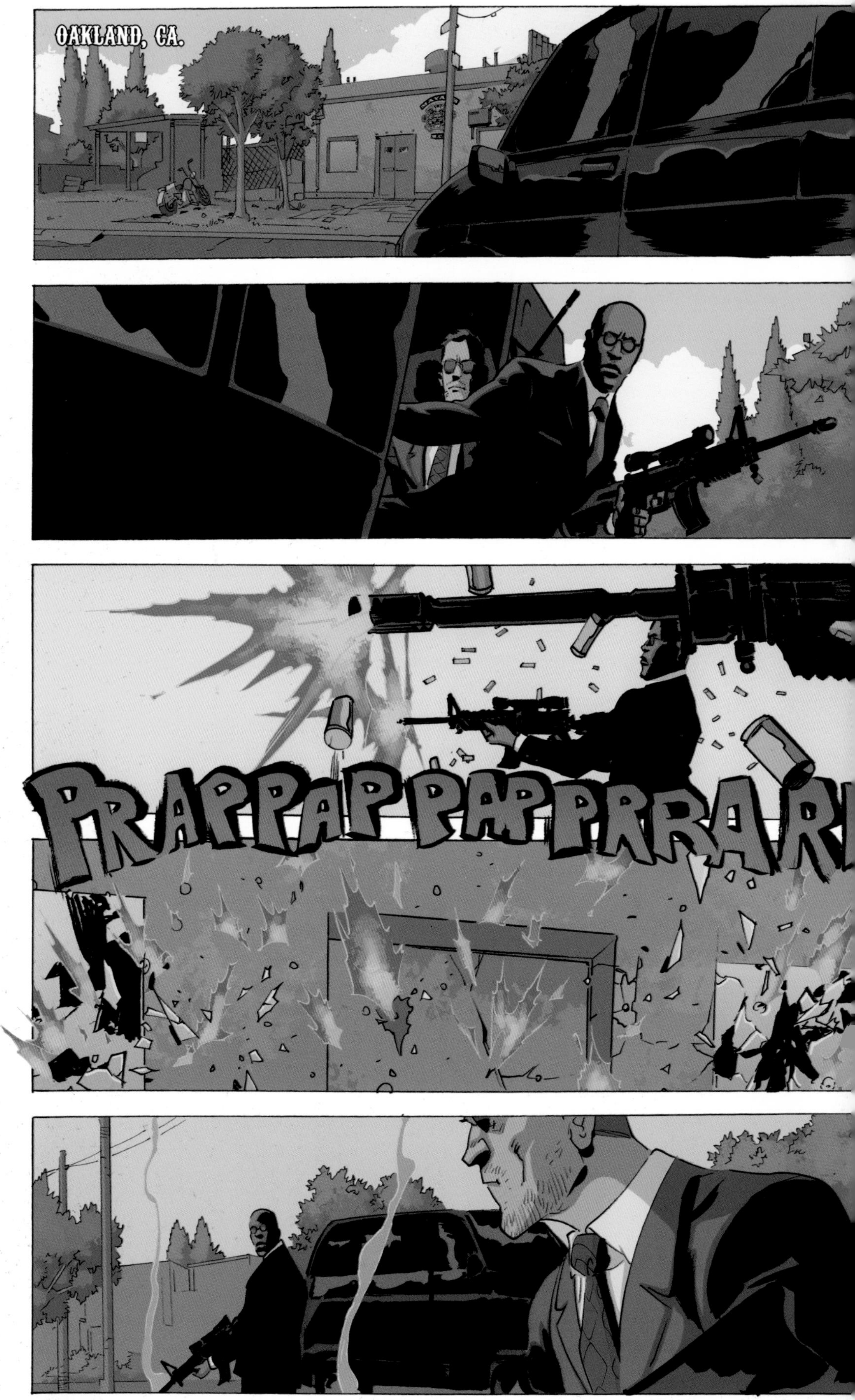
OAKLAND, CA.
PRAPPAP PAP PRRAR

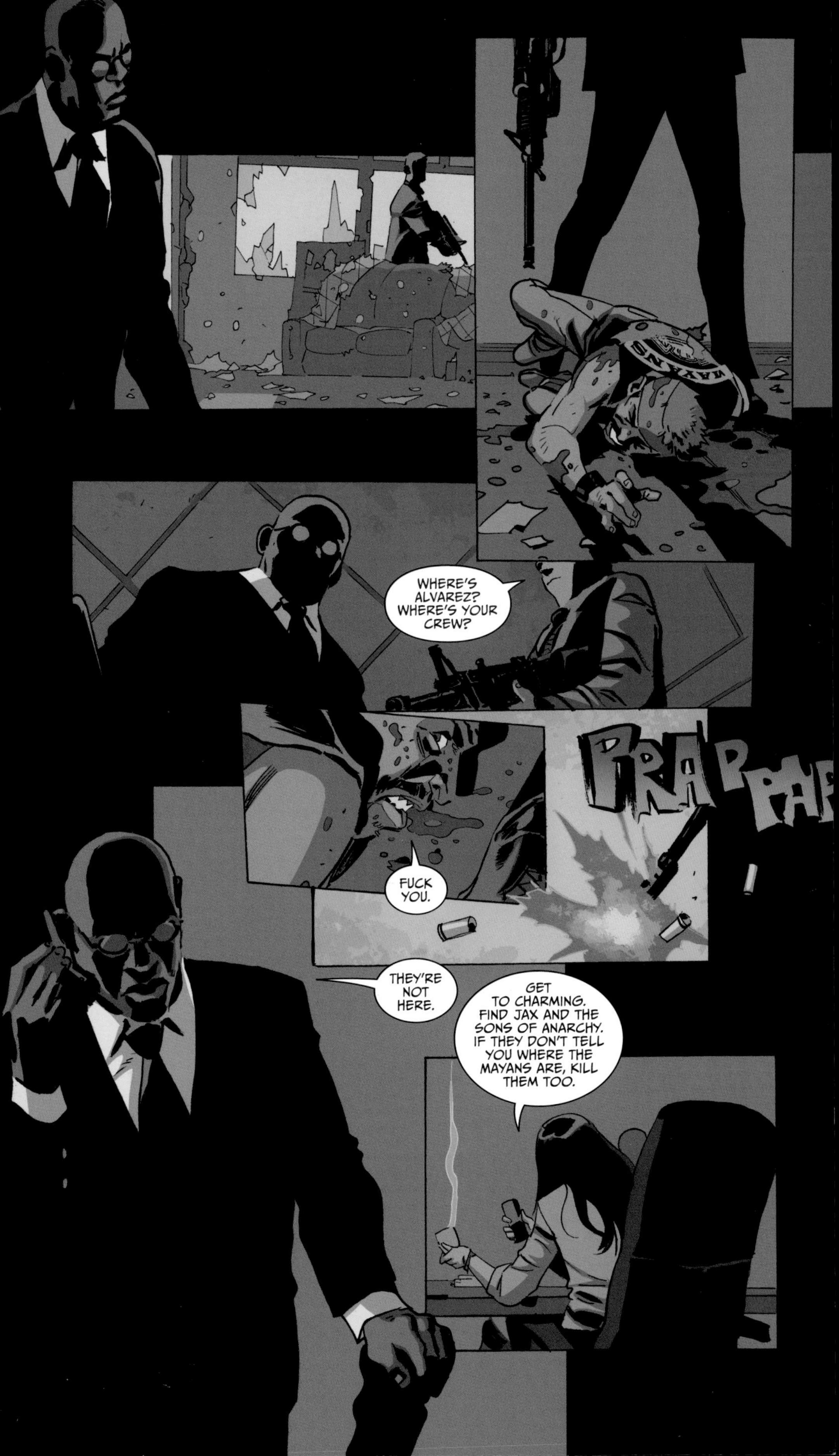
WHERE'S ALVAREZ? WHERE'S YOUR CREW?
FUCK YOU.
PRAP PAP
THEY'RE NOT HERE.
GET TO CHARMING. FIND JAX AND THE SONS OF ANARCHY. IF THEY DON'T TELL YOU WHERE THE MAYANS ARE, KILL THEM TOO.

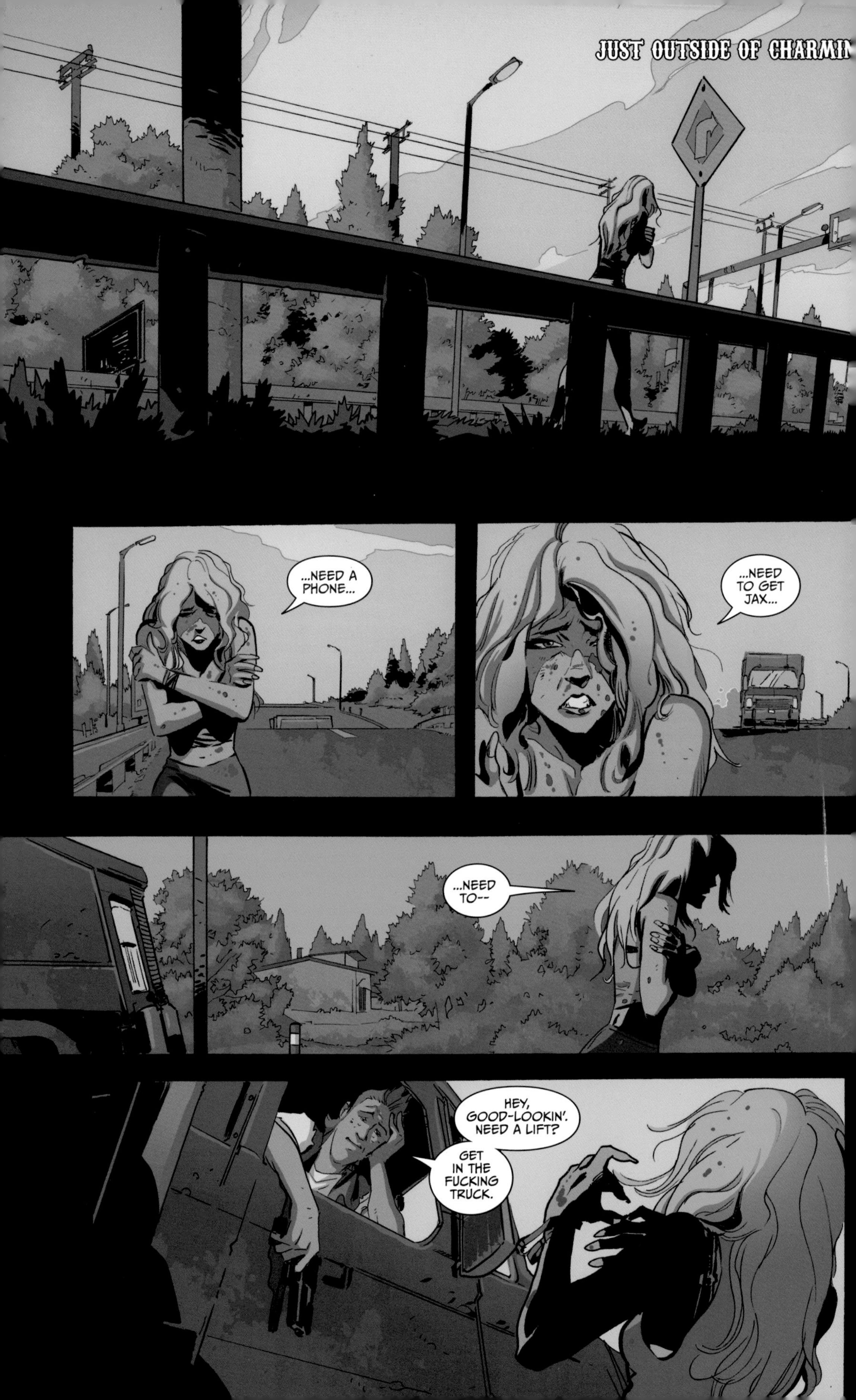
JUST OUTSIDE OF CHARMIN
...NEED A PHONE...
...NEED TO GET JAX...
...NEED TO--
HEY, GOOD-LOOKIN'. NEED A LIFT?
GET IN THE FUCKING TRUCK.

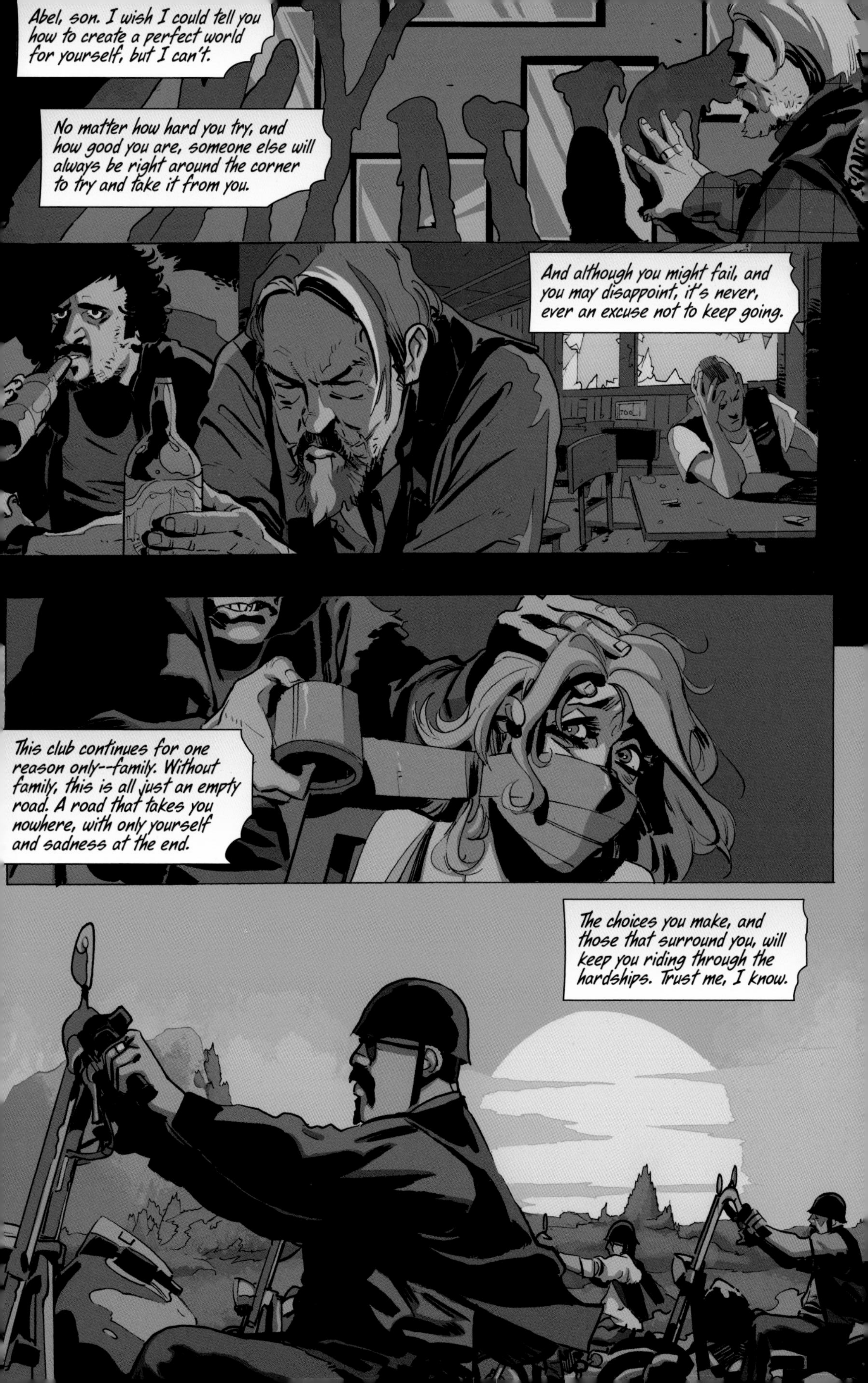
Abel, son. I wish I could tell you how to create a perfect world for yourself, but I can't.
No matter how hard you try, and how good you are, someone else will always be right around the corner to try and take it from you.
And although you might fail, and you may disappoint, it's never, ever an excuse not to keep going.
This club continues for one reason only--family. Without family, this is all just an empty road. A road that takes you nowhere, with only yourself and sadness at the end.
The choices you make, and those that surround you, will keep you riding through the hardships. Trust me, I know.

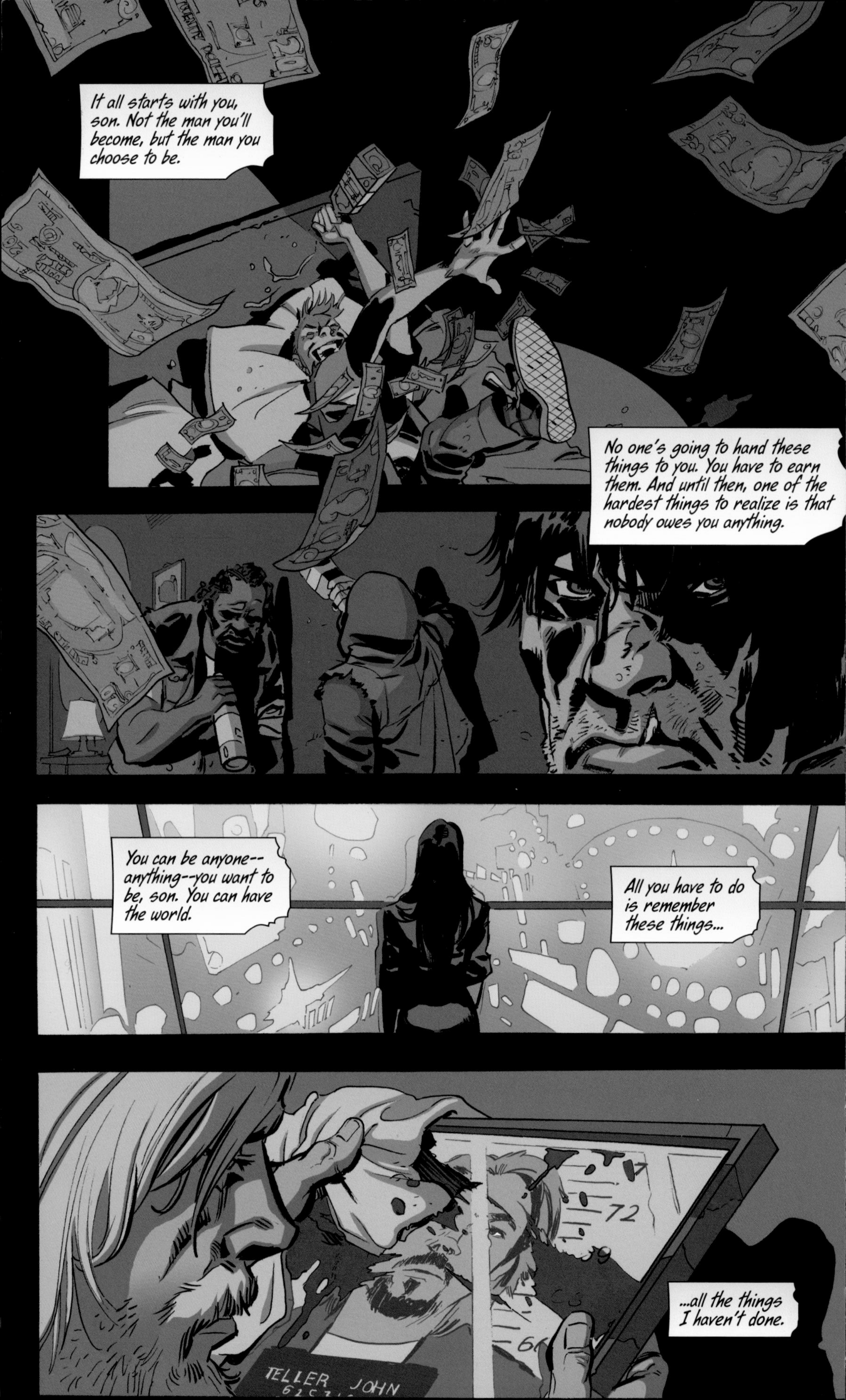
It all starts with you, son. Not the man you'll become, but the man you choose to be.
No one's going to hand these things to you. You have to earn them. And until then, one of the hardest things to realize is that nobody owes you anything.
You can be anyone--anything--you want to be, son. You can have the world.
All you have to do is remember these things...
...all the things I haven't done.
TELLER JOHN

CHAPTER 22

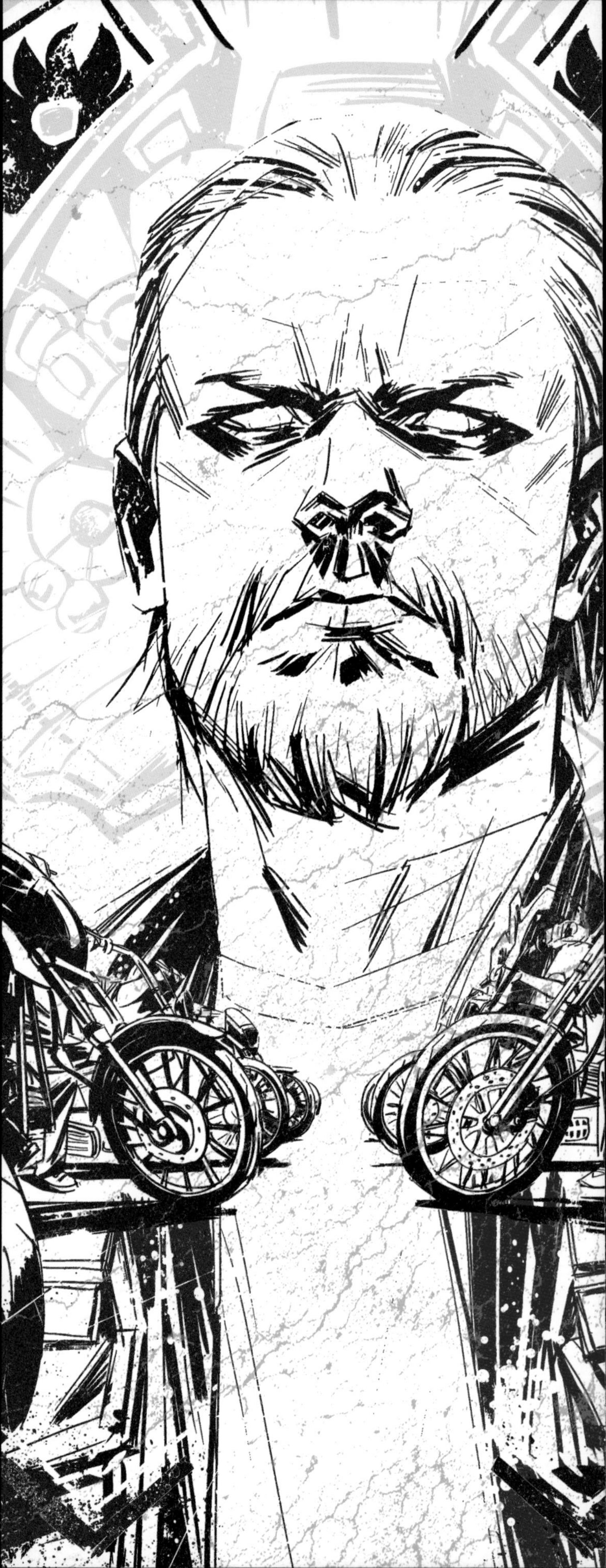

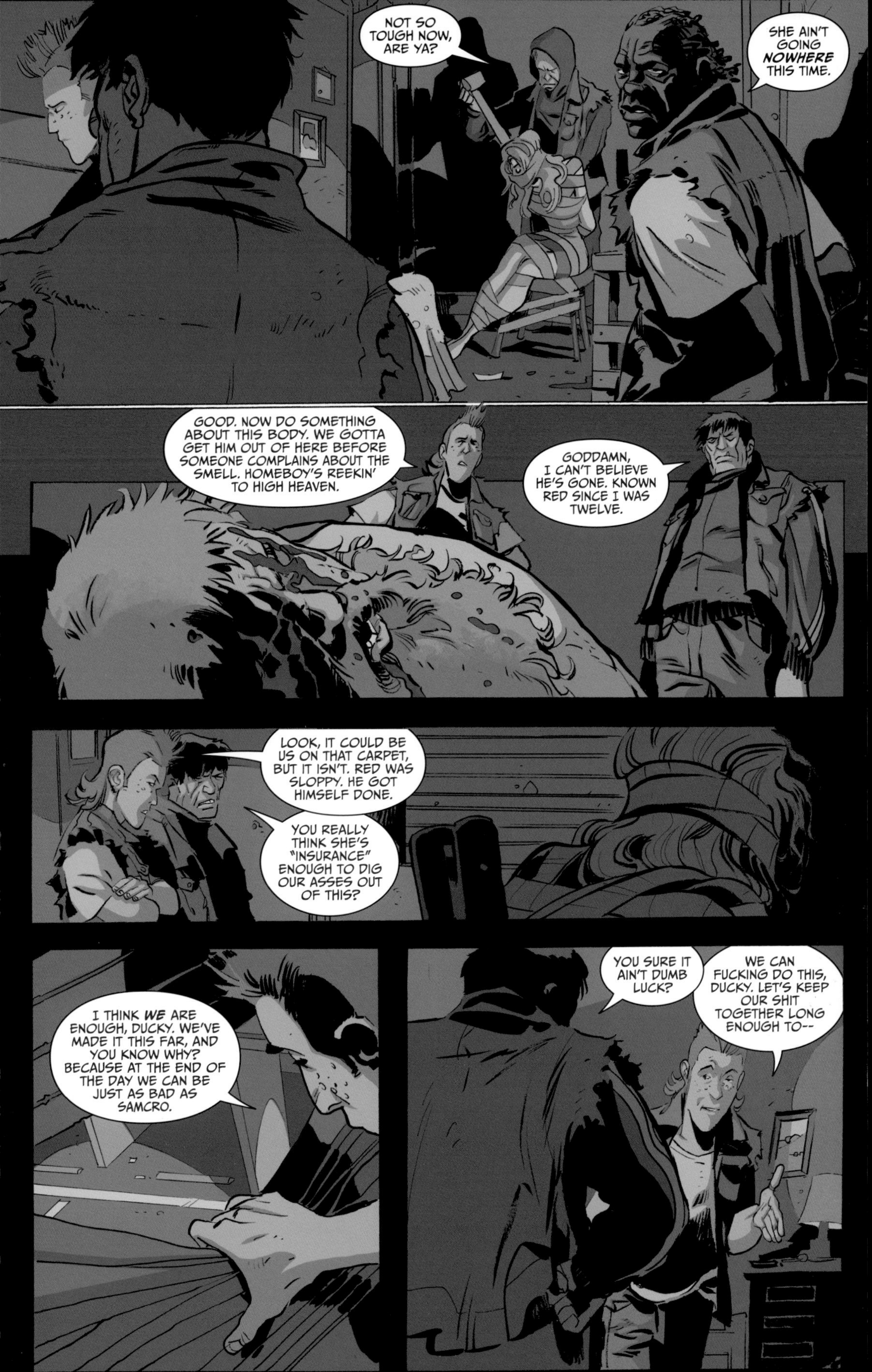
NOT SO TOUGH NOW, ARE YA?
SHE AIN'T GOING *NOWHERE* THIS TIME.
GOOD. NOW DO SOMETHING ABOUT THIS BODY. WE GOTTA GET HIM OUT OF HERE BEFORE SOMEONE COMPLAINS ABOUT THE SMELL. HOMEBOY'S REEKIN' TO HIGH HEAVEN.
GODDAMN, I CAN'T BELIEVE HE'S GONE. KNOWN RED SINCE I WAS TWELVE.
LOOK, IT COULD BE US ON THAT CARPET, BUT IT ISN'T. RED WAS SLOPPY. HE GOT HIMSELF DONE.
YOU REALLY THINK SHE'S "INSURANCE" ENOUGH TO DIG OUR ASSES OUT OF THIS?
I THINK *WE* ARE ENOUGH, DUCKY. WE'VE MADE IT THIS FAR, AND YOU KNOW WHY? BECAUSE AT THE END OF THE DAY WE CAN BE JUST AS BAD AS SAMCRO.
YOU SURE IT AIN'T DUMB LUCK?
WE CAN FUCKING DO THIS, DUCKY. LET'S KEEP OUR SHIT TOGETHER LONG ENOUGH TO--

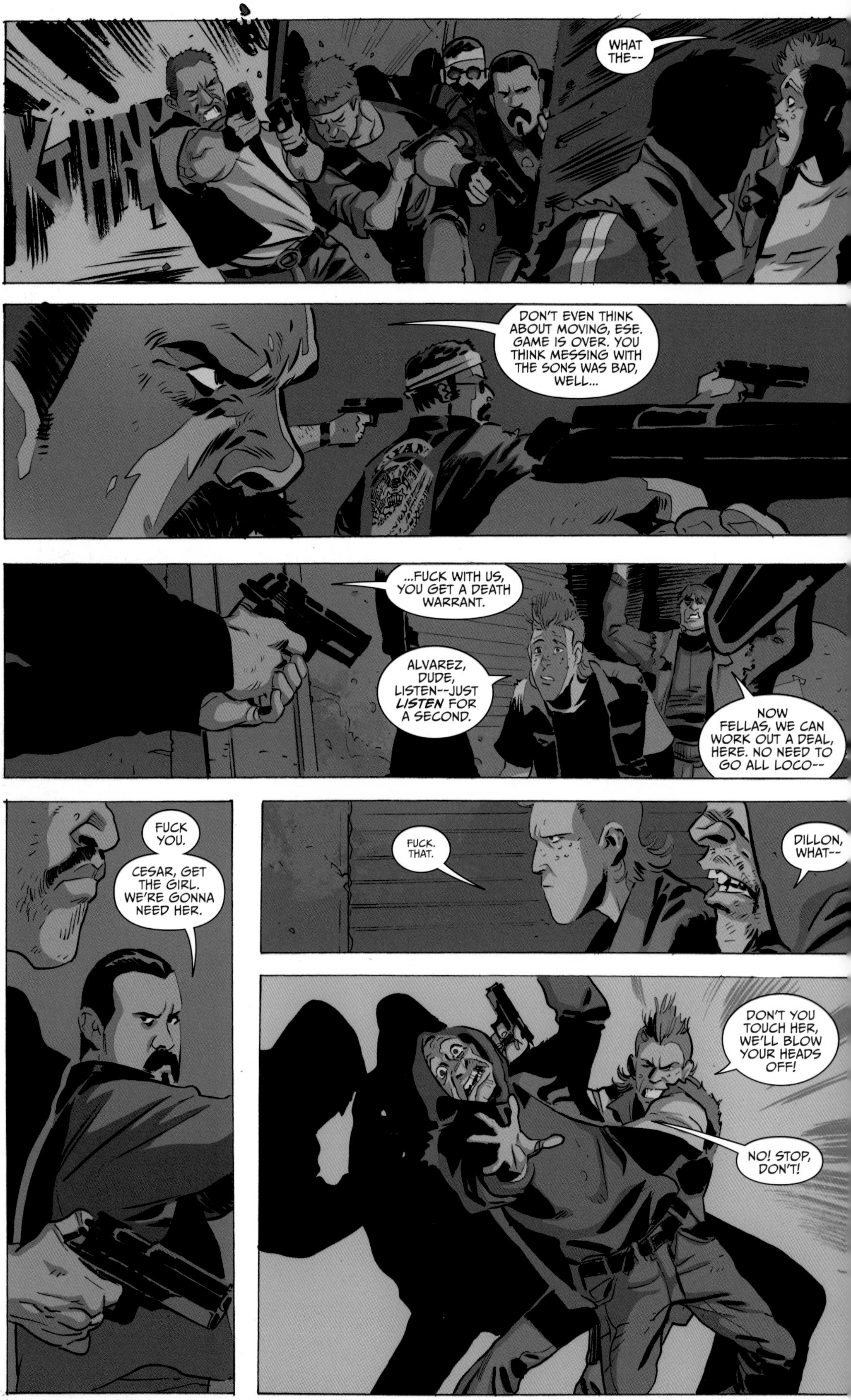
KTHAK
WHAT THE--
DON'T EVEN THINK ABOUT MOVING, ESE. GAME IS OVER. YOU THINK MESSING WITH THE SONS WAS BAD, WELL...
...FUCK WITH US, YOU GET A DEATH WARRANT.
ALVAREZ, DUDE, LISTEN--JUST *LISTEN* FOR A SECOND.
NOW FELLAS, WE CAN WORK OUT A DEAL, HERE. NO NEED TO GO ALL LOCO--
FUCK YOU.
CESAR, GET THE GIRL. WE'RE GONNA NEED HER.
FUCK. THAT.
DILLON, WHAT--
DON'T YOU TOUCH HER, WE'LL BLOW YOUR HEADS OFF!
NO! STOP, DON'T!

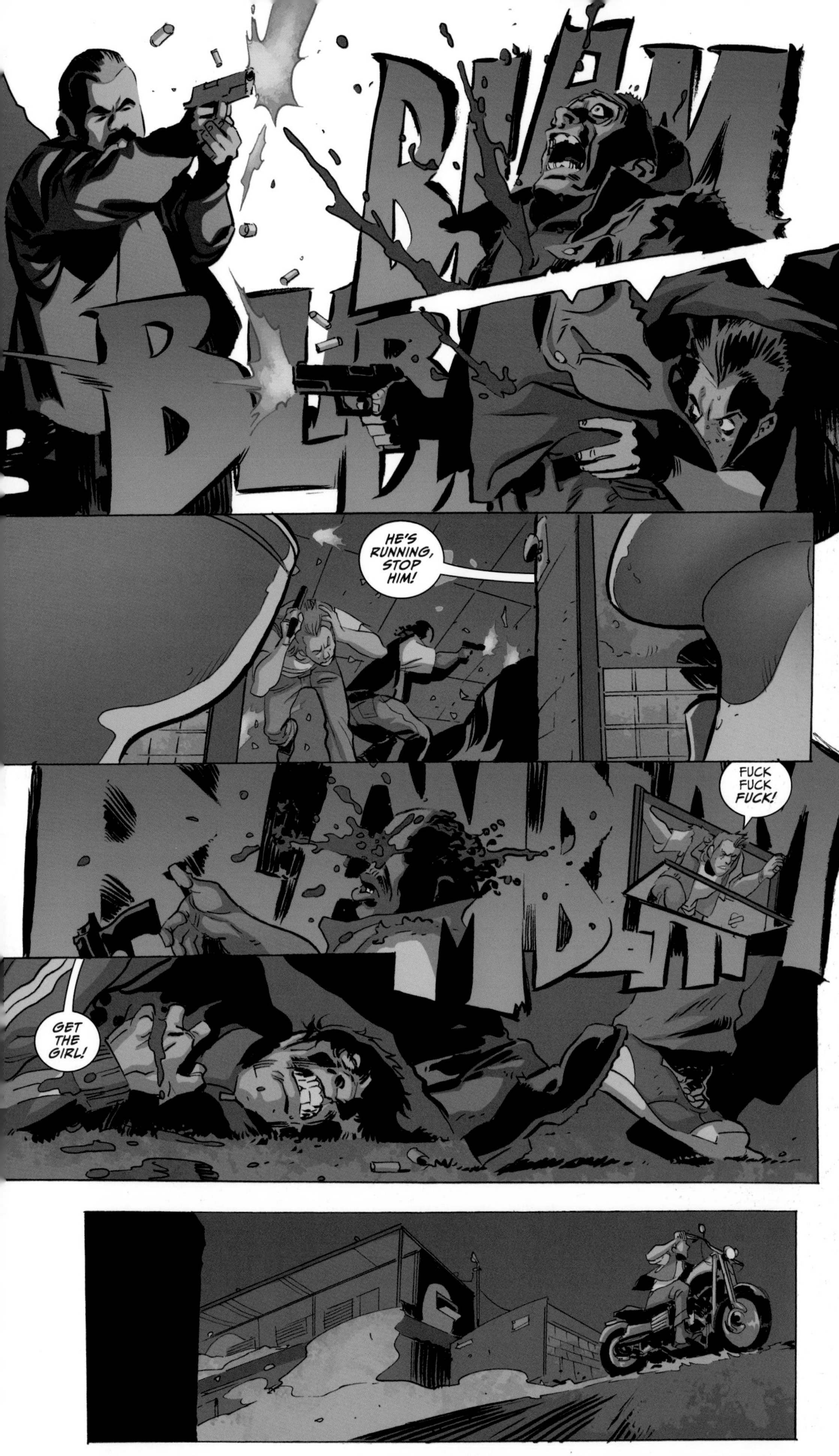
HE'S RUNNING, STOP HIM!
FUCK FUCK FUCK!
GET THE GIRL!

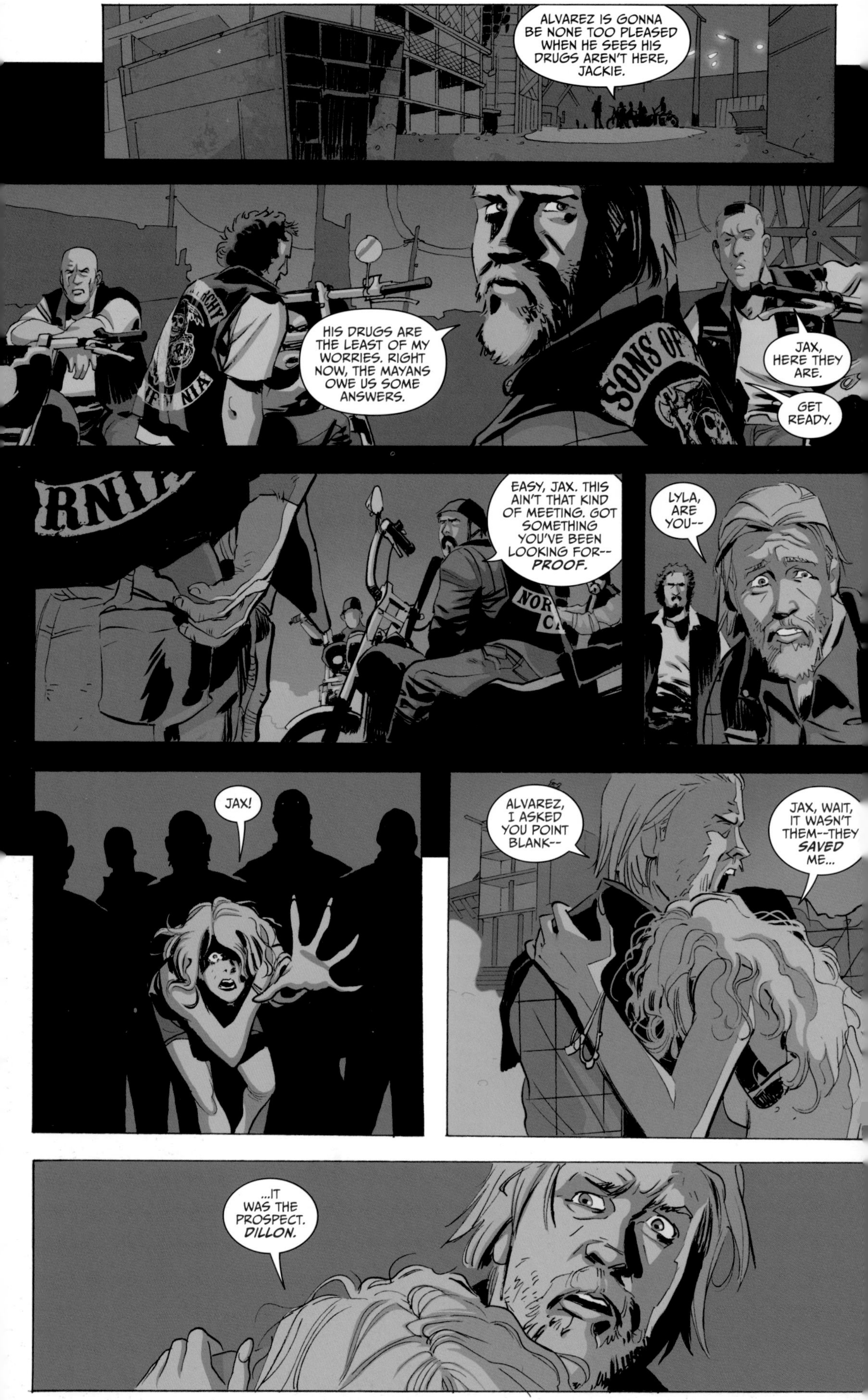
ALVAREZ IS GONNA BE NONE TOO PLEASED WHEN HE SEES HIS DRUGS AREN'T HERE, JACKIE.
HIS DRUGS ARE THE LEAST OF MY WORRIES. RIGHT NOW, THE MAYANS OWE US SOME ANSWERS.
JAX, HERE THEY ARE.
GET READY.
SONS OF
EASY, JAX. THIS AIN'T THAT KIND OF MEETING. GOT SOMETHING YOU'VE BEEN LOOKING FOR-- *PROOF.*
LYLA, ARE YOU--
JAX!
ALVAREZ, I ASKED YOU POINT BLANK--
JAX, WAIT, IT WASN'T THEM--THEY *SAVED* ME...
...IT WAS THE PROSPECT. *DILLON.*

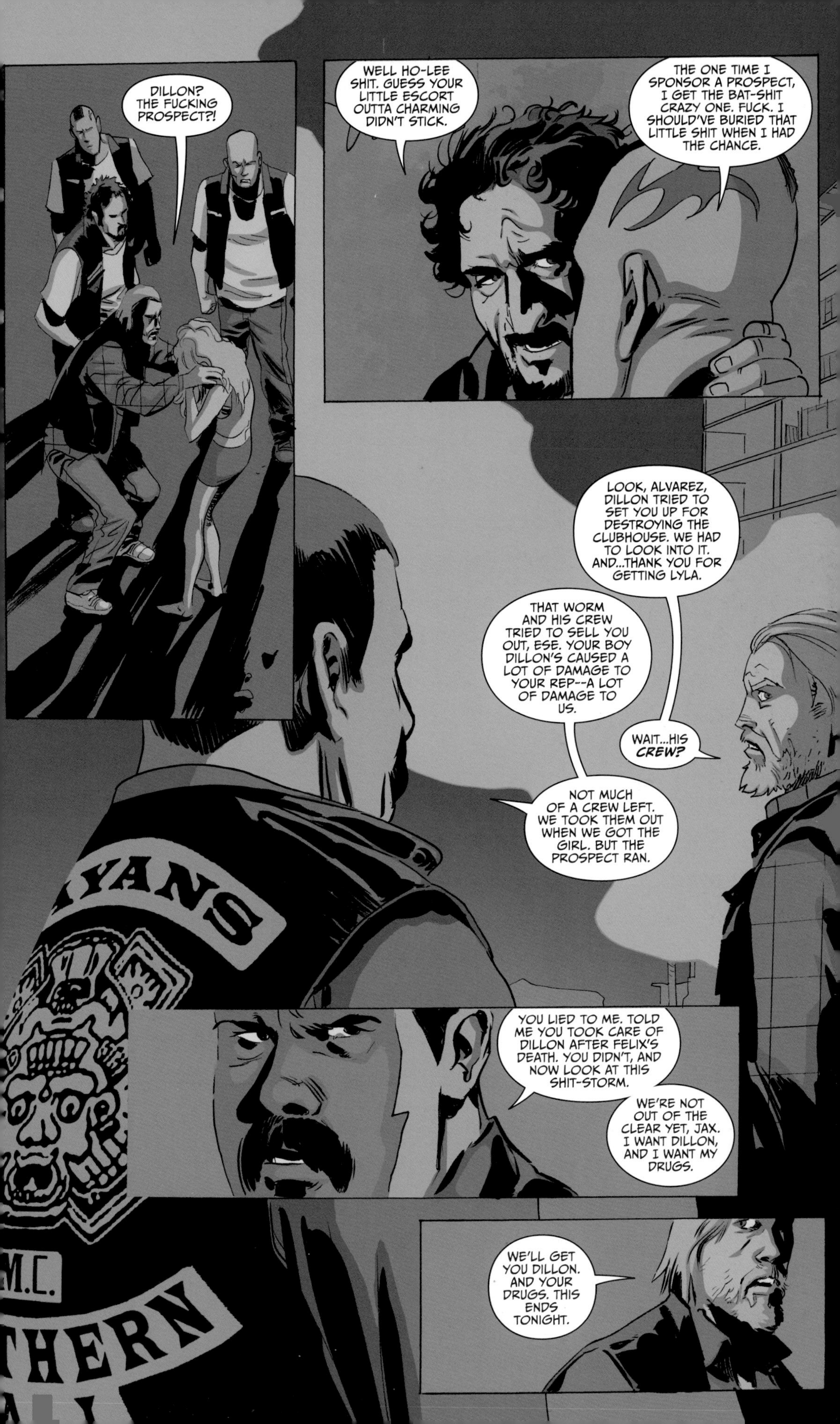
DILLON? THE FUCKING PROSPECT?!
WELL HO-LEE SHIT. GUESS YOUR LITTLE ESCORT OUTTA CHARMING DIDN'T STICK.
THE ONE TIME I SPONSOR A PROSPECT, I GET THE BAT-SHIT CRAZY ONE. FUCK. I SHOULD'VE BURIED THAT LITTLE SHIT WHEN I HAD THE CHANCE.
LOOK, ALVAREZ, DILLON TRIED TO SET YOU UP FOR DESTROYING THE CLUBHOUSE. WE HAD TO LOOK INTO IT. AND...THANK YOU FOR GETTING LYLA.
THAT WORM AND HIS CREW TRIED TO SELL YOU OUT, ESE. YOUR BOY DILLON'S CAUSED A LOT OF DAMAGE TO YOUR REP--A LOT OF DAMAGE TO US.
WAIT...HIS *CREW?*
NOT MUCH OF A CREW LEFT. WE TOOK THEM OUT WHEN WE GOT THE GIRL. BUT THE PROSPECT RAN.
YOU LIED TO ME. TOLD ME YOU TOOK CARE OF DILLON AFTER FELIX'S DEATH. YOU DIDN'T, AND NOW LOOK AT THIS SHIT-STORM.
WE'RE NOT OUT OF THE CLEAR YET, JAX. I WANT DILLON, AND I WANT MY DRUGS.
WE'LL GET YOU DILLON. AND YOUR DRUGS. THIS ENDS TONIGHT.

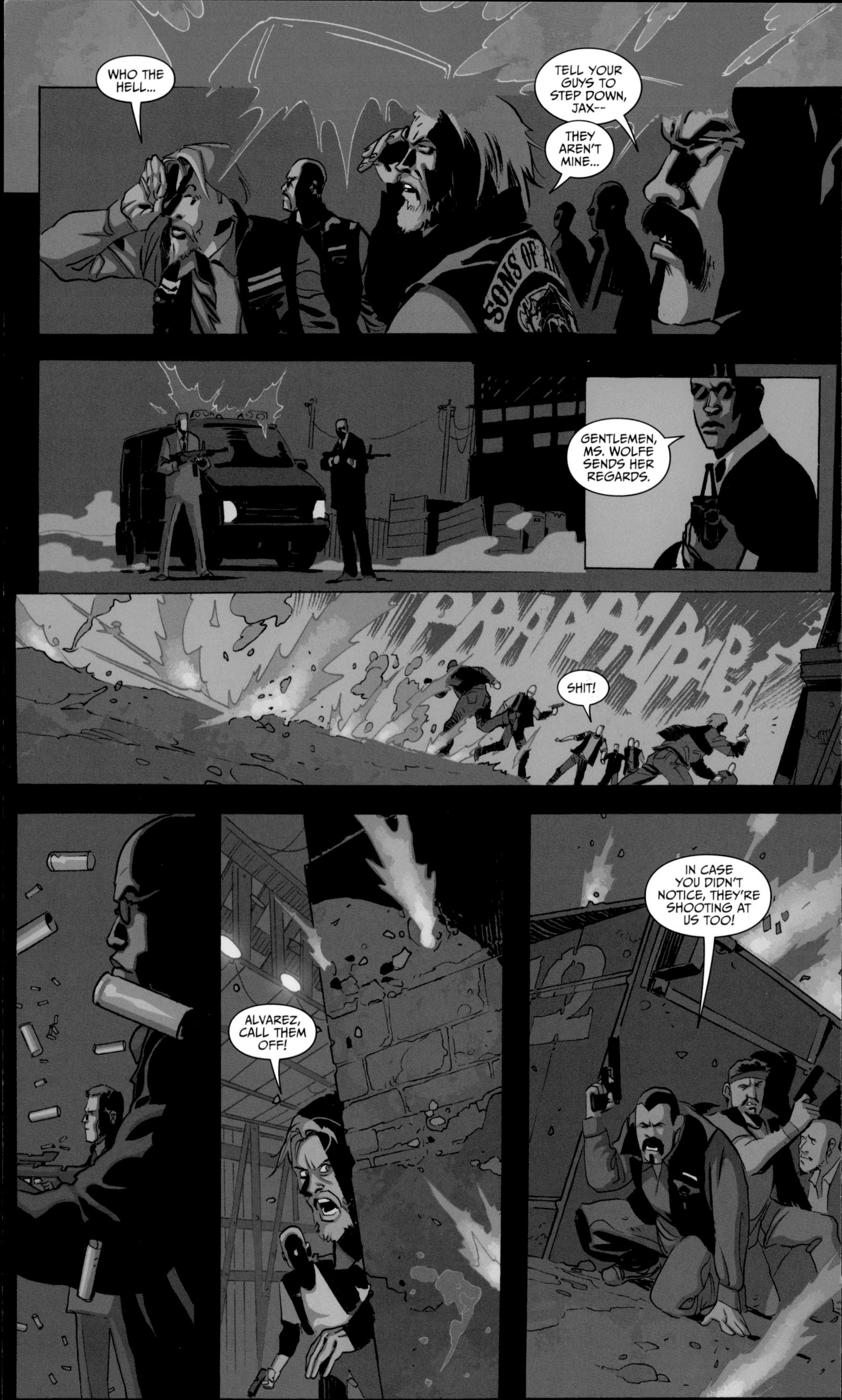
WHO THE HELL...
TELL YOUR GUYS TO STEP DOWN, JAX--
THEY AREN'T MINE...
SONS OF AN
GENTLEMEN, MS. WOLFE SENDS HER REGARDS.
SHIT!
ALVAREZ, CALL THEM OFF!
IN CASE YOU DIDN'T NOTICE, THEY'RE SHOOTING AT US TOO!

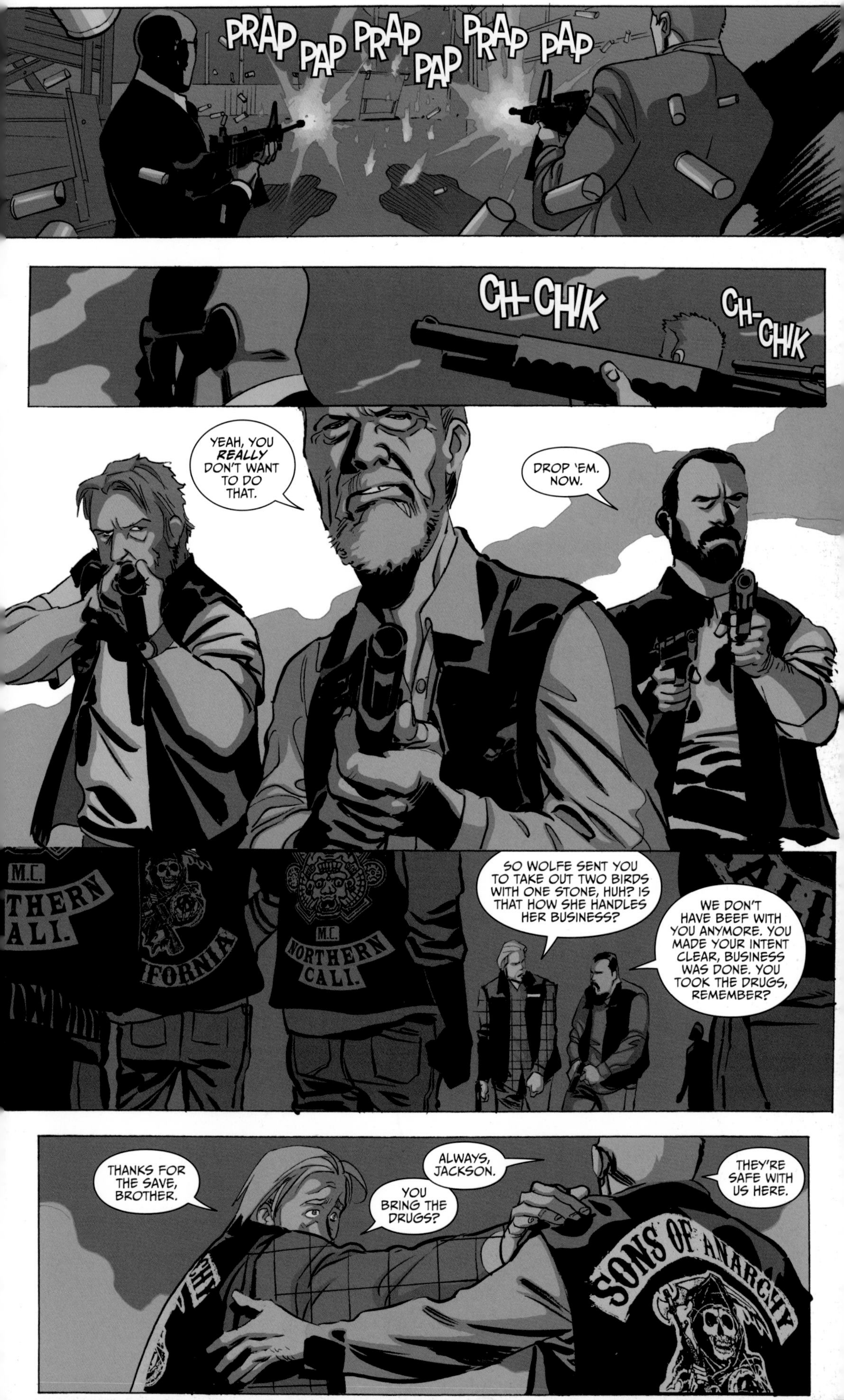
PRAP PAP PRAP PAP PRAP PAP
CH-CHIK
CH-CHIK
YEAH, YOU *REALLY* DON'T WANT TO DO THAT.
DROP 'EM. NOW.
M.C. NORTHERN CALI.
CALIFORNIA
M.C. NORTHERN CALI.
SO WOLFE SENT YOU TO TAKE OUT TWO BIRDS WITH ONE STONE, HUH? IS THAT HOW SHE HANDLES HER BUSINESS?
WE DON'T HAVE BEEF WITH YOU ANYMORE. YOU MADE YOUR INTENT CLEAR, BUSINESS WAS DONE. YOU TOOK THE DRUGS, REMEMBER?
THANKS FOR THE SAVE, BROTHER.
ALWAYS, JACKSON.
YOU BRING THE DRUGS?
THEY'RE SAFE WITH US HERE.
SONS OF ANARCHY

MIND TELLIN' US JUST WHAT IN THE FUCK YOU'RE DOING?

BEFORE WE PUT YOU DOWN.

GUYS, PUT YOUR GUNS DOWN. THIS IS A MISUNDERSTANDING.

WE HAVE SOMETHING THEY WANT, TOO.

I KNOW YOU'RE JUST DOING YOUR JOB AND RETALIATING FOR THE HIJACKING. I GET THAT.

PROBLEM IS, IT WASN'T ALVAREZ-- OR SAMCRO--THAT JUMPED YOUR SHIT.

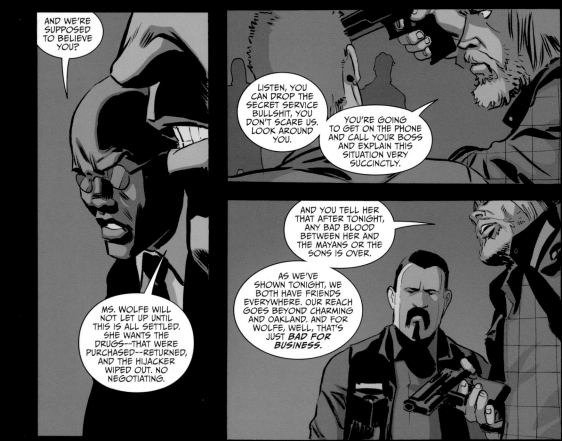

AND WE'RE SUPPOSED TO BELIEVE YOU?

LISTEN, YOU CAN DROP THE SECRET SERVICE BULLSHIT, YOU DON'T SCARE US. LOOK AROUND YOU.

YOU'RE GOING TO GET ON THE PHONE AND CALL YOUR BOSS AND EXPLAIN THIS SITUATION VERY SUCCINCTLY.

AND YOU TELL HER THAT AFTER TONIGHT, ANY BAD BLOOD BETWEEN HER AND THE MAYANS OR THE SONS IS OVER.

AS WE'VE SHOWN TONIGHT, WE BOTH HAVE FRIENDS EVERYWHERE. OUR REACH GOES BEYOND CHARMING AND OAKLAND. AND FOR WOLFE, WELL, THAT'S JUST *BAD FOR BUSINESS.*

MS. WOLFE WILL NOT LET UP UNTIL THIS IS ALL SETTLED. SHE WANTS THE DRUGS--THAT WERE PURCHASED--RETURNED, AND THE HIJACKER WIPED OUT. NO NEGOTIATING.

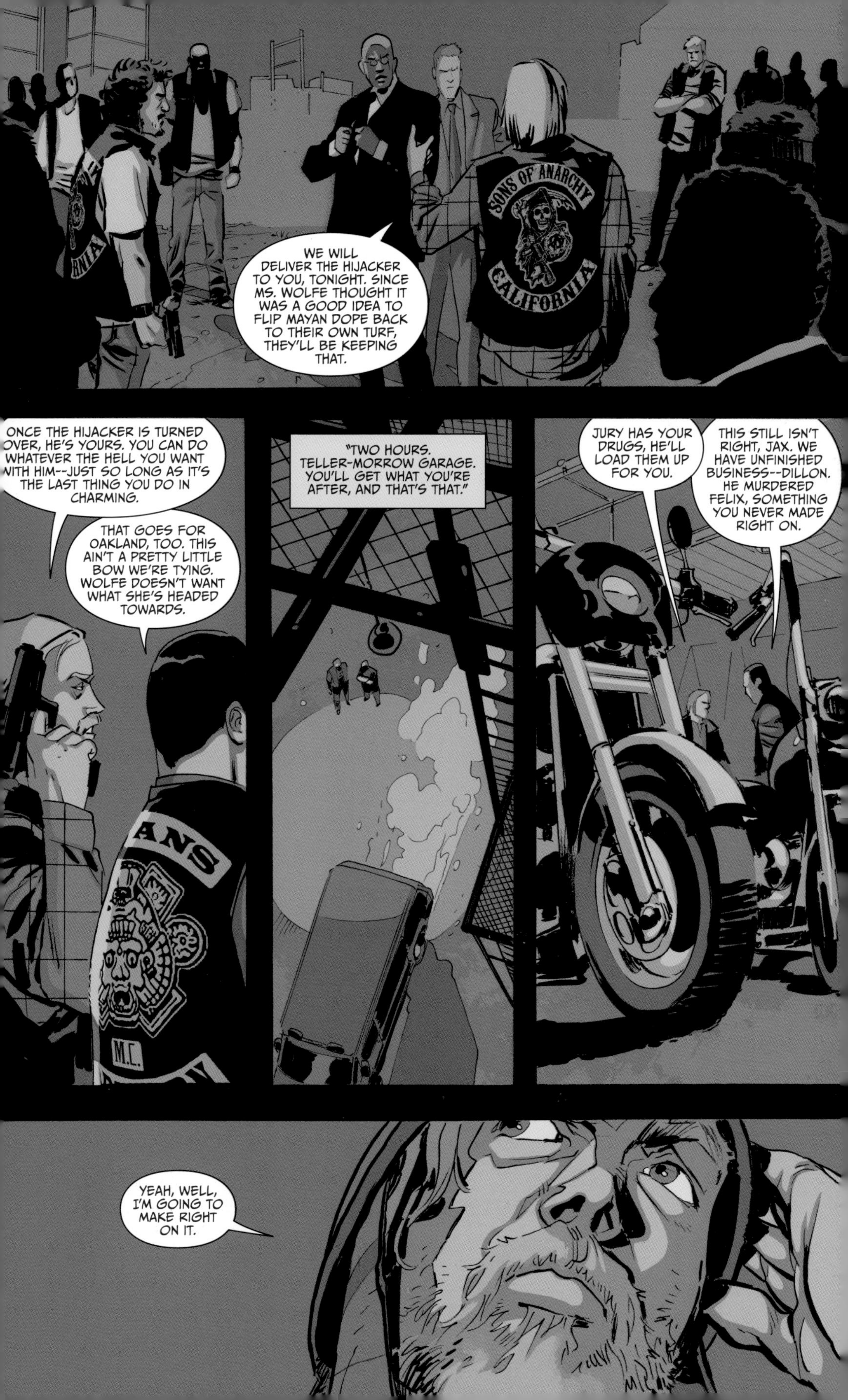
WE WILL DELIVER THE HIJACKER TO YOU, TONIGHT. SINCE MS. WOLFE THOUGHT IT WAS A GOOD IDEA TO FLIP MAYAN DOPE BACK TO THEIR OWN TURF, THEY'LL BE KEEPING THAT.
SONS OF ANARCHY
CALIFORNIA
ONCE THE HIJACKER IS TURNED OVER, HE'S YOURS. YOU CAN DO WHATEVER THE HELL YOU WANT WITH HIM--JUST SO LONG AS IT'S THE LAST THING YOU DO IN CHARMING.
THAT GOES FOR OAKLAND, TOO. THIS AIN'T A PRETTY LITTLE BOW WE'RE TYING. WOLFE DOESN'T WANT WHAT SHE'S HEADED TOWARDS.
"TWO HOURS. TELLER-MORROW GARAGE. YOU'LL GET WHAT YOU'RE AFTER, AND THAT'S THAT."
JURY HAS YOUR DRUGS, HE'LL LOAD THEM UP FOR YOU.
THIS STILL ISN'T RIGHT, JAX. WE HAVE UNFINISHED BUSINESS--DILLON. HE MURDERED FELIX, SOMETHING YOU NEVER MADE RIGHT ON.
YEAH, WELL, I'M GOING TO MAKE RIGHT ON IT.

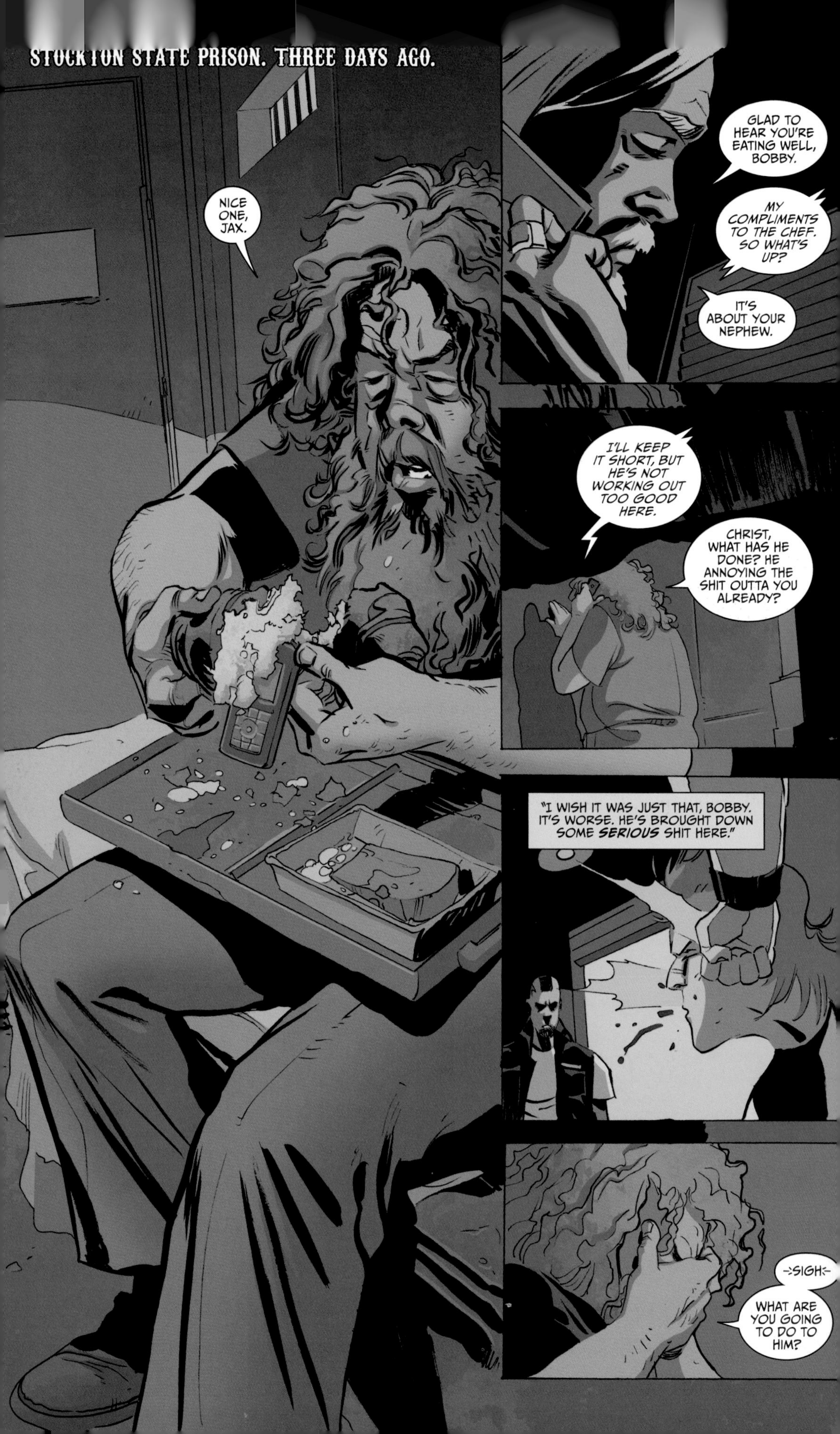
STOCKTON STATE PRISON. THREE DAYS AGO.
NICE ONE, JAX.
GLAD TO HEAR YOU'RE EATING WELL, BOBBY.
MY COMPLIMENTS TO THE CHEF. SO WHAT'S UP?
IT'S ABOUT YOUR NEPHEW.
I'LL KEEP IT SHORT, BUT HE'S NOT WORKING OUT TOO GOOD HERE.
CHRIST, WHAT HAS HE DONE? HE ANNOYING THE SHIT OUTTA YOU ALREADY?
"I WISH IT WAS JUST THAT, BOBBY. IT'S WORSE. HE'S BROUGHT DOWN SOME SERIOUS SHIT HERE."
-SIGH-
WHAT ARE YOU GOING TO DO TO HIM?

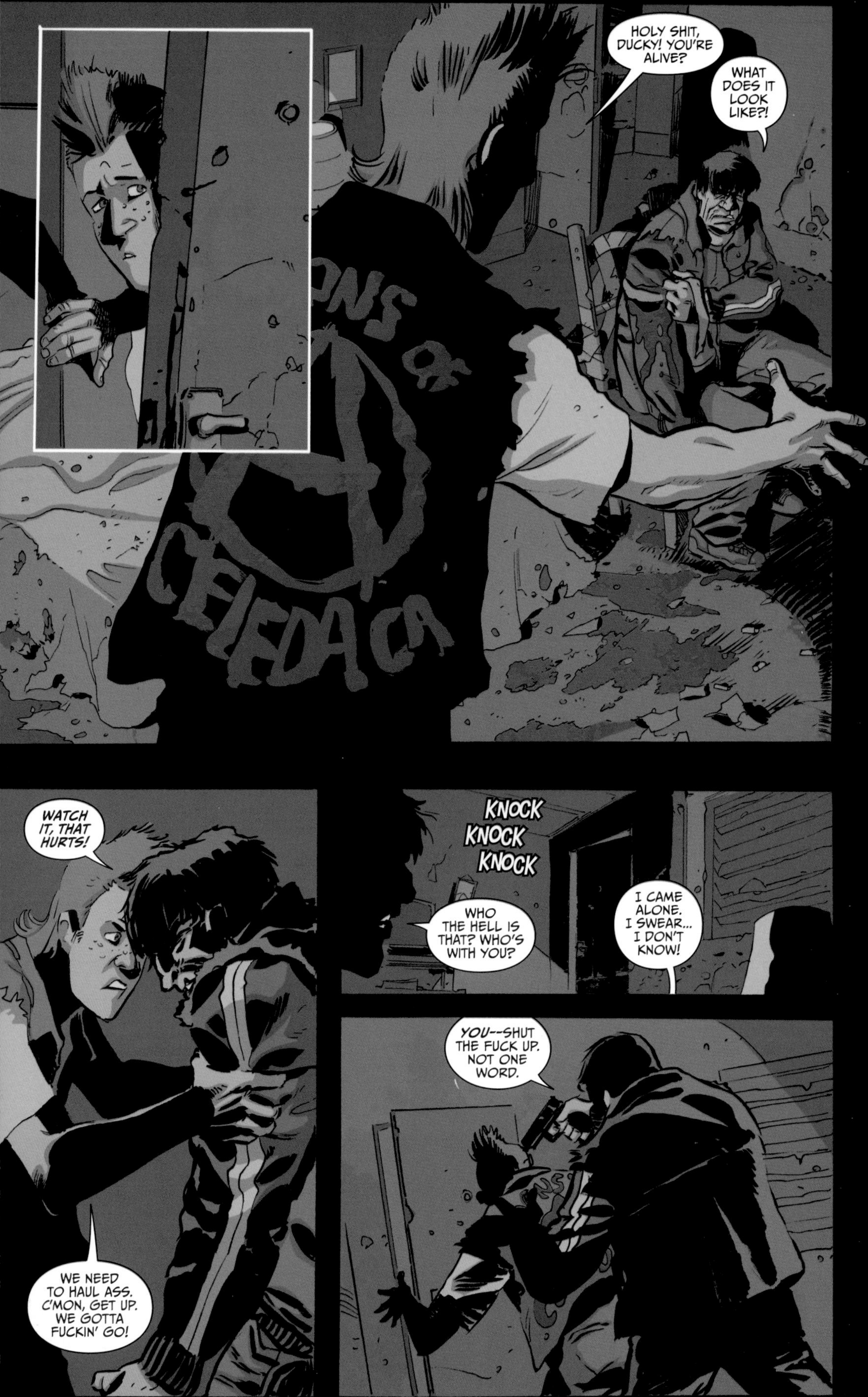

HOLY SHIT, DUCKY! YOU'RE ALIVE?
WHAT DOES IT LOOK LIKE?!
SONS OF CELEDACA
WATCH IT, THAT HURTS!
WE NEED TO HAUL ASS. C'MON, GET UP. WE GOTTA FUCKIN' GO!
KNOCK KNOCK KNOCK
WHO THE HELL IS THAT? WHO'S WITH YOU?
I CAME ALONE. I SWEAR... I DON'T KNOW!
YOU--SHUT THE FUCK UP. NOT ONE WORD.

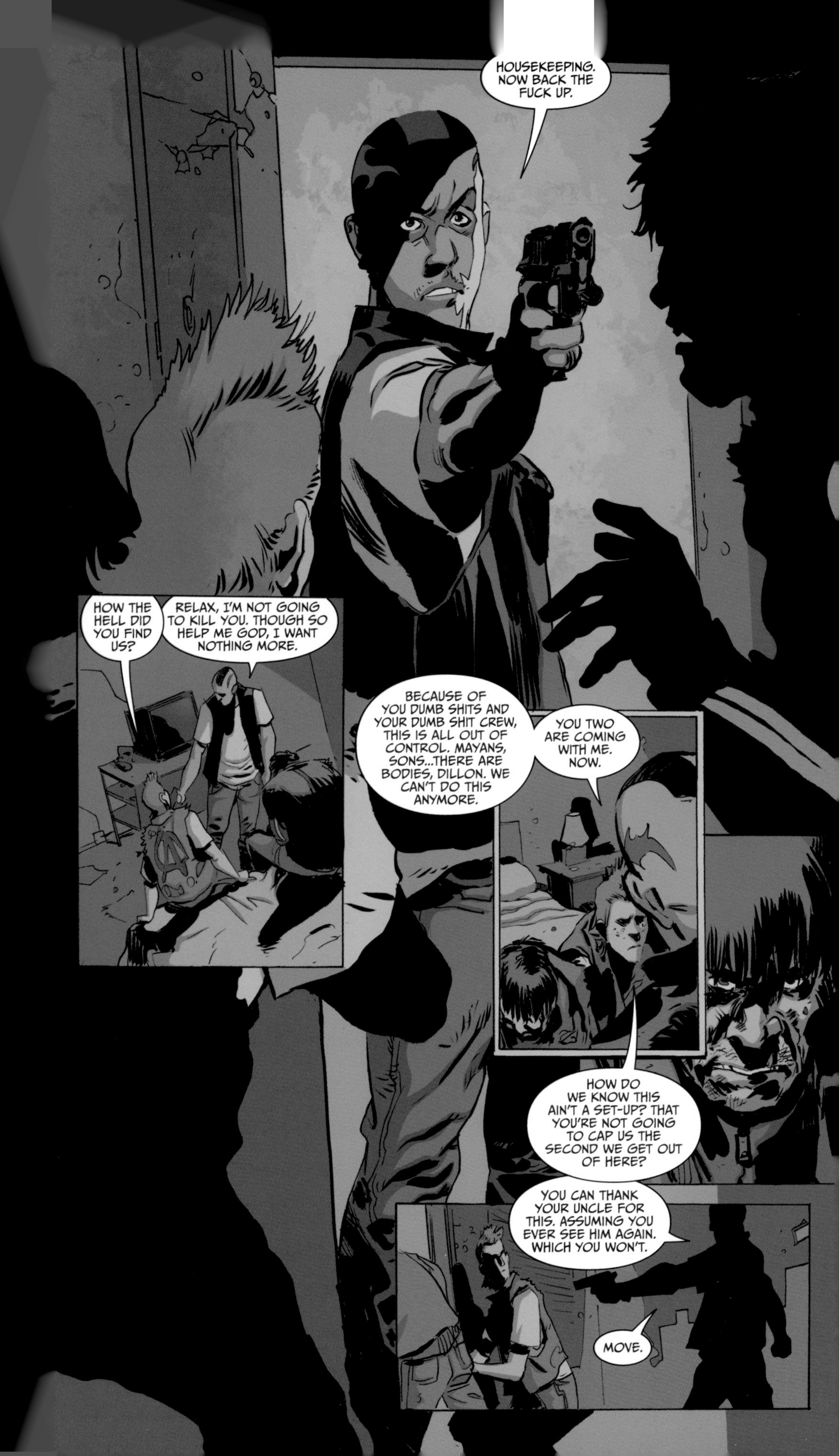
HOUSEKEEPING. NOW BACK THE FUCK UP.
HOW THE HELL DID YOU FIND US?
RELAX, I'M NOT GOING TO KILL YOU. THOUGH SO HELP ME GOD, I WANT NOTHING MORE.
BECAUSE OF YOU DUMB SHITS AND YOUR DUMB SHIT CREW, THIS IS ALL OUT OF CONTROL. MAYANS, SONS...THERE ARE BODIES, DILLON. WE CAN'T DO THIS ANYMORE.
YOU TWO ARE COMING WITH ME. NOW.
HOW DO WE KNOW THIS AIN'T A SET-UP? THAT YOU'RE NOT GOING TO CAP US THE SECOND WE GET OUT OF HERE?
YOU CAN THANK YOUR UNCLE FOR THIS. ASSUMING YOU EVER SEE HIM AGAIN. WHICH YOU WON'T.
MOVE.

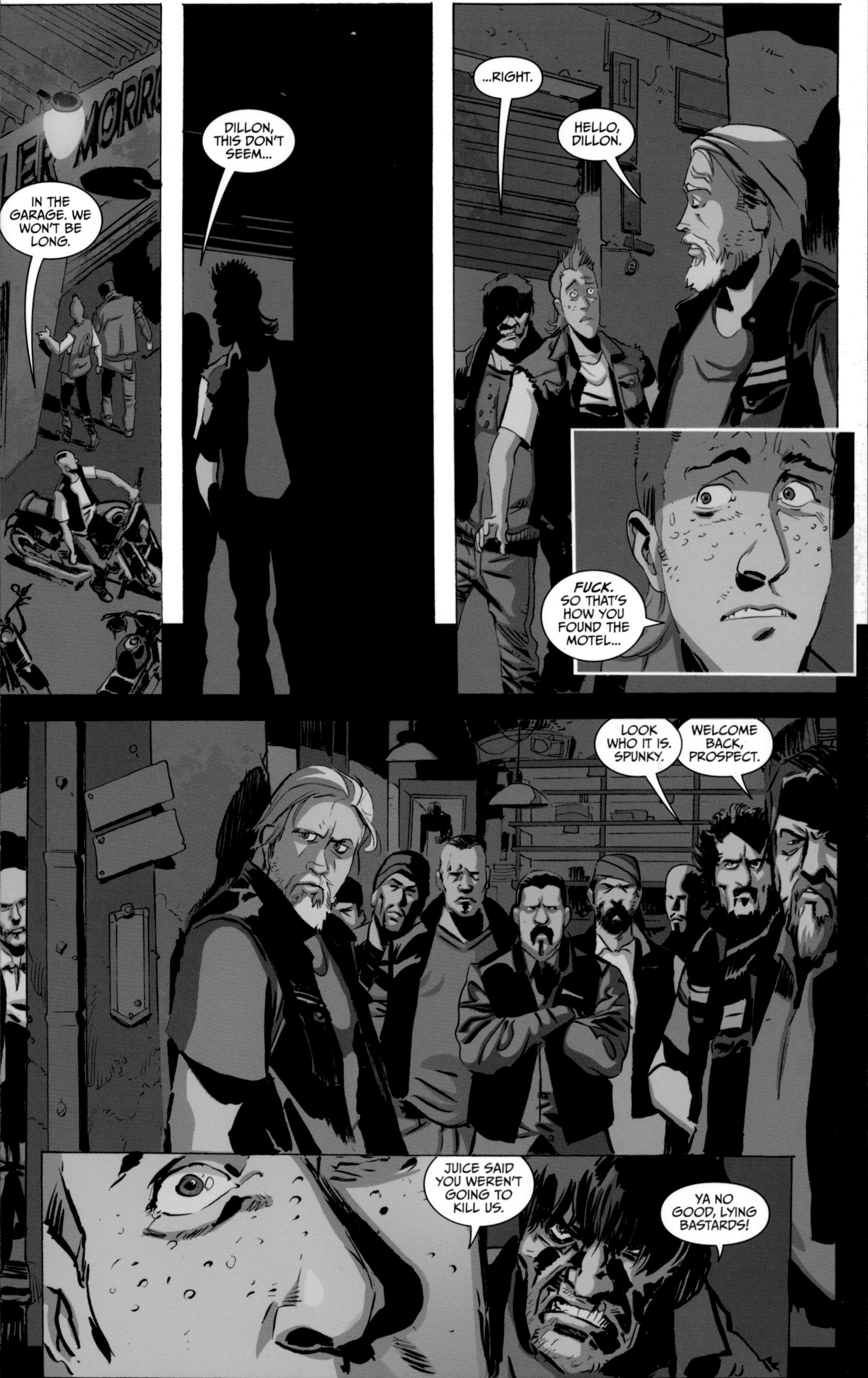
IN THE GARAGE. WE WON'T BE LONG.
DILLON, THIS DON'T SEEM...
...RIGHT.
HELLO, DILLON.
FUCK. SO THAT'S HOW YOU FOUND THE MOTEL...
LOOK WHO IT IS. SPUNKY.
WELCOME BACK, PROSPECT.
JUICE SAID YOU WEREN'T GOING TO KILL US.
YA NO GOOD, LYING BASTARDS!

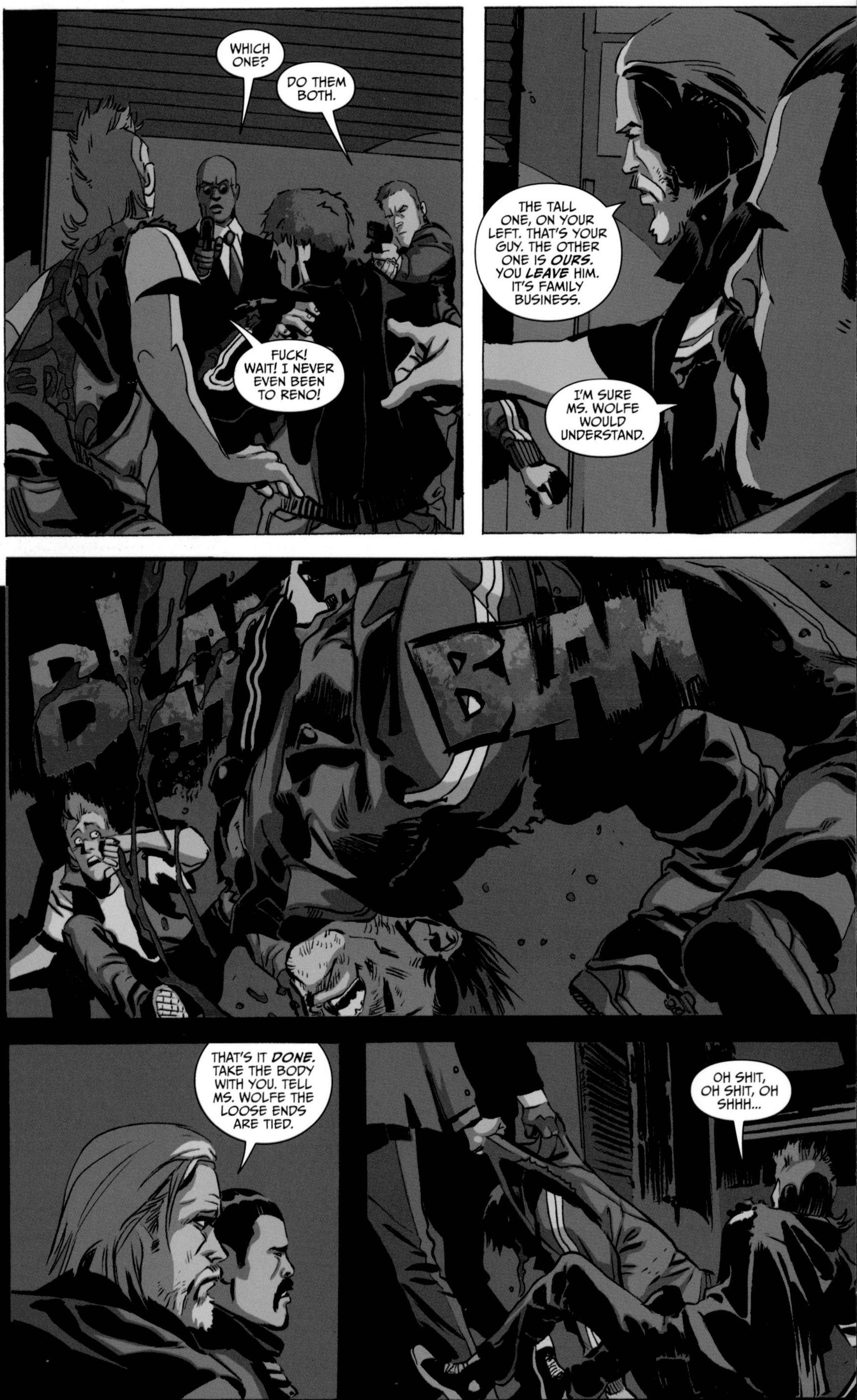
WHICH ONE?
DO THEM BOTH.
FUCK! WAIT! I NEVER EVEN BEEN TO RENO!
THE TALL ONE, ON YOUR LEFT. THAT'S YOUR GUY. THE OTHER ONE IS OURS. YOU LEAVE HIM. IT'S FAMILY BUSINESS.
I'M SURE MS. WOLFE WOULD UNDERSTAND.
BLAM
BLAM
THAT'S IT DONE. TAKE THE BODY WITH YOU. TELL MS. WOLFE THE LOOSE ENDS ARE TIED.
OH SHIT, OH SHIT, OH SHHH...

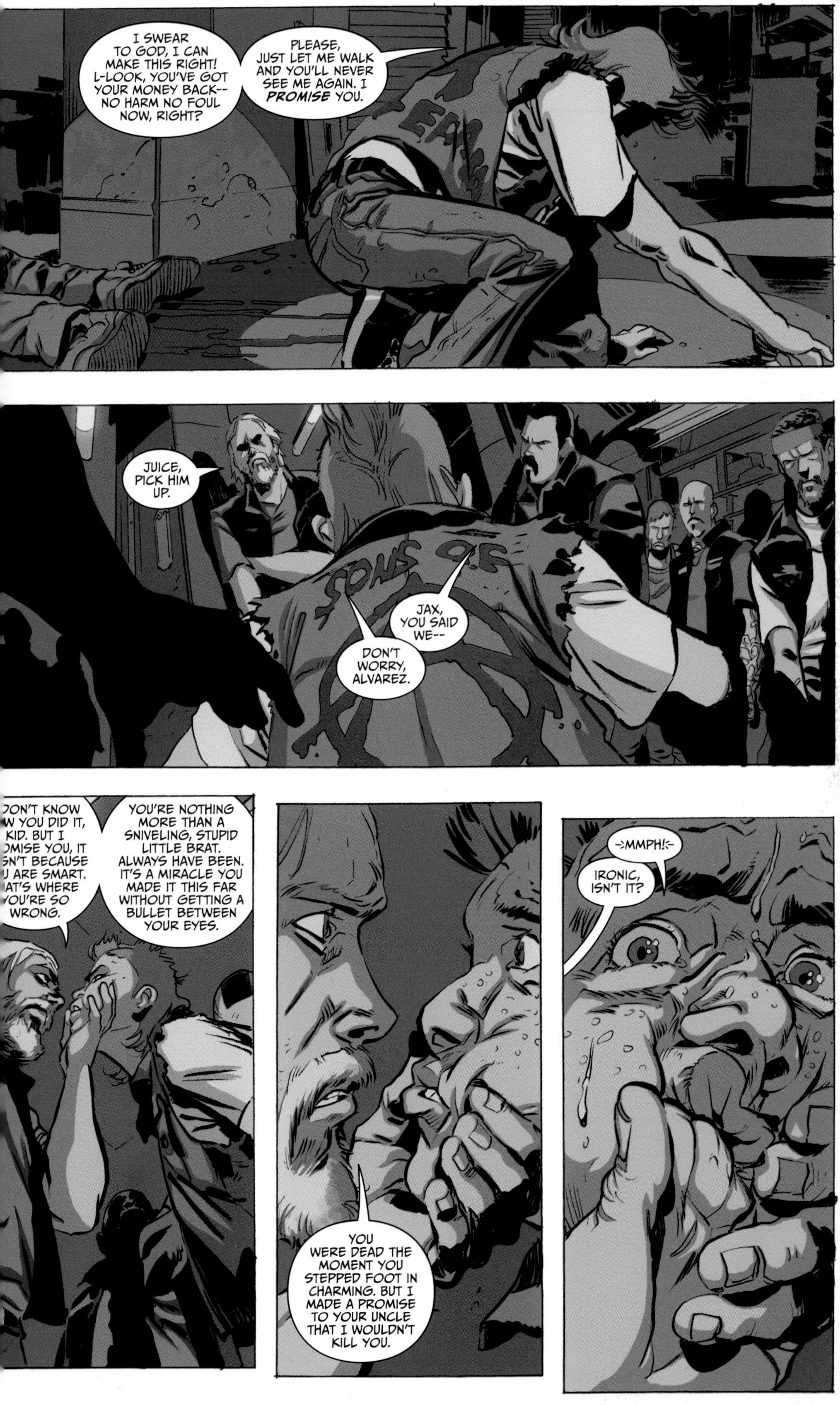
I SWEAR TO GOD, I CAN MAKE THIS RIGHT! L-LOOK, YOU'VE GOT YOUR MONEY BACK-- NO HARM NO FOUL NOW, RIGHT?
PLEASE, JUST LET ME WALK AND YOU'LL NEVER SEE ME AGAIN. I *PROMISE* YOU.
JUICE, PICK HIM UP.
JAX, YOU SAID WE--
DON'T WORRY, ALVAREZ.
DON'T KNOW W YOU DID IT, KID. BUT I OMISE YOU, IT SN'T BECAUSE U ARE SMART. AT'S WHERE YOU'RE SO WRONG.
YOU'RE NOTHING MORE THAN A SNIVELING, STUPID LITTLE BRAT. ALWAYS HAVE BEEN. IT'S A MIRACLE YOU MADE IT THIS FAR WITHOUT GETTING A BULLET BETWEEN YOUR EYES.
YOU WERE DEAD THE MOMENT YOU STEPPED FOOT IN CHARMING. BUT I MADE A PROMISE TO YOUR UNCLE THAT I WOULDN'T KILL YOU.
-MMPH!-
IRONIC, ISN'T IT?

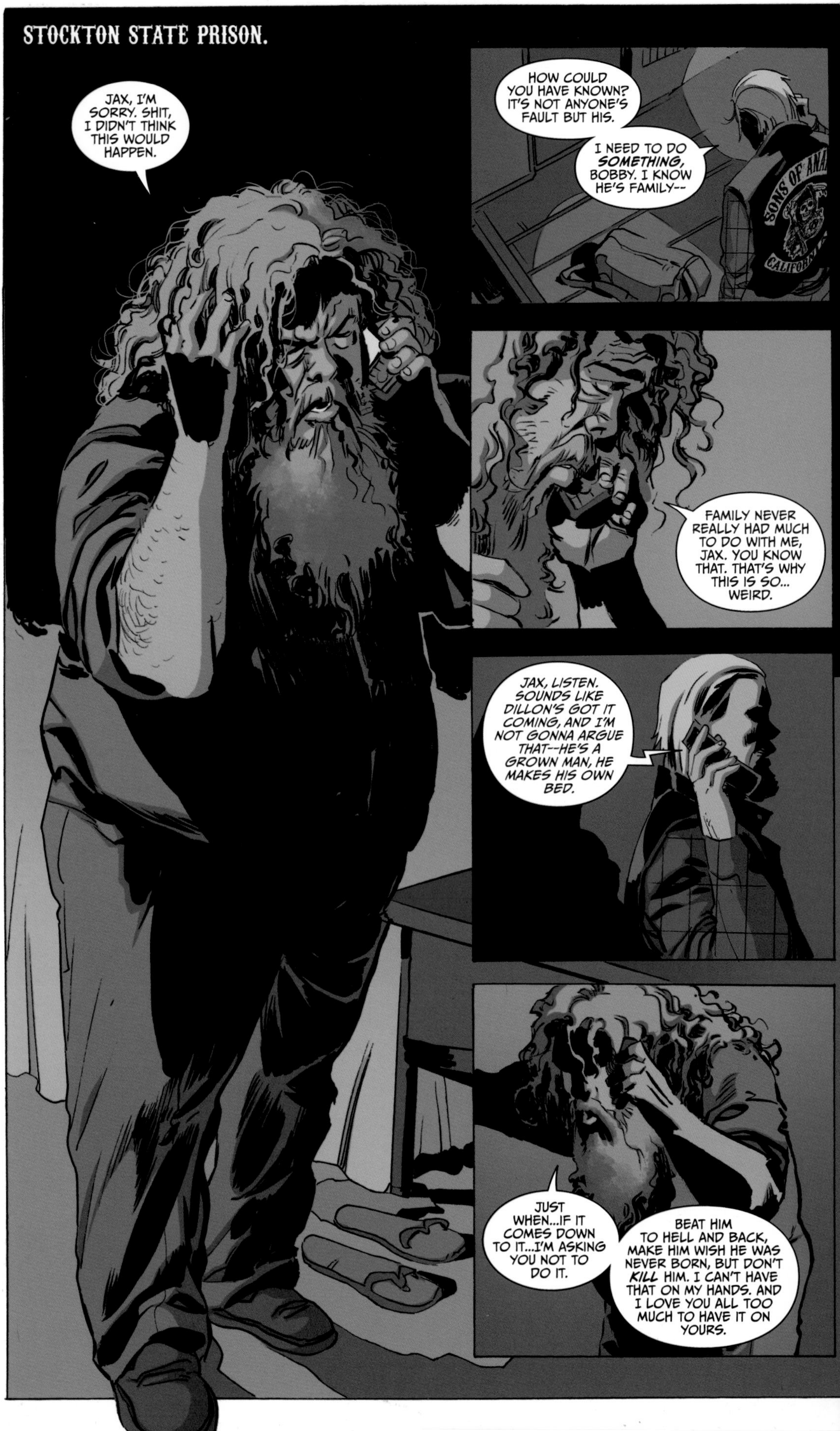
STOCKTON STATE PRISON.
JAX, I'M SORRY. SHIT, I DIDN'T THINK THIS WOULD HAPPEN.
HOW COULD YOU HAVE KNOWN? IT'S NOT ANYONE'S FAULT BUT HIS.
I NEED TO DO SOMETHING, BOBBY. I KNOW HE'S FAMILY--
FAMILY NEVER REALLY HAD MUCH TO DO WITH ME, JAX. YOU KNOW THAT. THAT'S WHY THIS IS SO... WEIRD.
JAX, LISTEN. SOUNDS LIKE DILLON'S GOT IT COMING, AND I'M NOT GONNA ARGUE THAT--HE'S A GROWN MAN, HE MAKES HIS OWN BED.
JUST WHEN...IF IT COMES DOWN TO IT...I'M ASKING YOU NOT TO DO IT.
BEAT HIM TO HELL AND BACK, MAKE HIM WISH HE WAS NEVER BORN, BUT DON'T KILL HIM. I CAN'T HAVE THAT ON MY HANDS. AND I LOVE YOU ALL TOO MUCH TO HAVE IT ON YOURS.

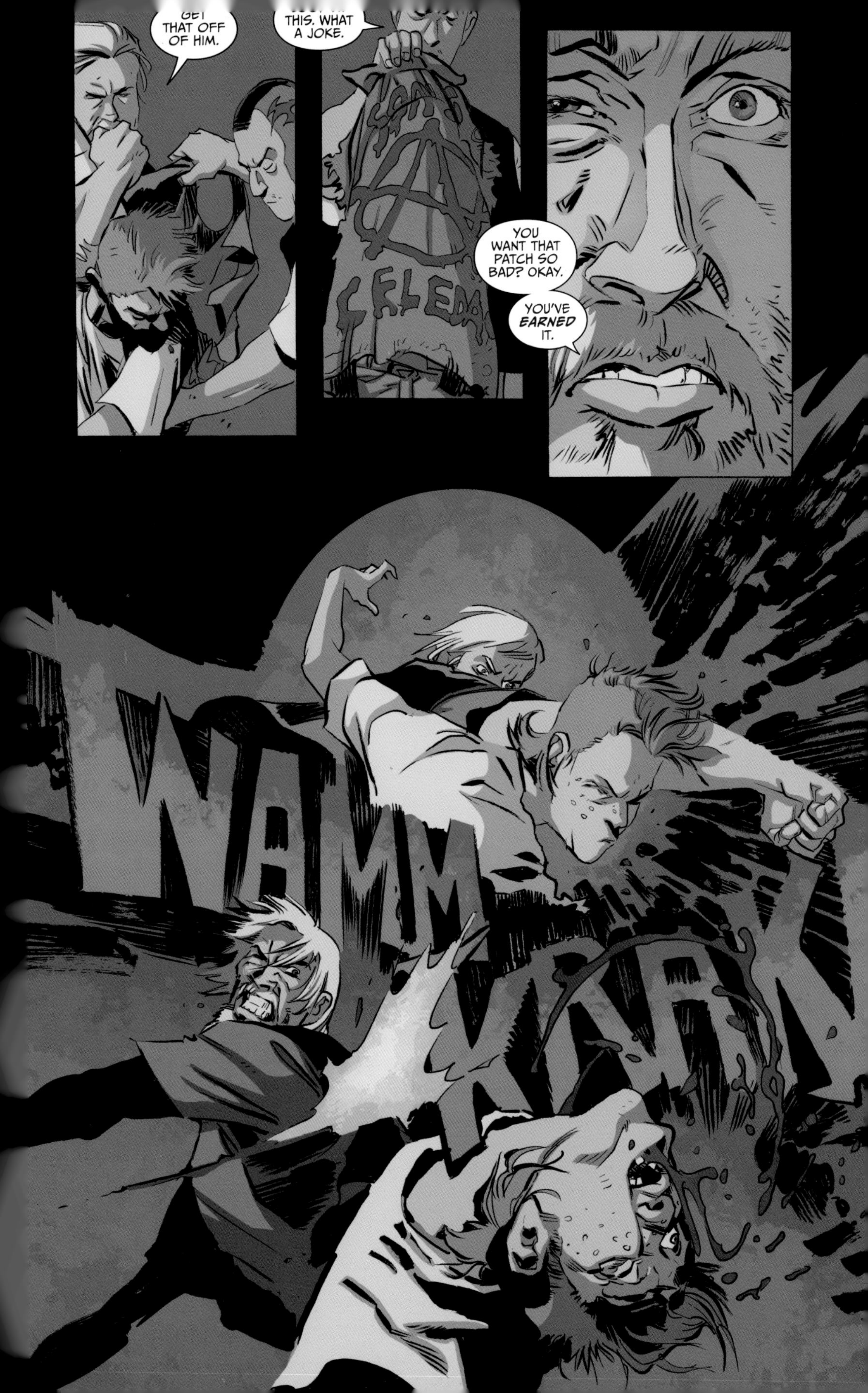

THAT OFF OF HIM.
THIS. WHAT A JOKE.
YOU WANT THAT PATCH SO BAD? OKAY.
YOU'VE *EARNED* IT.
WAMM

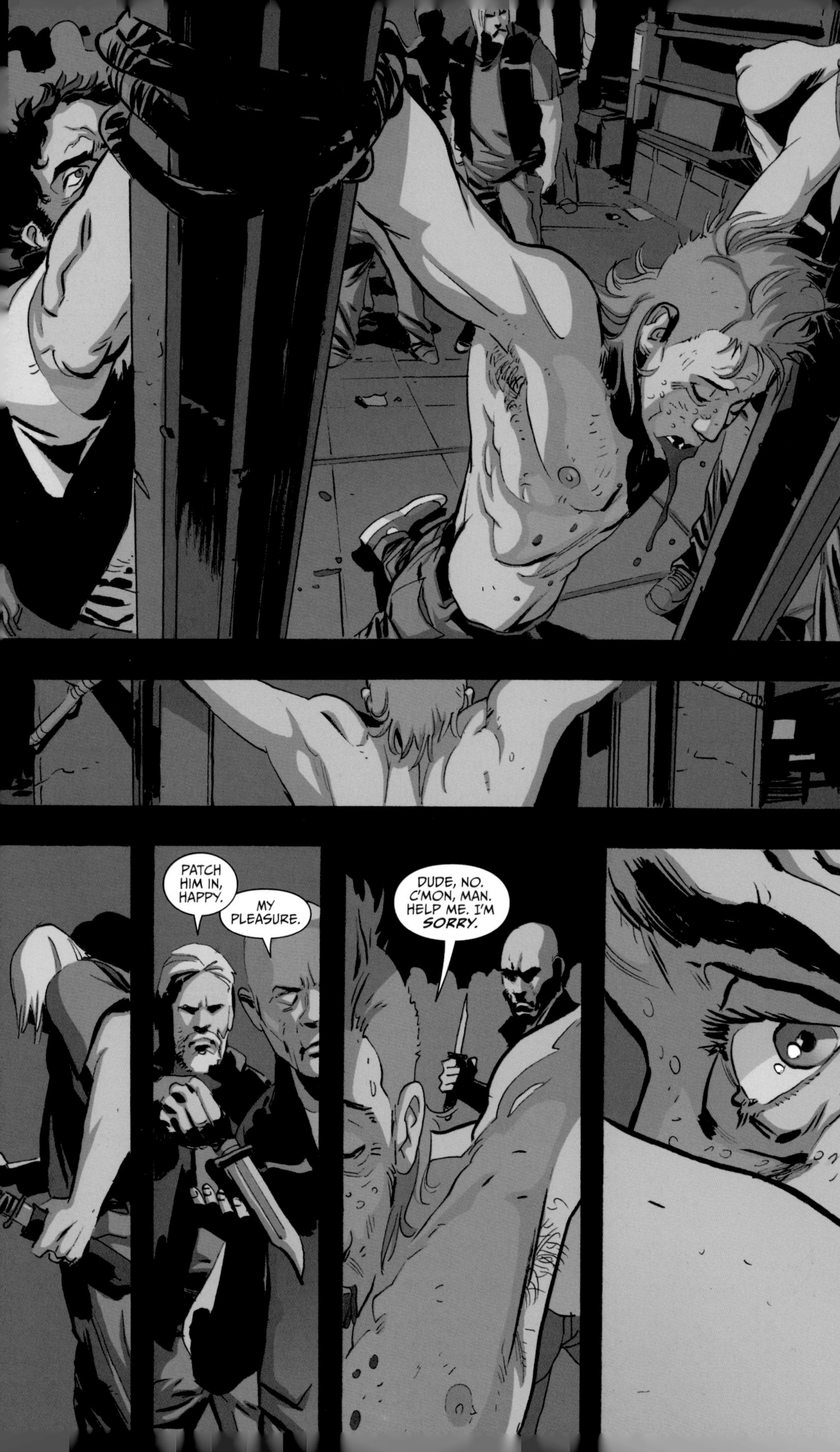
PATCH HIM IN, HAPPY.
MY PLEASURE.
DUDE, NO. C'MON, MAN. HELP ME. I'M SORRY.

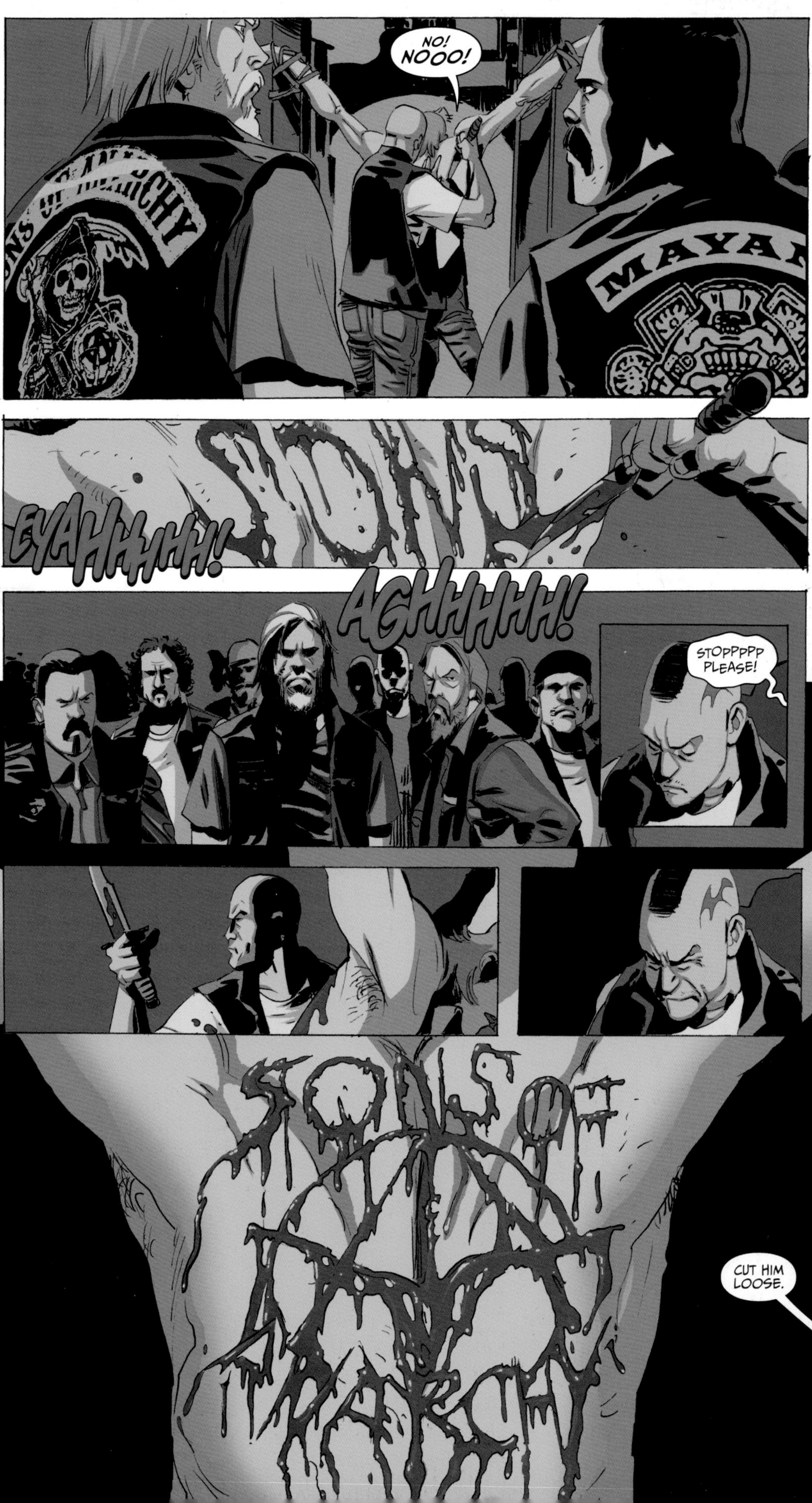
NO! NOOO!
EYAHHHHHH!
AGHHHHHH!
STOPPPPP PLEASE!
CUT HIM LOOSE.

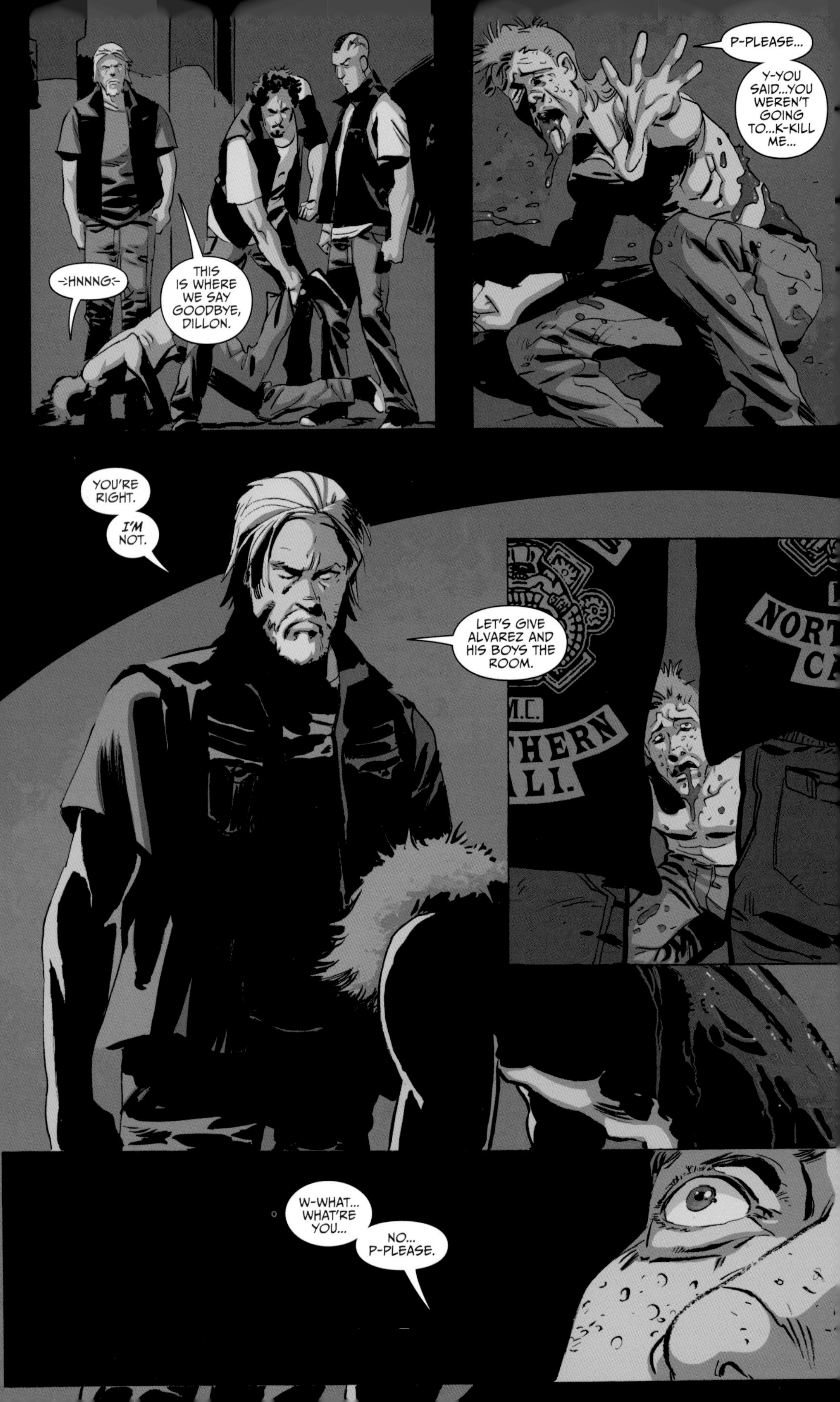
-HNNNG-
THIS IS WHERE WE SAY GOODBYE, DILLON.
P-PLEASE...
Y-YOU SAID...YOU WEREN'T GOING TO...K-KILL ME...
YOU'RE RIGHT.
I'M NOT.
LET'S GIVE ALVAREZ AND HIS BOYS THE ROOM.
M.C.
THERN
ALI.
NORT
CA
W-WHAT... WHAT'RE YOU...
NO... P-PLEASE.

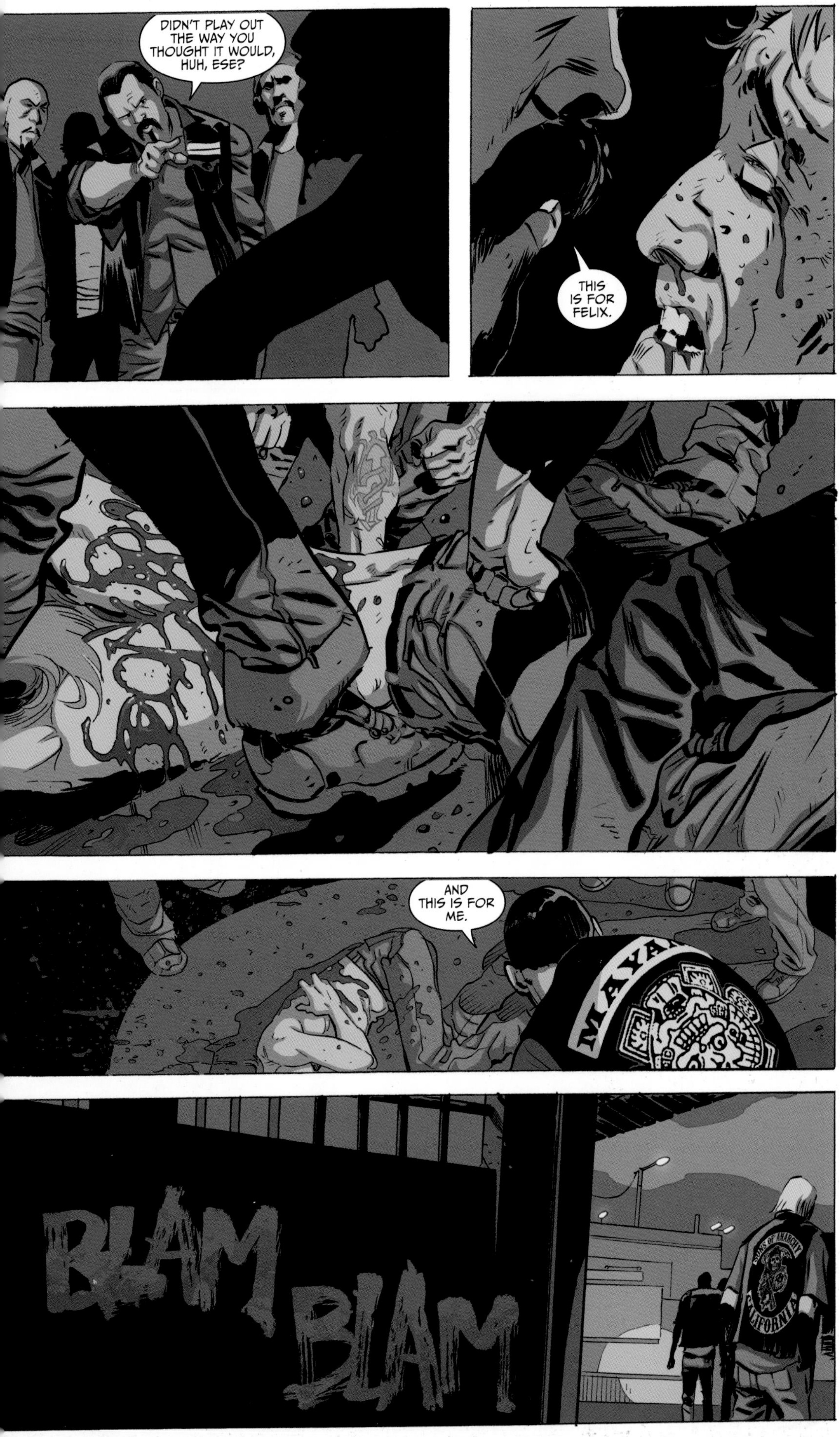
DIDN'T PLAY OUT THE WAY YOU THOUGHT IT WOULD, HUH, ESE?
THIS IS FOR FELIX.
AND THIS IS FOR ME.
BLAM
BLAM
SONS OF ANARCHY
CALIFORNIA

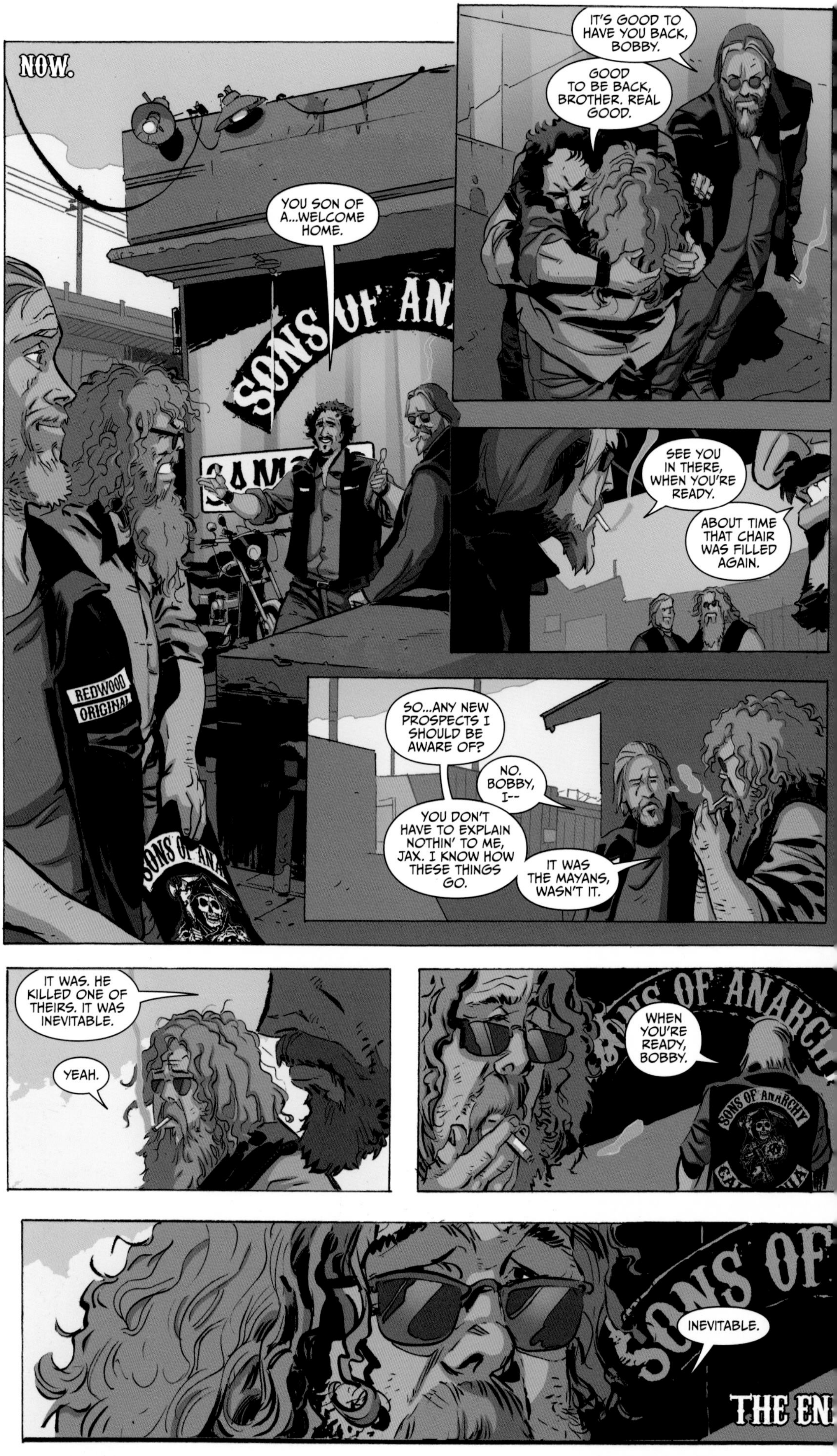
NOW.
YOU SON OF A...WELCOME HOME.
SONS OF AN
REDWOOD ORIGINAL
SONS OF ANA
IT'S GOOD TO HAVE YOU BACK, BOBBY.
GOOD TO BE BACK, BROTHER. REAL GOOD.
SEE YOU IN THERE, WHEN YOU'RE READY.
ABOUT TIME THAT CHAIR WAS FILLED AGAIN.
SO...ANY NEW PROSPECTS I SHOULD BE AWARE OF?
NO. BOBBY, I--
YOU DON'T HAVE TO EXPLAIN NOTHIN' TO ME, JAX. I KNOW HOW THESE THINGS GO.
IT WAS THE MAYANS, WASN'T IT.
IT WAS. HE KILLED ONE OF THEIRS. IT WAS INEVITABLE.
YEAH.
WHEN YOU'RE READY, BOBBY.
SONS OF ANARCHY
INEVITABLE.
SONS OF
THE EN

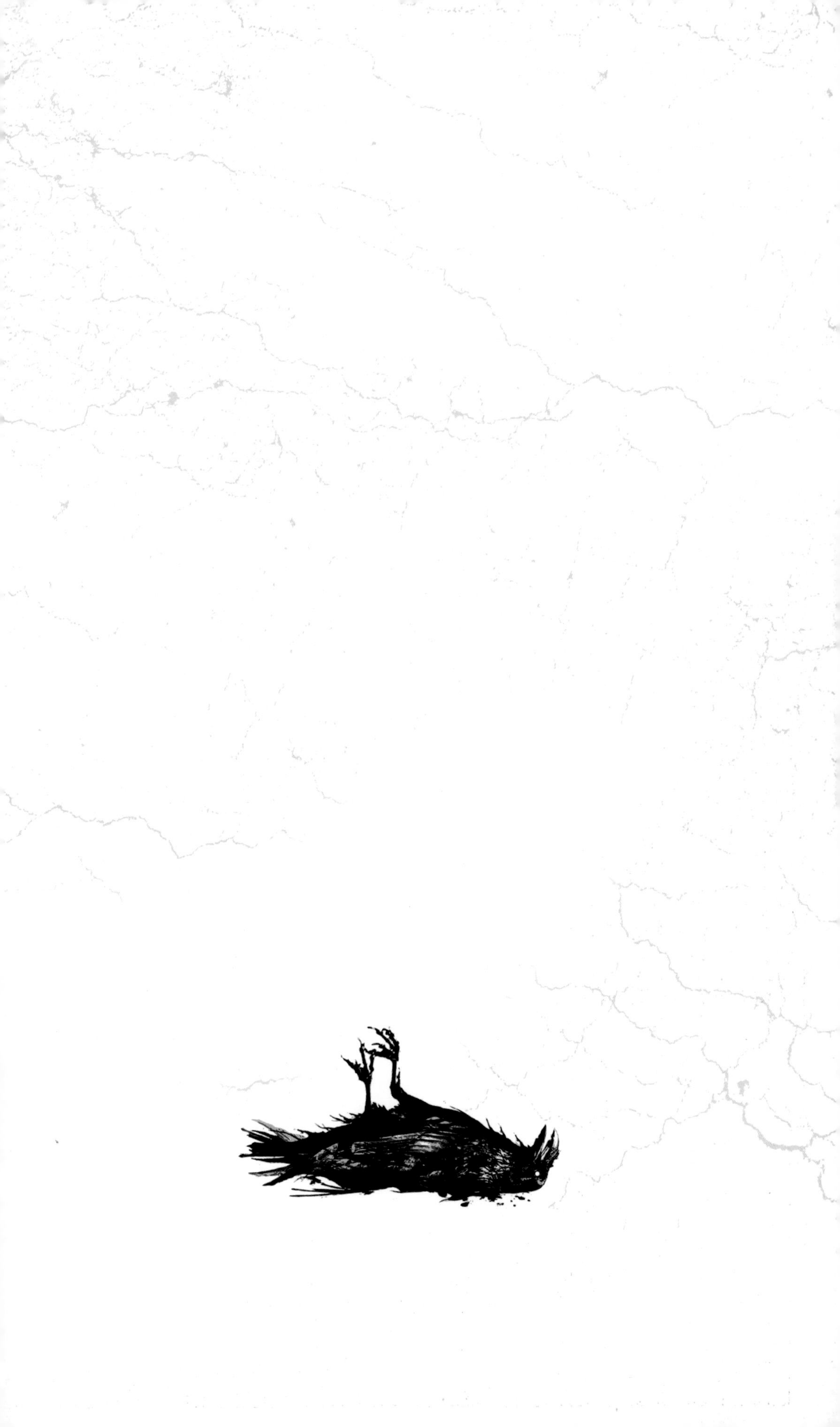

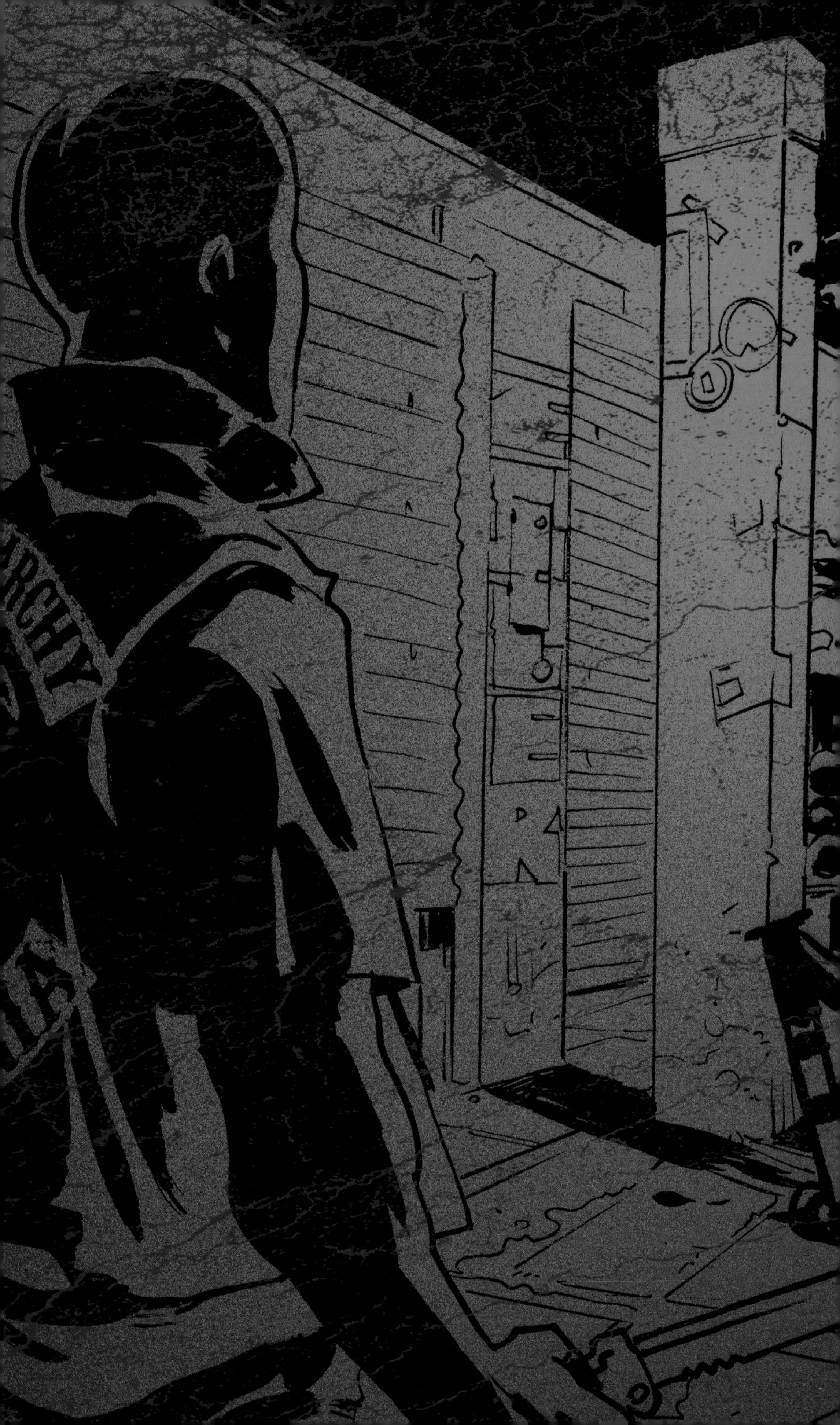

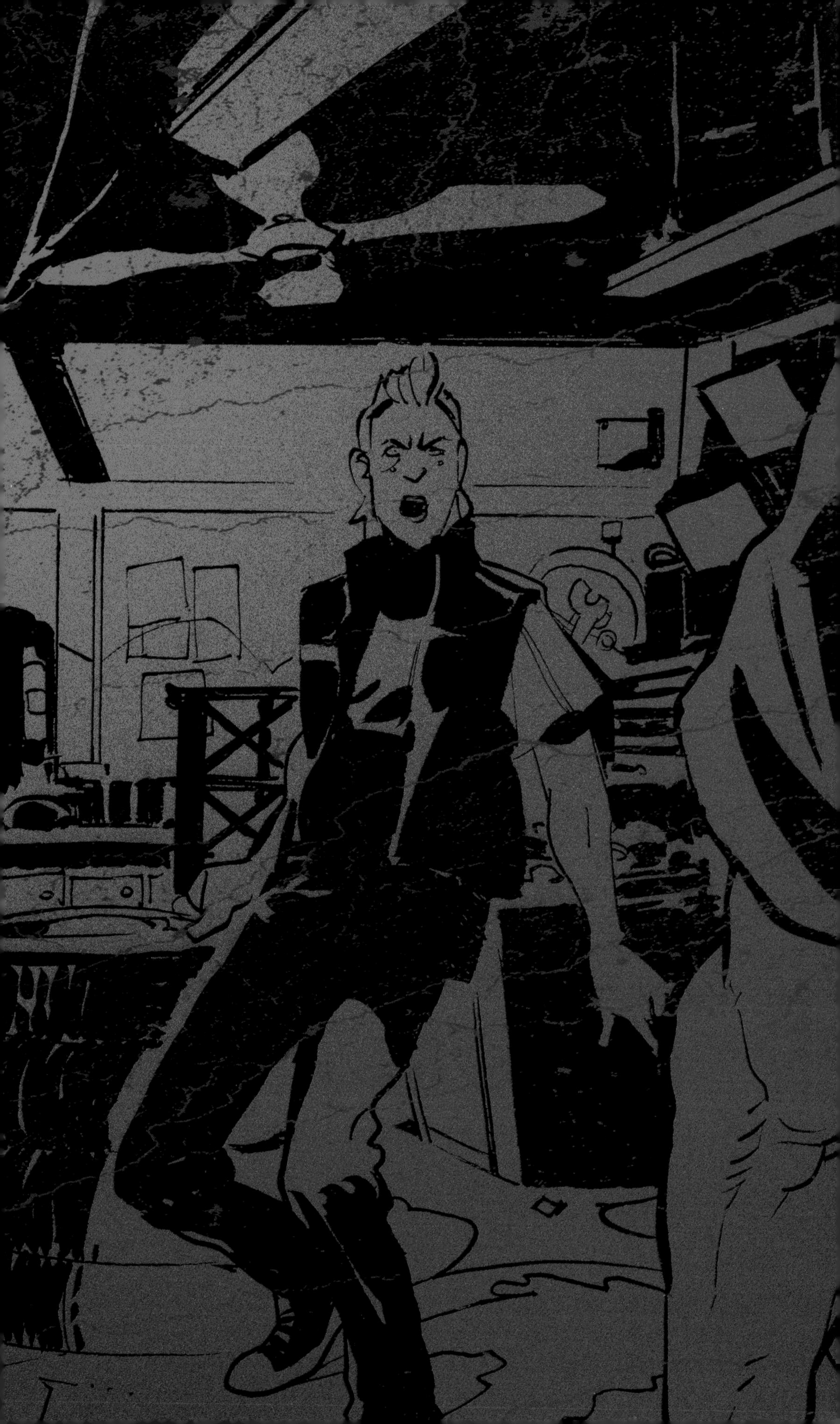

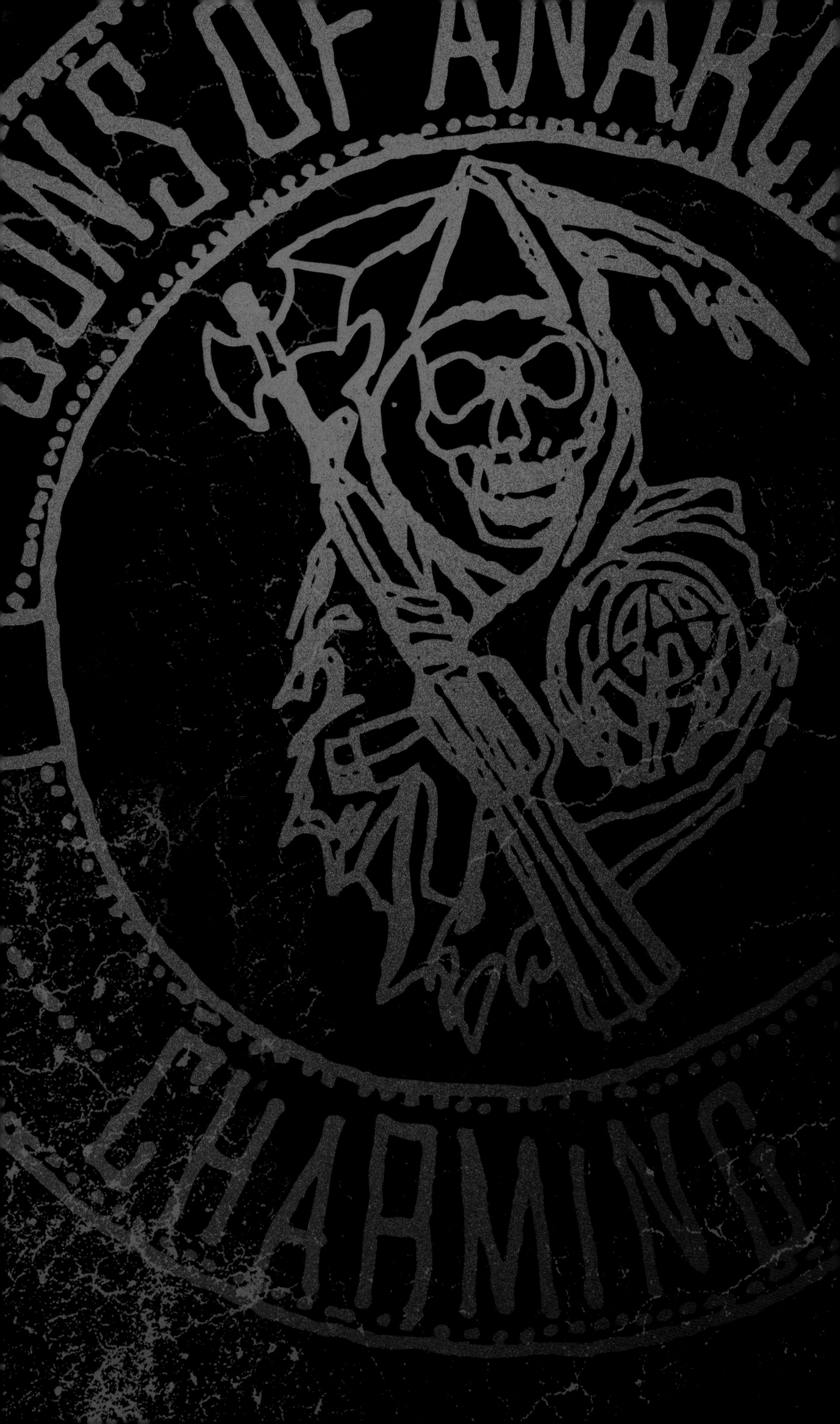
CHARMING

COVER GALLERY

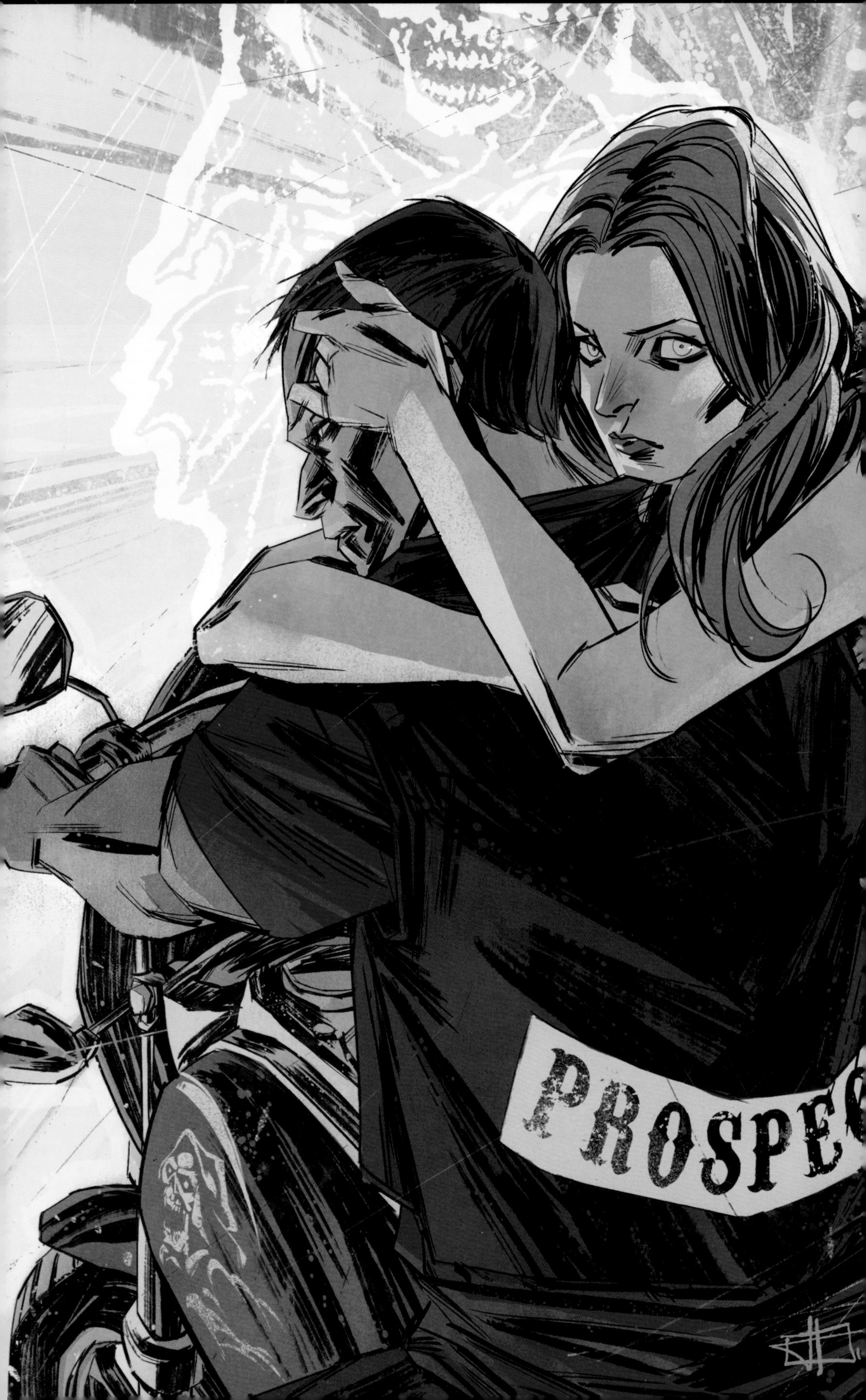
PROSPEC

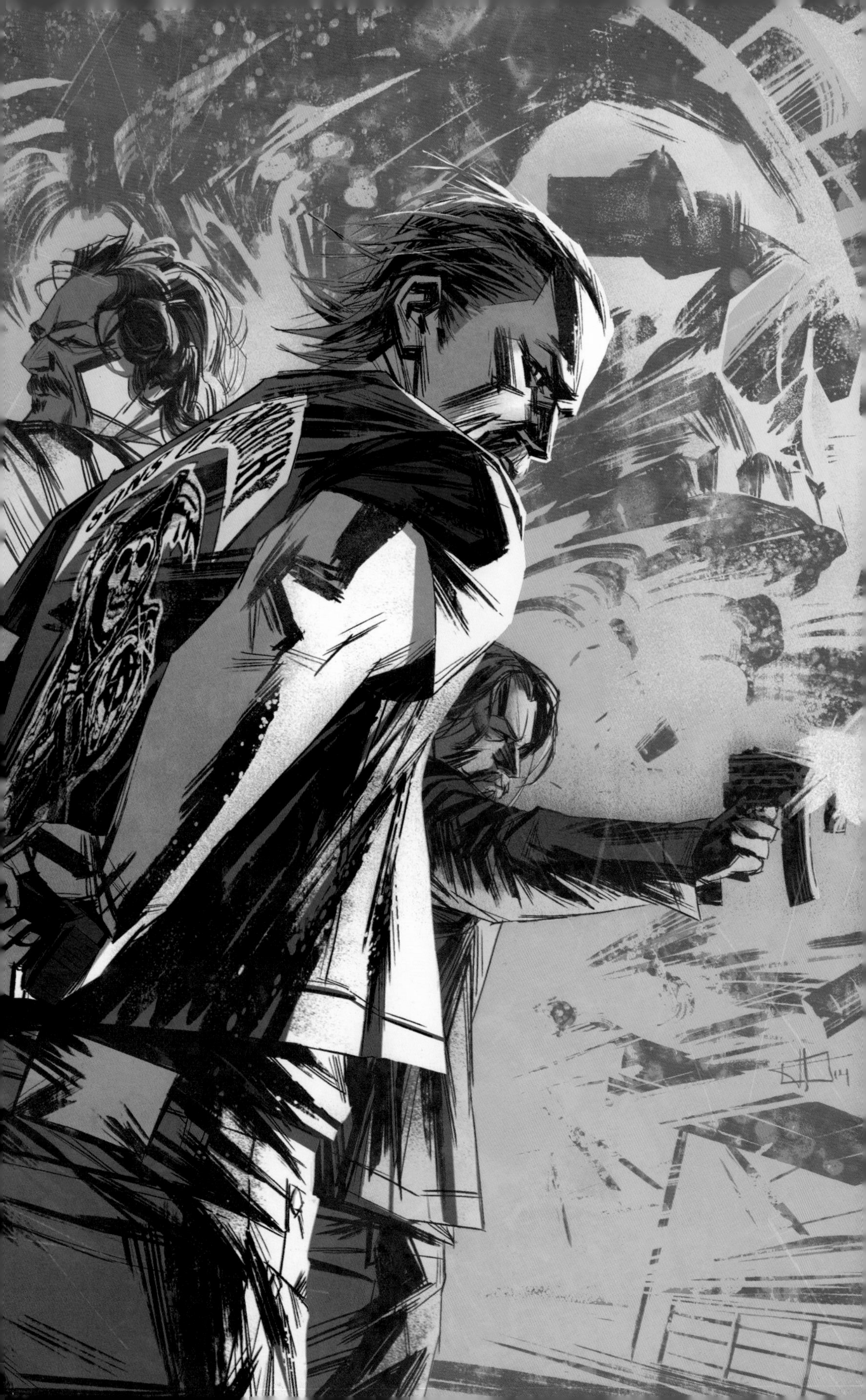

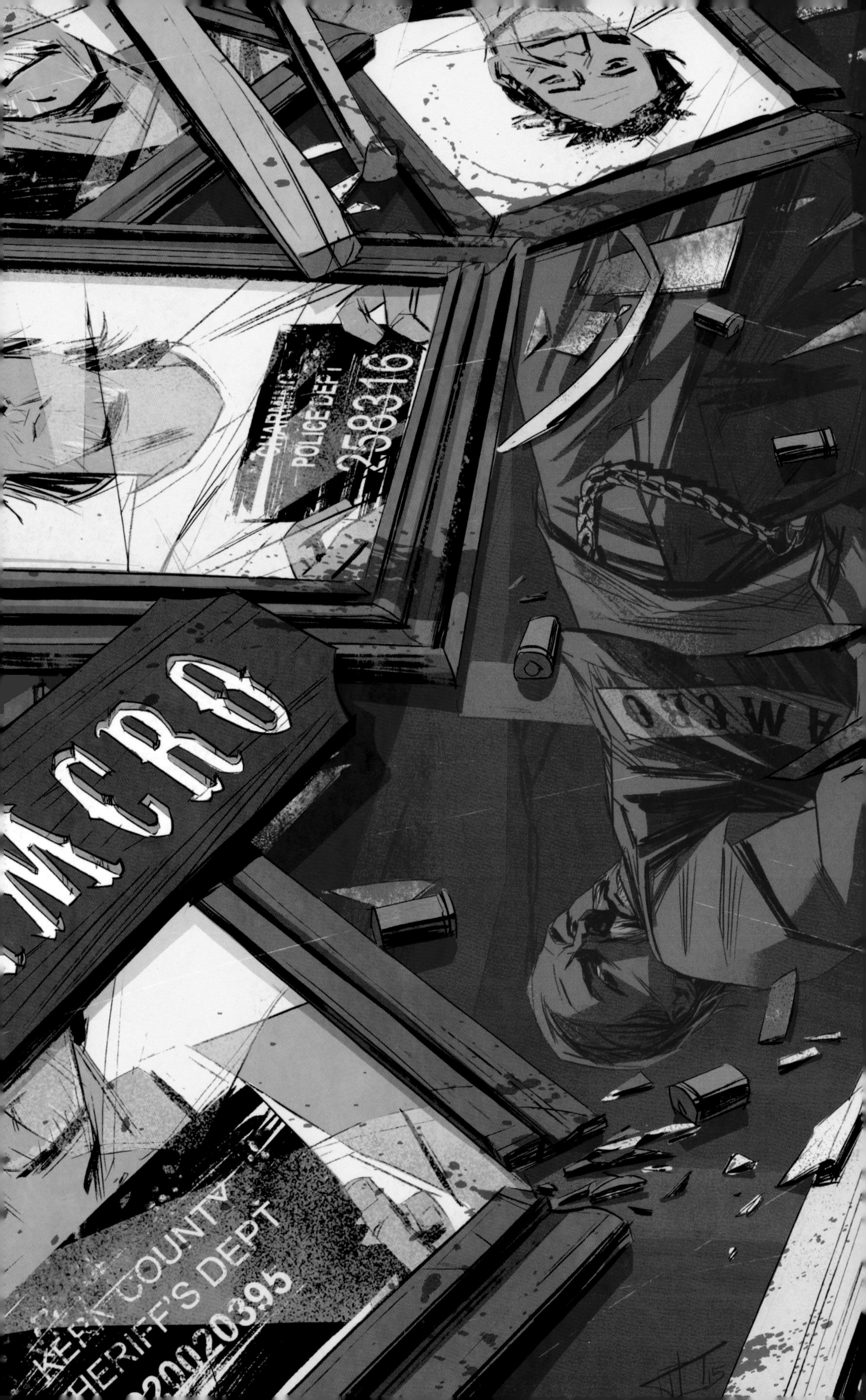
POLICE DEPT
258316
MCRO
COUNTY
HERIFF'S DEPT

ISSUE TWENTY-TWO **TONI INFANTE**

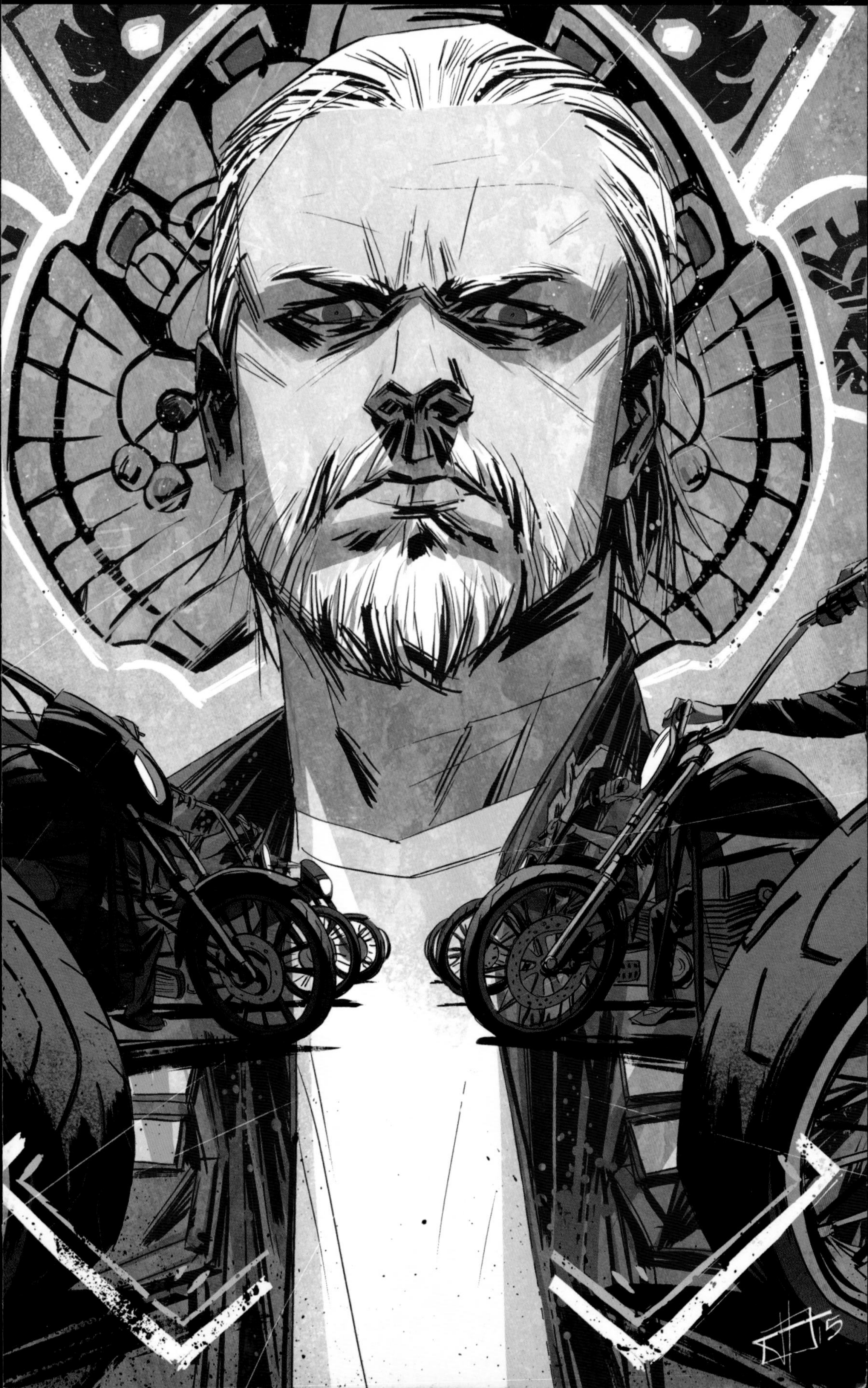

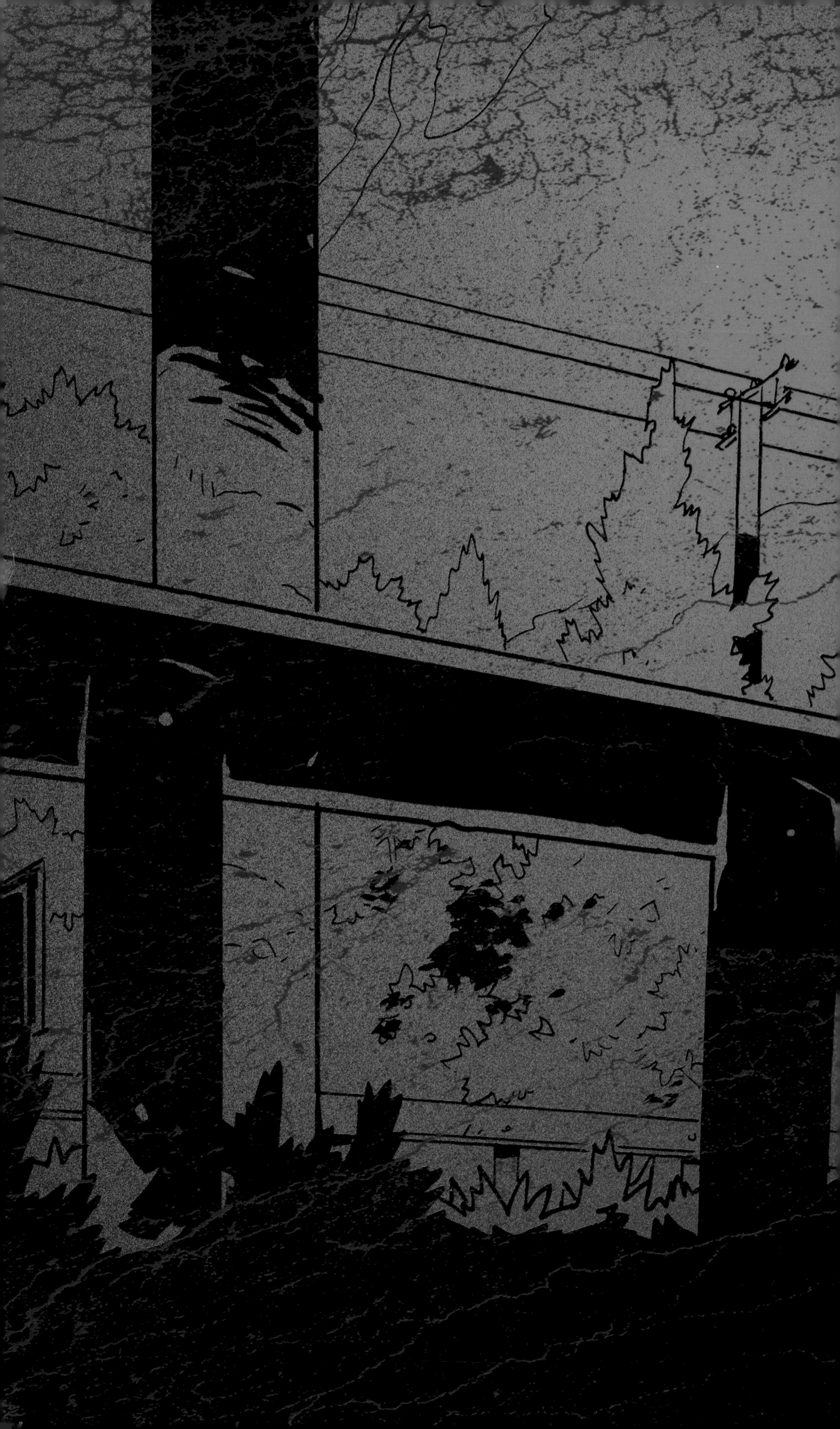

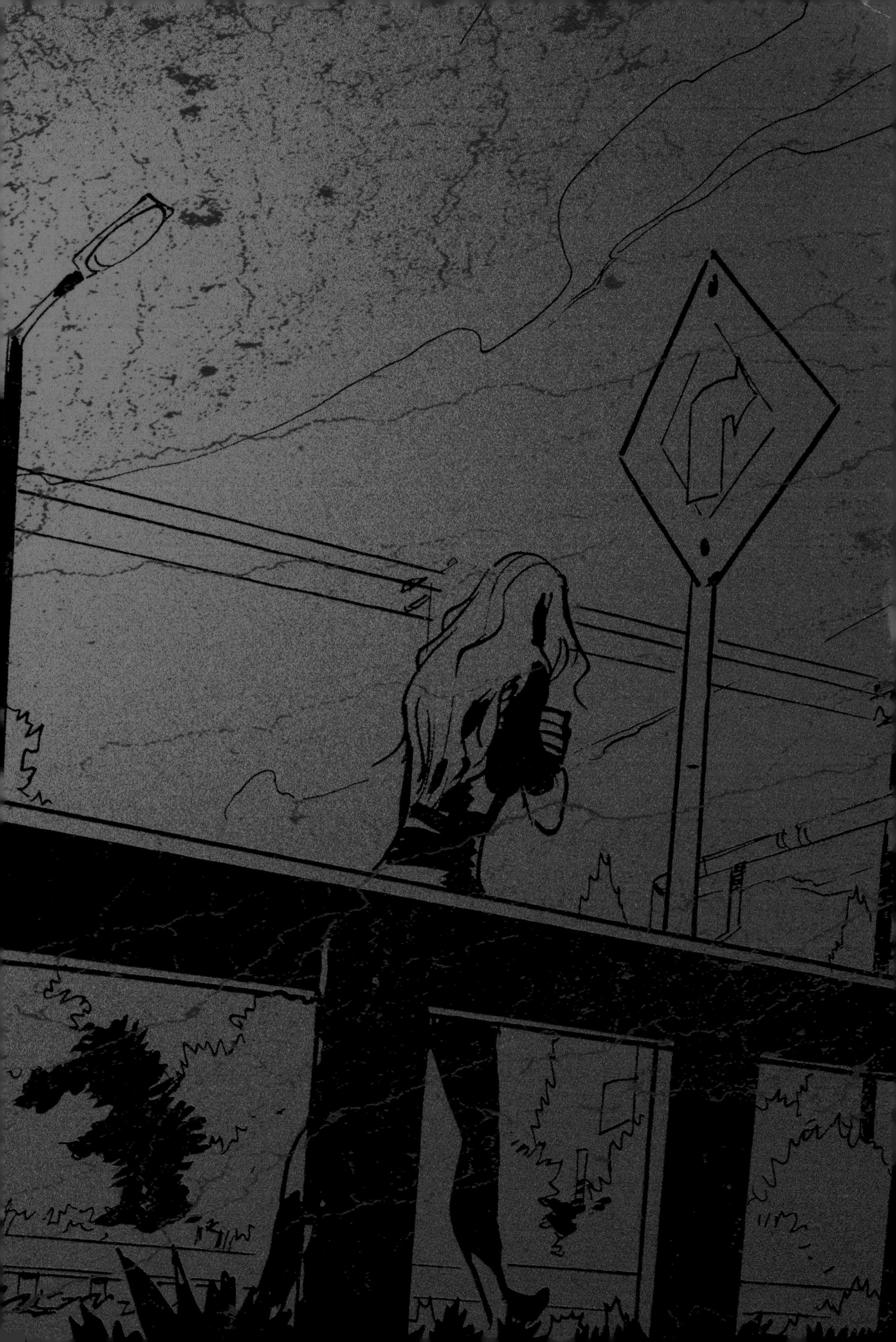

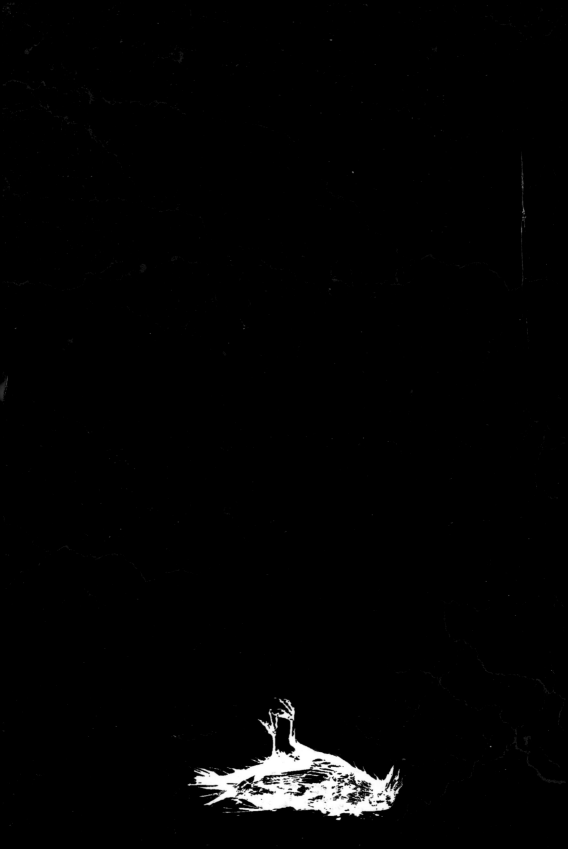